An
Italian
Odyssey

La Via Francigena

An
Italian Odyssey

**One Couple's Culinary &
Cultural Pilgrimage**

Julie A Burk & Neville J Tencer

Published by Verdera Media *vm*
British Columbia, Canada

Published by Verdera Media 𝑉𝑀
British Columbia Canada
www.verderamedia.com

Library and Archives Canada Cataloguing in Publication

Burk, Julie A.
An Italian odyssey : one couple's culinary and cultural pilgrimage /
Julie A. Burk, Neville J. Tencer.

ISBN 978-0-9865887-0-9

1. Burk, Julie A--Travel--Italy. 2. Tencer, Neville J--Travel--Italy.
3. Italy--Description and travel. 4. Pilgrims and pilgrimages--Italy.
5. Walking--Italy. 6. Food habits--Italy. 7. Cookery, Italian.
I. Tencer, Neville J. II. Title.
DG430.2.B87 2010   914.504'93   C2010-903033-8

Editing: Cathy Reed, C. Reed Writing & Editing
Cover and book design: Flash Lewis, ATR Design
Map of Via Francigena: Original artwork by Jannina Veit Teuten
Interior sectional maps: Kellie Burk
Interior photographic images: Julie A Burk, Neville J Tencer
Back cover photograph of authors: David Paleczny
Interior photographs of authors: Giuseppe Lavezzari, Cesare Cortesi
Cover photograph: Val d'Orcia by Neville Tencer

The authors kindly recognize and thank Richard Scott Mowrer,
son of author Paul Scott Mowrer; author Phil Cousineau; Tanisha Christie
on behalf of author Nelson Demille; and architect Hugh Newell Jacobsen
for permission to use their respective quotations.

To Maria:

May the spirit within you
and the mysteries that surround you
carry you forward on your chosen path.

Authors' Notes

This is a work of creative non-fiction. The authors have tried to recreate events, locales and conversations from their memories to the best of their abilities.

In preparing, researching and developing material for this book, the authors used a variety of sources of information including conversations with people they met during the walk and afterwards, public domain information from the internet, marketing material and literature provided by the various tourist offices, magazines, books and other printed material. Although the authors have made every effort to ensure that the information in this book was correct at press time, the authors and publisher do not assume and hereby disclaim any liability to any party for any loss, damage, or disruption caused by errors or omissions, whether such errors or omissions result from negligence, accident, or any other cause.

Table of Contents

The Road Not Taken

Two roads diverged in a yellow wood,
And sorry I could not travel both
And be one traveler, long I stood
And looked down one as far as I could
To where it bent in the undergrowth;

Then took the other, as just as fair
And having perhaps the better claim,
Because it was grassy and wanted wear;
Though as for that, the passing there
Had worn them really about the same,

And both that morning equally lay
In leaves no step had trodden black
Oh, I kept the first for another day!
Yet knowing how way leads on to way,
I doubted if I should ever come back.

I shall be telling this with a sigh
Somewhere ages and ages hence:
two roads diverged in a wood, and I —
I took the one less traveled by,
And that has made all the difference.

By Robert Frost

Acknowledgments

The authors wish to thank and recognize the following people for their assistance in various areas:

To Alex & Lola Chang for creating the spark that launched us on this path and Robert Ward who inspired us to write the book.

To the members of the Via Francigena Yahoo group, particularly Silvia Nilsen, William Marques, Ann Milner and Peter Robins, for your initial support and inspiration.

To Brandon Wilson, Paul Chinn & Babette Gallard, Alberto Conte, Eric Sylvers, James Martin, Jeff Sypeck, thank you for your valuable contributions, both prior to and after the journey.

We are indebted to Doctor Gillian Thompson, Professor Emeritus of History at the University of New Brunswick, for assisting us with Charlemagne's travels through Italy.

We are grateful to the various people we met along the Via Francigena and to those who bestowed sincere hospitality including: Gabriella; Herve and Luciana; Elisa and Graziana; the Gasparotto brothers (Roberto, Pietro Paolo and Giovanni) and Alessandra Costanza; Giancarlo Bindolini; Cesar Bolognesi and Riccardo Vignati; Pier Luigi Cappelletti; Danilo Parisi; Vittoria and Angelo; and Hilde. And a special recognition to all the people who work in all the *monasteri, conventi* and *ostelli*.

And a special appreciation to all the too numerous to mention friendly, helpful, and curious Italians who greeted us and kept our spirits high. This includes all those who made a special effort assisting us to get back on track when we were lost.

A special recognition to David & Mary and John & Ingrid, whom we met on the walk, and who later assisted us with the book; and to all the pilgrims we met along the way, especially Giuseppe.

We would like to honor our fellow pilgrim and friend, Cesare Cortesi, who acted as our guardian angel and blessed us with his friendship. He also assisted us with the Italian language.

A warm, extra special *buon giorno* and *grazie mille* to Maria, wherever you may be, for the fond memories we shared. We hope our paths cross again. *Buen camino e buon viaggio.*

To Antonella, Santi, Maria, and Ticks, a heartfelt thank you for your generosity and hospitality before, during, and after our journey—our home away from home. Antonella also helped us with the Italian language.

We are ever indebted to Cathy Reed for her tireless editing efforts and her valued feedback and support; and to Flash Lewis for his wonderful creative design work for this book. And thank you to Jennifer Louise Taylor for her valued comments and feedback on our book cover, and a big hug and thank you to Kellie Burk for creating the interior maps, even with her very busy schedule. A special thanks to Giuseppa Aurucci who was an excellent teacher and resource for the Italian language.

We are indebted to Jannina Veit Teuten who gave us permission to use her map of the Via Francigena. We kindly recognize and thank Richard Scott Mowrer, son of author Paul Scott Mowrer; author Phil Cousineau; Tanisha Christie on behalf of author Nelson Demille; and architect Hugh Newell Jacobsen for permission to use their respective quotations.

We would like to pay special tribute to our friends too numerous to mention (especially those who committed extra time and effort) and to our families, for assisting us in the preparation of this book and providing valuable feedback, comments, and continuous support. Without you, this book would not have been possible.

And finally, thank you to every single person who was, in any way, part of our preparation, our journey, and the development of this book.

Prologue

Sometimes in life, the reasons for doing something become clear only after you have had the opportunity to reflect.

"You're crazy!" one of our friends politely stated when we told him that we planned to walk the Camino de Santiago in Spain. Yet, like us, over a hundred thousand folks each year choose to walk, bike or push their way 800 km across the top of Spain, and each year the numbers grow. Over the past ten years, more than one million people have made that journey.

Why did we decide to walk the Camino de Santiago? As with many other people, it could have been our desire to see a foreign country, or to undertake a physical challenge, or maybe just a strong need to do something different. That said, the experience left a lasting impression on us that was hard to put into words.

Moreover, why, after that, did we decide to seek another "crazy" adventure?

"An Italian Odyssey" is the story of our "camino" through Italy on the ancient trail, the Via Francigena, perhaps Europe's oldest pilgrim path. It is a route that is less well known, not as well mapped or signed, and decidedly more arduous than the Camino in Spain.

Our initial plan was to complete a 1,000-kilometer cultural and culinary walk from Switzerland and through the heart of Italy to Rome. But our adventure quickly took on a life of its own.

After making the symbolic crossing over the Swiss-Italian Alps, it didn't take us long to discover the nuances of Italian life, and to enjoy fine Italian cuisine and wonderful hospitality. While we experienced so many magical moments, we soon encountered frustration and despair as we faced unexpected challenges of navigating an ancient and often elusive trail.

Ultimately, we discovered the meaning of our "camino" and we walked the final steps to Rome proud to be modern day pilgrims. In many ways, it was a classical journey.

So this is the tale of our bittersweet journey of eating and walking our way to Rome. It's our first book, co-written by the two of us, so you, the reader, can experience our story from two different points of view. We hope you enjoy sharing our adventure.

Buon viaggio!
Julie and Neville

Part 1

Ambitious Expectations on the Way of Gaul

Martigny

Bourg-St-Pierre

Gran San Bernardo

Saint Oyen

Aosta

Verrayes

Arnad

Bard

Pont-Saint-Martin

Ivrea

I

A Calling

*"The longest journey
starts with a single step."*
– Lao Tsu, Tao Te Ching

JULIE

It was destiny.

That was the only rational conclusion we could arrive at when we found ourselves standing on a long dirt track, surrounded by farmland that stretched into infinity. We spun around 360 degrees; not a single person in sight. Neville consulted his maps.

"What are we doing and *where* are we?" I asked.

"We're 'farm whacking,'" was Neville's reply.

We had left the Abbazia di Chiaravalle della Colomba in the tiny commune of Alseno, walking along a quiet gravel road and expecting to follow signs that would point us toward the Via Francigena. But as we followed the road further out of the village, we noticed that the official route crossed a busy highway overpass.

"This doesn't make sense," Neville reasoned. "The signs point north, but we want to go southeast." He pointed to his homemade maps. "We have to go this way."

Frustrated, Neville mapped out an alternative route, following a series of faint, crooked lines that were the demarcations of farmland. "To hell with the official route; we'll 'farm whack' our way to Fidenza," he announced.

There we stood, surrounded by empty, dirt-brown farm fields, with rain clouds brewing on the horizon. I felt alone and lost. I hoped we would get to Fidenza before dark.

I was worried about where we would sleep that night. I had phoned earlier in the day to book accommodations, but could not reach anybody. And by now, I was hungry, so I also worried if we would even find a place to eat in Fidenza.

"So whose crazy idea was this anyway?" I asked Neville accusingly. "What have we got ourselves into?"

⟲⟳

Since the day we met, Neville and I had always been what I would call modern-day travelers. Neville, born in Australia, had assimilated some of that Australian aboriginal spirit. He was always ready to go on a "walkabout." As for me, I read about solo women travelers and dreamt about being one of those adventurous women who traveled "off the beaten track." To satisfy our wanderlust, in the early 1990s, Neville and I backpacked for almost a year, taking planes, trains, and buses, and at times hitchhiking our way around the world. As we got older we continued to travel, but our travel escapades had become less exotic; more planned and predictable.

In early 2007, determined to reignite our spirit of adventure, we hiked the famous Camino de Santiago in Spain. The Camino is an old pilgrim trail that snakes across the top of Spain, ending in Santiago de Compostela some 780 km later. Regardless of religion or beliefs, for many the Camino has a certain magic that leaves a lasting impact. It certainly did for us.

⟲⟳

NEVILLE

It was on the Camino that I met Alex and his wife Lola. They are owners of Fresco Tours, an adventure travel company based in Bilbao,

Spain, that provides guided walking tours on the Camino. Alex gave me the impression that there was another "camino" in Italy.

Once back in Canada, I soon learned the other "camino" in Italy was called the Via Francigena, a broad network of trails originating in ancient Francia (now France) and part of the backbone of a string of Roman and medieval roads leading to Rome. Via Francigena meant the "way of the Franks" and was used to describe the route that people living in Francia would take to get to Rome.

From Francia, pilgrims would cross the Alps, enter Italy at Gran San Bernardo, and travel south through the Valle d'Aosta. They then journeyed along a series of medieval paths, passing through the western reaches of the Po River valley. Near Parma, they would head southwest, over the Apennine Mountains, crossing into Tuscany, toward the coastal port city of Luni, and from there they would continue south through the walled cities of Lucca and Siena and enter the region then known as Latium before finally arriving in Rome.

In the year 990, the English Archbishop, Sigeric the Serious of Canterbury, went to Rome to receive the pallium (religious garment) from Pope John XV. On his return trip to England, he recorded the route he took, providing the first written documentation of the Via Francigena.

⸎

JULIE

For the next few months, Neville sought to find out everything he could about the Via Francigena. He read about the trail's origins and about explorers and emperors who had traveled the route, including Charlemagne, Napoleon, and Hannibal. He discovered there were Etruscan, Roman and medieval sites along the route.

"It's fascinating," Neville would periodically exclaim, as he continued to enlighten me about his discoveries. "Can you imagine walking through Italy? Just think of the history. And all that great food and wine—you'd like that."

What most excited me was the diversity of food and wine in the five regions of Italy that the Via Francigena passes through. From Neville's research, I learned that Switzerland and France influence the cuisine of the distinct region of Valle d'Aosta, a small French-speaking corner of northwest Italy. Fine cheeses include *Toma, Fontina DOP*, and also *Fromadzo DOP* – which is a firm cow's milk cheese dating back to the 15th century. Meat dishes include beef stew called *carbonnade*, breaded veal cutlets called *costoletta*, spicy blood sausages called *boudin*, and *mocetta*, a rare *prosciutto* made of various meats such as chamois, ibex or beef.

The rice capitals of Europe, Piedmont and Lombardy are located in the Po River valley. Here you find *risotto* dishes such as *panissa*—a typical *risotto* from Vercelli, *salame d'oca*—goose salami from Mortara, and *Risotto alla Certosina* from the Carthusian monastery of Certosa near Pavia. Piacenza is a center for *salumi* such as *Coppa Piacentina DOP*, and bacon known as *Pancetta Piacentina DOP*. In Emilia, you find *Prosciutto di Parma DOP*, Italy's best-known meat, and *Parmigiano-Reggiano DOP*, the king of cheeses. DOP means *Denominazione di Origine Protetta*, or Protected Designation of Origin, a product from a specified region that is made using defined methods and that satisfies a defined quality standard.

Further south, as the Via Francigena crosses the Apennine Mountains and enters the remote and tiny region of Lunigiana, the local cuisine includes dishes made with chestnuts (*castagne*) and wild game. Traditional foods include herb tortes called *torta d'erbe, lasagna bastarde* (lasagna made with chestnut flour), lamb from Zeri, pasta crêpe served with *pesto* and local cheese called *testaroli*, and wild boar (*cinghiale*).

Further south is central Tuscany, home to *fava, toscanelli,* and *cannellini* beans, as well as pasta dishes such as *tagliatelle*, homemade wide-ribbon *pappardelle*, and "rustic spaghetti" called *pici*, all mixed with large amounts of extra virgin olive oil. Other popular dishes include wild game such as rabbit, pigeon, duck, thrush, and pheasant.

Finally, entering the region of Lazio, the Via Francigena circles the old volcanic Lake Bolsena. Here they serve fish soup called *sbroscia*, as well as *corégone*—a lake salmon eaten roasted or boiled and served with different kinds of sauces. Another common dish is eel, typically fried and pickled with herbs and spices.

"I think we should walk the Via Francigena," Neville finally told me one day.

"You know I love to walk, I'll go anywhere, any time," I replied.

Nevertheless, I thought, at the time, that it was one of those passing suggestions that we don't always act on. However, the more Neville told me about the Via Francigena, the more intrigued I became.

❧

NEVILLE

"But there's one thing you ought to know," I told Julie one day. "We'll have to make all our own guidebooks and maps. There's no English documentation on the Via Francigena. We can't walk into our local bookstore and buy a guidebook, like we did for the Camino de Santiago in Spain."

In early 2008, I concluded that we could walk from Switzerland to Rome, about 1,000 km, in roughly 50 days. This amount of time factored in extra days for visiting some of the historic cities and sites along the route. We also decided that we would make this a cultural and culinary walking adventure through Italy, much like the Camino in Spain but with a larger focus on food and history.

I merged and translated the information I had collected on the Via Francigena. The preparation included creating homemade guidebooks, a painstaking procedure that involved downloading Italian documentation from the Internet, translating the information into English, and repackaging it into a booklet-style personal guidebook. For each stage, I included the number of kilometers, the walking time, the change in elevation, the type of terrain, and the level of difficulty.

I found and downloaded a series of rather dated topographical maps, 300 in total, and repackaged them into two booklet-style map books. They were not the best, but at least I could make out the names of the towns and villages and see the various demarcations and shadings of black that represented a road, a cluster of buildings, or farm pastures.

I also made an accommodation guidebook with possible places to stay along the route. Finally, with Julie's assistance, I created a cultural and culinary guidebook, identifying the typical and traditional foods and beverages found in each region we would pass through. This would be Julie's specialty. As a self-described "foodie," she was always keen on trying, and learning about, as many different culinary delights as possible.

After assembling all the information, I told Julie: "It's not going to be easy. Many sections are unmarked, and along some sections, especially in the north, it's dangerous to walk and one should take the bus. The terrain and the changes in elevation will be more demanding than on the Camino in Spain."

"Are you sure you want to do this?" I asked her.

"Yes. Walking the Via Francigena is just the kind of journey we're looking for," she replied.

She was right. It made perfect sense. The Via Francigena offered all the basics of a great adventure. We could explore Italy's Etruscan, Roman and medieval history, experience first-hand Italy's modern-day culture, and enjoy the fine foods and wines for which Italy is so famous.

"You couldn't ask for anything better," we reasoned.

By midsummer, however, we were both a bit concerned. We weren't sure we had everything figured out or that this would work as expected. But underneath any misgivings, there was something bigger, a force pulling us, and we decided we were ready to embark on what we expected would be the cultural and culinary "camino" of our lives through Italy.

We heard the call and we heeded it.

II

In the Footsteps of Napoleon

*"There is nothing like walking to get the
feel of a country. A fine landscape is like a
piece of music; it must be taken at the right
tempo. Even a bicycle goes too fast."*
— Paul Scott Mowrer

JULIE

When I awoke on the first real day of our little adventure, I was tired and groggy from too little sleep.

I slipped down from the top of the bunk bed, stumbled over our packs and clothes in the dark, stuffy room, and eventually made my way to the communal bathroom.

Thank God, it was only a few meters away. I didn't have to worry about someone seeing me disheveled, bagged out (the way I always am when I don't get enough sleep), and dressed in my "skimpies."

It usually takes me a good half-hour to wake up and I'm never sure which part of me is going to kick in first, the body or the brain. But there was no doubt it was my brain when I opened the bathroom door.

I quickly turned and fled back to our tiny room where Neville was reorganizing the clothes in his pack. "Oh man, I can't believe it. What a rude awakening!" I shouted.

"What are you talking about?" Neville asked.

"Some naked guy was in the bathroom taking a pee. Why can't people lock the door?"

"He must be one of those young guys that kept me awake last night; they were still drinking at 2:00 am." Neville assumed the five guys in their early twenties were on a booze vacation and he was astonished that a short time later they were all up and ready to leave.

⚬⚬⚬

Neville

We took the train from Thun to Martigny the day before, having decided to start our walk in Martigny, Switzerland for a few good reasons. First, from Martigny, it was roughly 1,000 km to Rome. This was a lovely round number. Second, Martigny was an old Roman city, and since parts of the Via Francigena followed the old Roman roads, it made sense to start there. Third, the city is home to the famous Saint Bernard Dog Museum. And finally, by starting in Martigny, we could make that all-important symbolic climb over the Alps, and that just seemed the proper way to start our journey.

Martigny is in the remote southwest corner of Switzerland in the French-speaking canton of Valais. Originally named Octodurus, when a Celtic tribe, the Veragres, settled in the region in the 5th century BC, it was the site of the Battle of Octodurus in 56 BC. Later, when conquered by the Romans in 15 BC, it became an important Gallo-Roman center, sandwiched between the Celtic and Mediterranean cultures of Europe.

Today the sleepy little city of some 15,000 is the regional capital of Valais. Located at the southwestern end of the Chemin du Vignoble, a tourist wine route stretching from Leuk to Sion to Martigny, it is home to more than a dozen wineries that produce and sell mostly white wines and some fruit wines. The most famous winery is the Morand Distillery, which produces *Williamine*, a pear brandy unique to the area.

I had reserved two bunk beds at Camping TCS Les Neuvilles, a two-kilometer walk from the south end of town. Martigny is located at the base of the Swiss Alps, so I had visions of us bunking down for the night in a large wooden, dormitory-style Swiss chalet with a big fireplace in the center. I had visions of a campsite at the edge of town, pleasantly surrounded by trees and woods. Instead, the campsite, and our home for the night, was sandwiched between a busy industrial road and a major highway. To me, it looked more like a parking lot for camper vans with little patches of grass here and there.

The staff directed us to an aging gray concrete building just across from the main office. Inside there were four separate rooms: one with two single beds occupied by an older couple; another with four beds, also occupied; and a large room with dormitory style bunk beds, occupied by at least ten people.

The host guided us to the fourth room, which was the size of a walk-in closet, with two triple bunk beds and a small desk. It reminded me of an old joke: "The room was so small that you had to go outside to change your mind." There were three small, narrow windows at the very top of the wall, just enough for a hint of ventilation. I prayed that we did not have any roommates. So much for my dreams of lying around enjoying a big fireplace in a chalet surrounded by Swiss countryside.

≈≈≈

JULIE

Later that same afternoon, after dumping our bags at the campsite, we went into town to explore Martigny's rich Roman and medieval history. There were many sights to see, but our priority was to visit the famous Musée et Chiens du Saint-Bernard (Saint Bernard Dog Museum). Inside there were displays explaining the history of the dogs and an array of artifacts and information boards that described the history of Gran San Bernardo and the hospice. They told the tales of many explorers and travelers (including the French pilgrim Saint Martin, the emperor Charlemagne, and Sigeric) and their difficulties crossing the Colle (Pass) del Gran San Bernardo.

The history of the dogs dates back hundreds of years. Many believe that the dogs originated from Assyria and that a series of wars and trade brought some of the original dogs first to Greece, then later to Rome, and finally to this Valais region of Switzerland between 1660 and 1670. According to a document from 1708, the dogs were kept at the monastery at Gran San Bernardo. In 1867, a Bernese gentleman, Henry Schumacher, presented the San Bernardo dogs in Paris, and in 1884 he founded the Swiss Saint Bernard Club.

In January 2005, the Barry Foundation took over the breeding of Saint Bernard puppies from the friars of the hospice at Gran San Bernardo. The foundation became a major supporter of the Saint Bernard Dog Museum, which opened in 2006 and is located in the old military warehouse adjacent to the Roman amphitheatre. The foundation was named after Barry, the famous Saint Bernard dog that lived from 1800-1814 and was responsible for saving many lives. To this day, the hospice always keeps one Saint Bernard dog named Barry.

The highlight for me was seeing so many Saint Bernard dogs at one place. Normally the museum is home to eight or nine dogs, but on this day, there were more like twenty. We saw a number of kennels that housed three or four dogs, from puppies to six-year-olds, and every kennel had a plaque with each dog's name, age and other characteristics. There was an outdoor viewing area with mats, tubes and blocks for the dogs to amuse themselves, but most of the dogs just lounged around or slept. Only the puppies were active, playing with one another and doing their best to annoy the lazy older dogs, who tried their best to ignore the puppies.

One of the workers brought a big six-year-old male named Helios into the viewing area. Standing about three feet tall, Helios was in his glory, basking in the special attention from the worker who petted him and played with him. He even lay down in front of me on his back and let me rub his tummy.

I instantly took a liking to Helios. I asked him if he wanted to be my guide dog up to the pass. He just looked at me with his big sad eyes and snuggled his snout against my leg. I thought he would be much happier roaming the hills, climbing the mountains and aiding walkers like me.

⚭

The following morning, even though both of us were tired because of the all-night partying outside our window, the stuffy room, and the uncomfortable bunk beds, we were enthusiastic to embark on the first day of our long walk.

As we passed a Roman amphitheatre and the still visible sections of an old Roman road, I felt a sense of pride and honor that I was here to walk this historic route to Rome. Neville told me that we would be walking a section of the trail known as Route Napoleon. Napoleon, the famous French emperor, used this same route when he left Martigny on the night of May 19, 1800 to cross the Alps and invade Italy, following his army of 40,000 troops that had left Martigny four days before.

The route is also part of the Via Francigena, the old pilgrim path that we would be following south all the way to Rome. Other famous people who had traveled this section included Julius Caesar in 57 BC and Charlemagne in 800 and 801 AD.

This was the first day, the easiest, of a three-day hike to the pass. Today we would climb nearly 400 meters, taking about six hours to walk 16 km to reach our first destination, La Douay. Over the three days, we would climb a total of 2,000 meters to arrive at the Colle del Gran San Bernardo before crossing into Italy.

We sauntered through the narrow streets of Martigny-Bourg, a small picturesque hamlet just south of Martigny. I let the details of what Neville was telling me slip away as I admired the colors and architecture of the buildings and the views of the vineyards that lined the slopes of the western valley walls in the distance. It was a beautiful sight and I was excited!

About one kilometer past Martigny-Bourg, the trail cut sharply to the left and climbed gradually higher into the woods. The ascent was on a dirt and grass trail, slippery at times because of the previous day's rainfall. Sections of the trail hugged the precipitous hillside, and in some places, there were sharp drop-offs into the valley below.

When we crossed the narrow Les Trappistes Pass, just west of the town of Sembrancher, we encountered an especially tricky section, which was slow going for me. There were many steep sections as we descended the slippery shale path down the mountainside into Sembrancher. As Neville bopped down the steep trail with no worries, I was super cautious. I slowly and carefully put one foot in front of the other, making sure I set my foot down flat and evenly on the ground.

I was walking carefully because, two months before, I had badly sprained my ankle. After two sets of x-rays, the doctors told me that, besides my badly sprained ankle, I had chipped a small piece of bone and had a hairline fracture.

So our training regime for our walk had been derailed. I was in no shape to continue with biweekly walks of twenty kilometers with a pack on my back, as Neville had planned. For the balance of the summer, I hobbled around the house and then progressed from short walks to the car to one-kilometer walks, gradually increasing the distance over the balance of four weeks. When we left for Martigny, I was able to walk five to ten kilometers in one stretch with a light daypack on my back.

"It may take me longer than normal, but we have a *long way* to go and I have to get over the Alps," I said to Neville.

I was a little apprehensive about walking with a badly sprained ankle, but I knew I could do it. I had a plan. I would walk purposefully and carefully on rugged terrain and take my time. I would use any available cold water, from a village fountain, river, or canal, to soak my ankle during the day to prevent any potential swelling, and when I got to our accommodation, I would ask for ice.

❧

NEVILLE

The climb out of Sembrancher to La Douay was slow. It was due south and straight up, climbing 200 meters along a narrow valley floor. We passed by several mountainside farms and I was impressed to see that some people had taken full advantage of solar technology, using the sun's energy to electrify their homes and fences.

The views ahead and behind us were spectacular. I could see all the way back toward Sembrancher. Mountains to the north, east and west surrounded us, and beautiful Swiss wood farmhouses dotted the mountainside.

The first day of any hike is tough, especially if you haven't been doing any serious long-distance walking for a while, and this day was no exception. The afternoon temperature had risen to 25 degrees, and with the humidity, it felt more like 35 degrees. My muscles wanted an extra day or two to get into shape and they were letting me know. Toss in a steep mountain climb with the heat and humidity, and my whole body was complaining.

In my case, it was my lower back that complained the most. Days before leaving, an old lower back pain had resurfaced. I found it uncomfortable to sit for long periods and even more difficult to stand straight. The doctor had told me some time ago that a slight compression of my lower spine was pinching some nerves. Usually the pain disappeared after a few days, so I rarely gave it much thought. However, on this first day, the nagging pain had returned.

So here we were, two middle-aged Canadians planning to journey all the way to Rome, one with a bum back and the other with a bum ankle. I was starting to think the idea was just a little fanatical and I was apprehensive about how successful we might be. In fact, I had visions of our adventure ending abruptly and us finding ourselves flying back to Canada sooner than planned.

༄

We arrived at the small hamlet of La Douay in the late afternoon. From our vantage point on the top of a hill, we could see a café and restaurant, and the bed and breakfast that would be our home for the night was right next door. The hamlet of La Douay is such a small place that you might miss it if you were driving through on your way to Italy. It straddles the road that heads south and up to the Gran San Bernardo. One side consists of a narrow strip of houses and a cluster of old, dilapidated buildings, and on the other side is Le Gîte Serge Favez as well as Le Catogne café and restaurant, the only place to eat in the area.

We descended the hill and a lone man standing in the parking lot waved us over. Serge, the owner of the little B&B, greeted us warmly.

Serge ran the B&B while his wife Sylviane managed the café and restaurant. Serge was quiet, humble, and probably younger than he appeared. I had the thought that perhaps he had left the "rat race" and found peace and solitude in this little village halfway up the Swiss Alps.

༄

JULIE
Serge showed us to our room at the back of the hotel, away from the roadside traffic and overlooking the river rushing by. I was instantly joyful. The room was bright, comfortable, and airy, and the beds looked so inviting. I lay on the bed and enjoyed the luxury of it all.

After my shower, I decided to check out the river. Surrounded by forest, it was an ideal place to soak my ankle. The water was cold, and as I immersed my ankle for a few minutes at a time, I played my musical recorder. I love playing outdoors, alone and surrounded by the peacefulness of nature. I reflected on the walk that day and prided myself on taking good care of my ankle. It had held up well; it was going to be okay.

When it started to get cool, I returned to the room and told Neville I wanted to go and write in my journal over a coffee. He joined me on a cozy bench seat at the restaurant bar. I ordered two coffees and we made notes about our first day of hiking. The coffees tasted so good that I ordered two more. We were shocked to discover the bill came to 12.80 Swiss francs, about 10 American dollars.

"Uh, oh," I said to Neville, "We'll have to put a limit on coffees until we get to Italy."

Dinner that night was not as exciting as I had hoped. It was a set menu, which included a puff pastry with mushroom sauce, a tiny side salad and dessert. Water and coffee were extra. It was expensive by Swiss standards for what we got. And to top it off, I don't eat mushrooms.

The next morning, we left for Orsières, climbing steadily higher, crossing through patches of woods and farm fields. When we arrived, we bought a snack at the grocery store and then found a spot at the river Dranse where I could soak my foot while we ate our pastries and fruit. The water was so cold I could only keep it in for a few minutes but it was the best ice pack I could have had.

I told Neville I wanted to go and check out the old town with its large church and high steeple. But this meant going back one kilometer in the direction from which we had come. Neville was not keen to stop and didn't think there was anything interesting to see.

"We won't get to Bourg-St-Pierre until five o'clock if we stop," he complained.

"So? I don't care about keeping to the time that's in the book. I want to enjoy the scenery along the way. I'll meet up with you." He reluctantly followed me into the old part of the town.

I arrived at the old church, which was massive, and different from other churches I had seen. I walked up the steps, expecting it to be closed, but it was open. Inside were many stained glass windows, gigantic columns, the ceiling restored with beautiful paintings, and the altar attractively decorated with artwork. I just stood there alone, in awe. I had never been in a church alone and it was dead quiet. It was a special feeling and a moment I will always remember.

Leaving Orsières, we climbed higher and higher. We stopped to look back at the views of the town and the valley with all the little villages dotted throughout the slopes against the backdrop of the high mountains. I was in heaven. I pinched myself and said to Neville, "I can't believe we're here, finally walking in Switzerland!"

There was something special for me about walking in Switzerland. My grandparents were born there, and since the first time I had visited the country I had dreamed of hiking it some day. Now here I was, passing through little Swiss villages full of distinctive old buildings, and throughout the valley, I saw those dark wood Swiss houses you see on postcards, complete with brilliant red geraniums on the windowsills. Lush green forests and never-ending farm fields

Chemin Historique-Route Napoléon – Switzerland

and pastures surrounded us. As I continued to walk and enjoy the physical beauty, I had a deeper appreciation of the land and people.

⊙☙⊙

NEVILLE

We continued our trek upwards. All the time we could see Orsières below us. We followed old farm tracks, still used today to move farm equipment, so they made for easy walking. We passed the small hamlet of Dranse, named after the river that flows through the valley and then made a steep climb to reach the small village of Liddes.

Once there, we sat on a bench outside a closed hair salon, eating a snack and watching the rain clouds close in. It became windy and started to rain. My past hiking experience reminded me that in the mountains the weather could be fickle. Unprepared modern-day hikers, and pilgrims in past years, have perished from what Mother Nature has thrown at them. We suited up, donning our rain gear and extra layers for warmth. Soon after, the rain stopped, the wind subsided and the sun was back out again. It was too hot to hike with all that gear, so off it came. Nevertheless, we kept it close by, just in case Mother Nature changed her mind.

It was already getting dark when we arrived in Bourg-St-Pierre. The clouds had moved back in again, accompanied by a light rain. I had expected Bourg-St-Pierre to be a "mini Whistler," similar to the famous ski resort north of Vancouver in Canada, dotted with trendy cafes, shops and boutiques. Instead, under a canopy of gray clouds, it looked barren and desolate, with almost all the shops closed and nobody on the streets.

The little hamlet of Bourg-St-Pierre dates from the year 800 AD. However, some experts say that a "Roman mansion" or roadside hostel first existed here in the first century. There is evidence of a Roman style fort built on top of a Celtic *oppidum*, or settlement, on the hill above the town.

I was hoping for a quaint bed and breakfast overlooking the valley, but all I saw was a campsite in the field below the main road. We went to investigate, but they had no rooms or beds for us; just plenty of tent sites, should we decide to pitch a tent. We walked through the old part of town and found a bed and breakfast but nobody answered the door. We passed a couple of closed hostels. This left us with our last alternative, the Hôtel & Restaurant du Crêt, and they gave us a room at the back of the hotel away from the road.

"I hope we get something more interesting than last night," I said to Julie as we entered the dining room. It was a set menu included with the cost of the room.

"It appears the menu of the day is *croûtes aux champignons*," Julie replied, making a face. Mushrooms again.

Though the meal was unexciting, our server was a cheerful young woman who took an immediate interest in us.

"Where are you from?" she asked. We hardly looked Swiss or Italian.

"We're Canadians," we told her. "We've been walking from Martigny for the past two days."

She responded in mock shock and told us with a smile, "You must be crazy."

"We plan to walk all the way to Rome," we then said.

"You are definitely crazy!" she announced. The smile was gone. I think she was serious this time.

She returned to our table a few minutes later and peppered us with questions about the route, the distance we would cover each day, and why we were doing it. Even though she thought we were crazy, she was obviously excited about "our little adventure."

The first two days of walking up the Swiss Alps had gone better than expected. In fact, I was not sure what I had expected; the thought of walking up and over the Alps had never crossed my mind until we decided to walk the Via Francigena to Rome. All in all, the experience was working out well: a well-marked trail, spectacular views, and even the weather had held up.

However, I was genuinely concerned about tomorrow's hike to the summit. The weather had turned sour and unless it improved overnight, we might find ourselves walking the entire day in the rain as we climbed another 800 meters. I prayed that it would not rain and particularly that it would not snow.

III

The Initial Test

*"Obstacles are those frightful things you see
when you take your eyes off the goal."*
– Hannah Moore

JULIE
Neville was already awake and organizing his pack when I woke at
7:00 am. He's always been the early riser. As I struggled to get out
of bed and mobilize my brain and body, he told me he was going
downstairs to see if breakfast was available. I heard him bound
down the stairs.

As I thought about breakfast, I was looking forward to fresh
warm croissants and a selection of French and Swiss cheeses and
meats. I wanted a hearty breakfast because I knew there would be
nowhere to get food along the way.

Neville came back to the room and announced there was a bus-
load of French seniors in for breakfast.

My heart skipped a beat. "Oh no! Does that mean they've eaten
everything?"

"I don't know but let's get down there," he replied.

I got myself together and we rushed downstairs, saying a quick
"Bonjour" to the owners as we passed through the bar, and made our
way into the large dining room.

I couldn't believe my eyes. The room where we'd eaten in solitude the previous night now hosted a large, boisterous crowd of seniors.

We found the last set of seats in the restaurant and sat down waiting for service. Impatient, I surveyed the dining room looking for food and saw a table near the dining room entrance, tucked away in the corner.

"Over here," I motioned to Neville as I made my way to the table, "This must be our breakfast, or what's left of it."

It looked like there had originally been a grand selection of items including cold cereal, French bread, fruit preserves, honey, and a variety of meats and cheeses. We picked through the remaining bits of food, splitting the last three pieces of cheese, two pieces of meat and some bread. "The croissants are all gone," I sniveled, glancing at the empty basket. So I politely stopped the server, who was rushing back and forth between the bar and the dining room with cups of coffee and tea for the seniors.

"Plus des croissants, s'il vous plaît?" I asked him.

He just looked at me as if I had my nerve to ask. Then he picked up the basket and walked away.

"Just because these people have devoured them, it doesn't mean I should go without," I whispered to Neville. "Besides, they're not walking any great distance today. Do they really need that many calories to climb back on a bus and sit in comfortable seats while sights whiz by?"

The server returned with an empty wooden basket and told us there were no more croissants. I was *très misérable.* "I can't believe it," I said as we returned to our seats.

Neville was calm. "Forget it," he said. "Let's just eat what we can and get going."

I continued to sulk.

We ate our scraps, anxiously waiting for our coffee to arrive. The same server passed us by several times, but with no coffee. He was obviously preoccupied with the group.

"But when do we get served?" I asked Neville. "We can't sit here all morning."

Finally, I got the waiter's attention. He took me over to a small machine sitting on the counter behind the group of seniors. It was noisy and I couldn't hear anything he said, but I understood what he was getting at.

"Great!" I grumbled under my breath, returning to the table. "We have to settle for machine coffee, while the group of seniors got special coffee. How can they do this? First, they cheated us of croissants, then coffee. The nerve!"

"Let's just eat and get going!" Neville repeated.

He's so logical and accommodating!

"Well I wonder if these people would appreciate it if they knew we were walking up to the Col today," I added. I gulped the rest of my bland machine-made coffee and said. "Okay, then, let's go!"

⁂

Before we left, we made a stop at the hotel gift shop, as there would be nowhere to get food along the way. With no food shops open in the village that morning, we had to choose from whatever was available in the gift shop.

We looked for some decent snacks to sustain our energy over the next several hours during our ascent to the Col, but all we found worth eating was a small bag of cashews, a fruit bar, and one Snickers bar for each of us. The cashews and fruit bar were a good choice. The Snickers bars, well...even though they were my favorite chocolate bar when I was a kid, I don't eat them now unless I have no choice—I feel they don't have any nutritional value. However, today they would have to do as our only other source of energy.

On our way out of town, we passed by the historic church and the old hospice building that Napoleon had apparently slept in on his march to Rome. We crossed the Dranse River over an old stone bridge after passing remnants of an old castle, and I stopped to

Misty clouds – En route to the Great St Bernard Pass

take photographs looking back at Bourg-St-Pierre. The mountain scenery was incredible: situated on the slope of a mountain and tucked into a little valley, the village looked serene. Rolling green pastures, dotted with the occasional Swiss mountain hut, surrounded us. Because it looked so natural and untouched,

I couldn't imagine skiers or busloads of tourists swarming the place.

Soon the clouds started rolling in. I definitely did not want it to rain today. Trying to remain positive, I sang: "Blessed are we, it will be rain free; blessed are we, it will be rain free."

"This hiking is easy," I thought. Today's climb would be our steepest yet, an 800-meter ascent, according to our travel notes. "But this is not so bad—it's been a gradual incline so far. If the walk is like this, it should be a cinch walking to the Col," I continued thinking.

Just before Lac des Toules, the reservoir and dam, the clouds got heavier and darker and it started to sprinkle. We donned our pack covers and ponchos, just in case, but after 20 minutes it was nothing more than a light drizzle. "That's good, but I'll leave my poncho on anyway," I said to myself.

I stopped to take in the views and for what would probably be my last photo-taking opportunity. We were deep in the heart of the mountains now. The Alps loomed around us and we were surrounded by thick forest and occasional sections of green pasture. I watched the heavy mist and clouds roll in and cling to the side of the mountains, camouflaging the snowy peaks. "Mmm, it better not rain!"

Walking blissfully along, I made up and sang my own French tune, to ward off rain: *"Partez, nuages, partez. Je voudrais le soleil. Montre-toi s'il te plaît! Je voudrais le soleil."*

❧

Neville
We climbed a muddy hill that skirted the construction going on at the dam. When we reached the top, I saw a group of hikers, guided by a short young man with a donkey, coming down the hill. As the group came closer, I noticed that each hiker was carrying a light daypack while the balance of the gear was piled high onto the donkey's back.

I stopped and talked to a few of the people as they passed by. I asked them what they were doing.

"We're on an organized tour heading for Martigny," an older couple told me. They were making their way down from somewhere high in the Alps above us.

Julie, keen to practice her French, jumped into the conversation and asked, "*Est-ce qu'il pleut là où nous allons*—is it raining up ahead?"

"Not at this moment," the young man replied in English. He had a serious, almost blank expression and continued to walk on without saying anything else.

After we parted, Julie turned to me and said, "That was too funny."

While Julie thought it was too funny, I had visions of it raining and even snowing up further. I was trying to figure out how far we had come and how far we had to go before reaching the Colle del Gran San Bernardo.

⊱⊰

The Colle del Gran San Bernardo (Great St Bernard Pass) is one of the oldest Alpine routes in Europe and has been in use at least since the Bronze Age. Tribes, armies, wayfarers, emperors, saints, popes, and simple pilgrims have crossed over the pass. Back in 387 BC, Brennus led his army of Cisalpine Gauls over the pass and on to Rome. Brennus successfully attacked and defeated Rome, capturing the entire city except for the Capitoline Hill. In the year 217 BC, Hannibal, with a team of elephants and 50,000 troops, purportedly crossed the Alps, though there is little evidence suggesting that he crossed at the Colle del Gran San Bernardo. In 57 BC, Julius Caesar's army crossed the pass to defeat the tribal peoples of Martigny, who worshipped the Celtic god Poenn. Centuries later, in the spring of 773 AD, an army led by Charlemagne (Charles the Great), crossed into Italy to conquer the Lombards. Charlemagne's uncle, Bernard, led one division across the Alps at this location while Charlemagne crossed the Alps at another location. Charlemagne returned to Rome in 800 AD and was crowned Imperator Augustus, or Holy

Roman Emperor. He returned to his home town of Aachen in 801 AD, crossing the pass for the final time.

I gazed back from where we had come. We were not carrying much water and our meager snacks were not going to last long, especially if the weather got worse. As we climbed higher, the air was damp and cool, and there were heavy misty clouds swirling around the nearby mountains. The light drizzle had turned into a steady, soft rain and the wind was picking up, blowing directly toward us. We had to keep our heads down to avoid getting our faces lashed by the rain and wind.

Up ahead, just beyond the reservoir, I spotted an old stone cabin and we made a dash for it. The little doorway into the cabin was bolted shut so we huddled as close to the wall as possible, taking shelter from the wind and rain. My worst fears about the weather turning sour were coming true. I estimated that at this rate it would take us perhaps four more hours of hiking before we reached the pass. I was worried.

⌒⌒⌒⌒⌒

JULIE

It was about noon. "Time for a snack," I said eagerly, feeling I deserved some food after three hours of hiking. I convinced Neville that we should indulge.

Dropping my heavy wet pack, I waited for Neville to pull out the fruit and nuts. Reluctantly, and with a certain amount of grumbling, he took off his pack and pulled off his poncho and pack cover. He fished into his daypack and eventually dug out our meager snack of cashews and fruit bars. I gobbled them down. Then I suggested we share a Snickers bar. As he mumbled something, another human being came up behind us.

"I can't believe there's someone else out here," I said.

The man approached us and I motioned for him to take refuge beside us, suggesting there was plenty of room. I tried to communicate with him but my French was poor, and it seemed he only spoke French. But when I commented on the lousy weather, he understood that much and agreed. I offered him some of our snacks, but he declined. I had a feeling he wished he wasn't there, or he wanted to be alone, but probably, like us, he was thankful for the shelter.

I turned back to Neville and asked him again for a Snickers bar. Either he had chosen to ignore me or he had forgotten about it, because he had already zipped up his bag and was securing the pack cover. I knew I was out of luck; he wasn't going to open it again. Clearly, he wanted to get going. I pouted as I struggled to put on my backpack.

We left our stone cabin refuge and the Frenchman and plowed our way through the increasingly relentless rain and wind.

The narrow stone path wound up the mountain and the terrain became more desolate. It was foggy and difficult to see. We passed black and white cows grazing high up on the misty slopes of the farmstead La Pierre. Their heavy cowbells clinked and clunked as they moved about, seemingly unfazed by the weather. It was a brief but welcome diversion during our lonely walk through the driving wet wind. For me, it temporarily broke the isolation I was feeling.

The rain got heavier and heavier, endlessly pelting us. I took breaks often, turning around to look back at where we had come from—my back was my only shelter.

Water was creeping through my poncho and jacket and I felt the cold moisture against my skin. I was becoming irritable and unhappy.

Half an hour later, we arrived at a spot where several trails intersected. We stopped and squinted through the heavy rain and fog to read the signs and figure out which way to go. As we stood there, the Frenchman, whom we had left behind at the shelter came up behind us and just kept walking. "The nerve," I thought, "How dare he leave us behind?" Now we were truly alone.

We squinted to see the signs for Chemin Historique—Route Napoleon, the route we were looking for. My heart skipped a beat.

Beside the words, "Route Napoleon" were the words: "2 hours—Colle del Gran San Bernardo." I couldn't believe it.

"Oh, my God! Two more hours of walking in this lousy weather!" I felt discouraged and miserable.

As we descended toward the Dranse Valley, I saw the trail continue into oblivion. Two hours felt like an eternity. The reality of our situation really sunk in.

We passed a collection of old buildings that looked like they'd been there for centuries. I think it was the locale of L'hospitalet and I imagined Napoleon and his army resting there. I would have loved to rest there too, but the weather was not cooperating, so I plowed on. I stopped several times to look back at the buildings, imprinting their image in my mind. The relentless rain and wind thrashed against my face.

My spirits were beginning to fade, so I started singing: "We must keep going on, just like Napoleon." And I just kept singing it to drum up the energy and perseverance to battle the horrific conditions.

About fifteen minutes later, I stopped to catch my breath. Neville was ahead of me. Beyond him in the distance, I saw a bus pass by. I assumed it was heading up to the pass; there was only one way to go, and that was up.

After twenty minutes, I watched the same bus return, but this time it was full of passengers. I smiled and waved as it went by. Part of me felt a moment of satisfaction and pride for having the willingness and spirit to be walking to the pass in this godforsaken weather and I wanted the passengers to know. But in reality, they probably thought I was crazy.

Not long after the bus was gone, I was back to feeling miserable again. When I crossed over the mountain road, Neville was already on the other side. He shouted back to me that he could see the trail going straight up the side of the mountain.

My heart sank to the bottom of my soaked hiking boots. I

looked up at the steep climb ahead. It hadn't occurred to me that we still had to go higher, that it would actually get steeper! I had just been concentrating on walking, one step at a time. I was completely disheartened.

I just wanted the rain and wind to stop but I knew this wasn't going to happen. I had had enough; I didn't even have the energy to speak. I felt like a soaked, weak, helpless idiot.

I noticed off to the right of the trail, a huge, tall (maybe 20 meters high) cement structure that looked like a Martian spaceship with four legs and a large round head. With barely enough energy to say the words, I squeaked out to Neville, "I'm going to take shelter under this thing. I have to stop. If I'm going to climb this steep mountain, I need something to eat, *now!*"

Neville reluctantly followed me. As soon as we got underneath the spaceship, I demanded a Snickers bar. Neville didn't move.

"*The Snickers bar!*" I repeated firmly.

"Okay, okay," he said, relenting, "but we can't stay here long; we have to keep moving or we'll freeze to death."

While Neville fought with his pack to pull out the bars, I tried pulling off my waterlogged gloves, which seemed to be molded permanently to my hands. I tried to ring them out, but I had so little strength. Then I pulled off my drenched poncho to shake it off, thinking that would help but it only made matters worse. Seconds later, I was freezing cold.

"Aren't you glad we didn't eat these earlier?" Neville said smugly. "Now, hurry up. We've got to get moving!" he added anxiously.

"I know, I know," I replied, inhaling the Snickers as fast as I could.

I got ready to brave the elements again. Having fuelled myself physically, I mustered up some positive energy to continue. "All right," I said to myself. "You can and you must do this; just keep on moving."

I tried hard but I lacked the mental energy. I tried to remain positive and appreciate the fact that we had gotten this far. I even tried thinking about all the people in the past—Hannibal, Caesar, and Napoleon, and all those before us who had braved these mountains in possibly worse conditions.

I waffled back and forth between positive and negative thoughts. At times, it seemed I was floating in and out of reality, hallucinating, believing that this really could not be happening. To keep sane, I sang aloud my favorite yoga chants. I mustered all the energy I had, releasing my loudest yoga mantra ever— *"Sat Nam"*—thinking the Gods would give me a break. But they didn't. So I trudged on, floating in and out of this state for what felt like an eternity.

Then I looked ahead and saw another sign: "4 km." I froze, my heart sank, and I nearly collapsed.

Surrounding me were raw, appalling conditions—cold vicious wind and heavy rain. Mucky water gushed down between the rocks, creating little rivers that flowed over my boots. With every step I took on the jagged, rocky terrain, the trail became steeper, more rugged and more slippery. I stumbled often, cautious of trying not to twist my injured ankle. I stopped every few moments to compose myself before continuing.

"Alright," I yelled out, "I've had enough punishment for one day. Please have mercy on me. I can't go on like this. I just want it to end."

Tears streamed down my face. I stopped and turned around with my back to the wind and rain, breathing heavily. I broke down, crying and sobbing, and heaving uncontrollably. I became fearful for my own survival, as if God was punishing me.

Then I yelled at the top of my lungs, "Please let this stop! I don't want this anymore. I can't go on. I am so f…g tired of this. Please God; just let me be at the monastery."

Neville had stopped and was staring back at me with a worried look on his face. "What's wrong? Are you alright?"

"No…you *bloody Martian,* I'm not!" I sobbed loudly. *"I can't take this anymore!"*

❦

NEVILLE

It was at that moment I realized Julie had lost it, gone completely crazy. The wind and rain and cold—everything was too much for her.

"She's freaking out!" I thought to myself.

I tried to calm her down: "It's okay. It'll be alright, we don't have much longer." It was a lie because I really had no idea where we were and how far it was to Gran San Bernardo.

She just stood there stunned, not saying a word. I wasn't sure if she'd heard me with the wind howling all around us or if she was trying to make sense of what I had just said. Then she gave me a nudge to motion me forward. She wanted to get moving.

After about ten minutes, I turned and said, "Let's walk on the road." It only made sense. The path had turned into a swollen creek and it was getting impossible to walk. Eventually, one of us would slip and twist an ankle or, worse, break something.

"What, are you crazy?" Julie shouted back. "Then we have to deal with the cars on this steep and winding road in addition to facing the wind and rain. And there's no shoulder on the road! I don't think so!"

"It will be easier," I protested. "It will be flat, easier to walk on, no wet rocks, and the terrain will be consistent."

I'm not sure if she agreed with me or was just too stunned to protest, but she followed me onto the road.

Shortly after, I heard Julie chanting to the rhythm of our poles hitting the pavement. At least she was chanting, but then maybe she was slowly going insane. I told her to stay right behind me, so I could block the rain and wind.

"One footstep at a time," I called out, and we marched bit by bit up the road.

We passed another sign: "2 km." Julie broke down again. She sobbed and yelled. I knew how she felt. Our gloves and boots were soaking wet, our hands and fingers were frozen. It was pouring rain, and the wind was blowing directly into our faces. There was heavy fog, so we couldn't see more than twenty meters ahead. Under these conditions, two kilometers felt like two hundred kilometers. Then I heard thunder, not once but twice, and I wondered what was coming next—snow, hail, what? Would it ever end?

I yelled out, "Just think of walking to the 'Roost' in the rain." Julie laughed, and I am sure this helped lift her spirits. I chuckled too. When we had done our practice walks at home, the Roost Farm Bakery was often our destination for a snack or lunch. It made the walking worthwhile, especially if it was raining.

⁕

JULIE

Neville lifted my spirits a little. I thought about our indulgences at the Roost Farm Bakery: the hot Montreal smoked meat sandwiches, the great homemade soups, and the delicious sweet treats. I could just taste them in my mouth.

We plodded slowly along the shoulder of the road. I kept close behind Neville, grateful he was in the front, taking the full brunt of the storm and sheltering me. I pushed on, one little step at a time. I chanted to myself and hummed. I was thankful there was little traffic on the road as we inched our way up toward the pass. I had just gotten into a good rhythm when I heard a vehicle coming up behind us.

We both turned and Neville said, "There's a bus coming up the road."

We stopped and moved over to let the bus pass by, but instead it stopped just behind us. We looked at the bus driver and he looked back at us. He motioned us over.

In an instant I thought, "We can't be that far now! I'm sure if we've made it this far, we can walk the rest of the way."

One part of my brain told me that I was too proud to get on the bus. I wanted to get to our destination on my own feet. But the other side of my brain said, "Of course, you fool, get on that bus."

Neville shouted back at me, "Let's go!"

We dashed across the road and jumped on. We thanked the bus driver profusely. What a relief!

We stood for the short two-minute bus ride. It felt very strange, almost surreal, to be suddenly in a vehicle traveling twenty times faster than we had been walking only a moment earlier. I felt all the people on the bus staring at us. They probably wondered what crazy fools we were to be walking this road in such terrible weather.

It was only about a kilometer to the monastery. "Darn, I had a feeling we were that close," I said to Neville. It was one of those moments when you are forced to make a split-second decision. Was it right or wrong? I wondered. I reassured myself it was the right thing to do at that time.

❦

At the monastery, I pushed open the ancient, heavy wooden doors, passed through a second set of doors that helped keep out the bitter cold wind and the snow, and entered the hospice with a huge sense of relief. I was waterlogged from head to toe and chilled to the bone. All I wanted to do was get out of my soaking wet clothes and boots, and collapse.

A plump woman in her 60s, wearing large-framed glasses, was standing in the long, wide hallway talking to other guests. She looked up and greeted us.

I found a spot against the wall to put my pack down. I started digging into my pack to get some dry clothes when the woman interrupted me. She had something different in mind for me. She turned to us, speaking what seemed to be a combination of German and French.

"Mi dispiace! No comprendo," I said to her, mixing up my Italian and Spanish. I'm sorry but I don't understand.

I continued to burrow in my pack, frantically fishing out my fleece and other dry clothes. The woman kept talking, this time in German and Italian. I looked up at her dumbfounded, and she motioned us to follow her to another door.

But I didn't want to follow her. All I could imagine was stripping off my wet clothes, jumping in a hot shower, and putting on warm dry clothes. I was shivering. "Why doesn't this woman understand?" I thought.

But she ignored me and opened a short creaky door to a set of stairs below. She explained something, but still I didn't understand. Then a man emerged at the bottom of the stairs. It was the Frenchman.

He called us down to the basement. It was huge and, surprisingly, warm, with an ancient look and feel about it. Thousands of racks lined the whole space. There were more than enough hooks for an army to hang their wet clothes. A collection of clothes, skis, boots and other old items from over the years had been stashed in corners and along the walls.

The Frenchman, in a combination of French and hand signals, explained the routine. He motioned us to take off all of our wet clothes and then showed us where to hang them. He took old newspapers and stuffed them into one of our boots. This would help sop up the water. I certainly hoped they would be dry by morning.

"Okay, now I want to go back upstairs and have a shower and get into my dry clothes," I said to Neville.

But again the plump woman had something else in mind. She led us into the *salle à manger* to have tea with one of the monks.

I wasn't interested in having tea with the monk; I wanted to get my soaking clothes off! A young woman emerged from the *salle à manger*. She spoke English, so I told her I needed to have a shower and get into some dry clothes before having tea. She conveyed this to the woman and the monk and they both agreed I could go.

The older woman gave us directions to our room and I was in awe as I entered it. We had a large, spacious room all to ourselves. It was decorated simply with old, chunky, dark wooden furniture and two huge antique beds covered with bright orange bedspreads. We quickly stripped off our wet clothes, changed into some dry clothes, grabbed our skimpy, hi-tech "shammy" towels and some soap and headed for the showers, only to learn we needed a key.

We returned downstairs, and the same plump woman nearly pushed us into the *salle à manger* and made us sit down for tea.

"But what about my shower?" I asked.

We finally gave in and sat down opposite the monk. He served us lukewarm, weak tea. Even so, I felt privileged to have the opportunity to talk with a monk. We were interested to hear what he had to say and we had plenty of questions.

We had read earlier about the hospice. We knew it was more than 1,000 years old. In the early 900s, the Huns and Saracens swept through the region, terrorizing travelers, raping, pillaging, destroying everything in their path, and demanding steep payments for safe passage. Anxious about the disruption to merchants and pilgrims, King Rudolf III of Burgundy booted out the Huns and Saracens. He asked the Archdeacon of Aosta, Bernard of Menthon, who had spent

The hospice at Great St Bernard Pass

years aiding travelers, to manage the construction of a hospice at the pass. The hospice of the Colle del Gran San Bernardo became a welcome refuge, offering safety, shelter and food to pilgrims, clerics, and travelers on what was an extremely dangerous mountain route.

The monk was just starting to tell us a story about the hospice when a middle-aged woman with white hair, wearing a long, cream-colored, heavy woolen full-length dress that looked more like a robe, appeared at the doorway. She wore a large metal cross around her neck and large wide-framed glasses and held a walking stick. She greeted the monk with a friendly, warm smile, speaking to him in Italian.

I understood a few things she said. She was asking for a place to eat and sleep for the night.

At first, I was a little annoyed. We were summoned to appear before the monk, and now a woman, who had suddenly appeared out of nowhere, had interrupted us.

There was something mysterious about her. She certainly didn't look like she had hiked up the Col in the rainstorm. Where had she come from, and how did she get here? Where was she going? The woman and the monk kept talking. I expected the conversation to finish quickly, so we could continue our visit with the monk, but that didn't happen. The woman had stolen the monk's attention. He got up from the table to fetch something for her and never returned.

So I jumped up from the table, and said to Neville, "I'm outta here—I'm going for my shower."

At 7:30 pm, a bell rang loudly throughout the hospice, calling us to dinner. We entered the *salle à manger* and saw the Frenchman and a young man with the young woman who had helped translate our conversation earlier. But there were no monks. I was under the impression we would be eating with them, but the table was set for only six, so I knew that would not be the case. I was extremely disappointed. A few minutes later, the Italian woman with the woolen dress appeared.

The dinner conversation was a lively mix of languages. The young couple did most of the talking, flipping between Italian, French, and English. We learned the young woman was an American living in Lausanne with her Swiss boyfriend, who was a student. They liked to travel and they were hiking a small region of the Alps. She had taken some time off work, and he had a break from medical school.

When we told them we were surprised to learn that wines were produced in the same region we had just walked through, the young man told us that his parents had a vineyard and produced wine nearby. He said that part of him wanted to be on the farm helping his parents, but he thought the proper thing to do was to go to medical school. As he talked about their vineyard and about how he loved to be involved with the wine business, I could hear the passion in his voice. Neville, with his business background, suggested there was a way he could still work in the vineyard and study business and economics with the wine business in mind.

I tried to strike up a conversation with the Frenchman using my poor French, but I didn't get far. He was quiet and seemed shy. I assumed he didn't want to talk much or else he was embarrassed about conversing with someone who spoke poor French.

Instead, I tried my Italian with the Italian woman. Her name was Maria. She told me she had walked to Santiago de Compostela. I wanted to ask her how she had come to the hospice and where she was going next. I had many questions for Maria, but she left dinner sooner than I expected. There was definitely something mysterious about Maria.

It was 9:00 pm when I settled into bed. I was tired and ready for sleep. As I attempted to write the last few words in my journal, I reflected on the day.

Why did we have to endure such a horrific hike? Was it a test, a punishment, a message?

This had been the worst and most difficult hike in my life. For all my singing, humming, chanting and positive thinking, it did not change the outcome. The hike influenced my psyche in a way I had never experienced before.

After such a grueling physical and emotional challenge, I came to realize that I had chosen to hike this challenging, isolating, demanding mountain pass knowing the possibility of vile weather. I had taken that chance, and I had to face the consequences of taking on something that I knew was unusual and difficult.

"Merci pour mon existence." Thank you for my existence. God bless me, I made it here!

As I closed my eyes, I couldn't help but think about the history of this place and all those it had served in the past, including crazy adventurers like us. I imagined how Charlemagne, Caesar, and Napoleon must have felt crossing the pass at Gran San Bernardo and entering the hospice centuries ago. I felt like I could truly appreciate what it must have been like to climb these mountains—to be an explorer or pilgrim in such forbidding conditions without the modern conveniences we enjoy today. I admired their courage.

Well, I guess I had some too!

I closed my eyes and I remembered Napoleon's words: *"What is possible is within everyone's range—I want to attempt the impossible."*

IV

Welcome to Italy

*"For once you have tasted flight you will
walk the earth with your eyes turned
skywards, for there you have been and
there you will long to return."*
– *Leonardo da Vinci*

JULIE

"What a glorious morning! Yes, we have been blessed," I shouted
with glee as I stepped outside the hospice and was greeted by
absolutely clear skies. It was stunning how different it was—so
brilliant with the sunlight reflecting off the snow-capped mountains. The air was a cool, crisp and dry six degrees Celsius. We could
see mountains and more mountains all around us—north, south,
east, and west—with their peaks covered with fresh snow about 300
or 400 meters above us. Looking north towards Switzerland, we
could see all the way down to the valley floor.

As I stood on the rocks, captivated by the majestic 360-degree
view, I wondered why it couldn't have been this beautiful the day
before. It was almost impossible to imagine how it was yesterday,
walking up to the Col in the "storm from hell"—the pelting rain,
the violent winds whipping the rain into our faces like pellets, and
the temperature dropping to almost zero. Now I felt like walking

back down the road to where we had jumped on the bus, just so I could say I walked the whole way!

We rambled around on the rocks and outcrops, like kids in a playground, checking out everything we hadn't seen the day before. Located 2473 meters above sea level, the hospice sits on barren, rocky terrain, half surrounded by tourist kiosks. We snapped photo after photo of the mountains and views of Switzerland from where we had come, and then more photos of the lake and mountains of Italy where we were heading.

Before leaving, I went back to stand on the highest plateau of the rocky outcrop near the hospice to imprint the entrancing view into my memory one more time. Wisps of clouds coming up from the valley floated from one mountaintop to another, like a veil opening up to expose the scenery and then closing. There was something special about this place. It was peaceful and serene.

I now felt on top of the world, physically and mentally. I was ready for Italy—ready to begin our cultural and culinary walk along the Via Francigena all the way to Rome.

"This is going to be great," I exclaimed with excitement to Neville. "If we can survive that hellish experience yesterday, we can survive anything."

Entering Italy was more casual than we expected. Being an honorable and honest Canadian, Neville thought we should go and see the Italian border guard to show our passports and clear customs.

"Nev, I don't think we need to do that; I'm sure he'll come out to see us."

"No, I think we should go," Neville reiterated.

Neville approached the passport control booth, which was the size of a telephone booth. The middle-aged Italian border guard stood inside looking through the small window and waved him on. He wasn't the least bit interested in checking our passports or knowing who we were.

"See, I told you so." I said.

Neville on top of the Italian Alps – Colle del Gran San Bernardo

"Yeah, I know, he must have thought we were just those crazy people who walk up and down here," Neville replied.

Neville still thought this was odd, though—out of character for Italian border guards. The many times we had visited Italy, they had always enforced strict rules regarding visitors reporting to the authorities.

"So here we are in Italy, as easy as a stroll in the park," Neville commented.

"Well, it depends on how you look at it," I reminded him, thinking of what we had been through to get to this point.

We rambled around a bit, climbing some small rocky hills to take pictures of the mist rising from the valley floor and lifting higher and higher to meet us. We looked back toward the Swiss Alps and relished that special feeling of having the place all to ourselves.

"It's astonishing how a designated physical border high in the Alps can signify a change in cultures," I commented to Neville. We hadn't gone more than 500 meters from the Swiss-Italian border before we knew that we were definitely in Italy!

Deeply absorbed in a quiet, peaceful walk descending the old Roman road, we were suddenly "yanked" back to reality. We heard a strange noise and looked around to see a bus whizzing up the twisting road from the valley below, blaring its horn as it rounded every bend in the road. The sound of the horn blasts reverberated off the mountains and across the plateau.

"Welcome to Italy," I said to Neville.

⁓

We descended into the deep valley along a well-graded mountain path not far from the windy switchback road, occasionally passing old, dilapidated, slate-covered buildings. The shifting light made the surrounding mountains take on different shapes and images, and the landscape became greener, more treed and less barren. It was such a complete and welcome change from the day before.

After an hour, we had to leave the grassy track and walk on the road that led into the pretty little village of Saint-Rhémy, located adjacent to a narrow mountain river. There was not a soul around; walking through the village felt like walking through the stage of a movie set. Symbols of the Via Francigena pilgrim were sculptured into the metal street lamp poles. I snooped around down little alleys, taking pictures of the characteristic slate-roofed and dark wood houses decorated with bright red and pink flowers.

In the small village square, I noticed a tiny white church tucked between other buildings. It looked so inviting that I stepped inside. It appeared that it could only accommodate about twenty people. Every square inch of the interior was ornately decorated with religious art and gold-colored, framed paintings. Standing in the solitude and the stillness of this little oasis, I absorbed all the colors, textures and images.

I emerged from the church to see Neville standing in the village square looking at his homemade map book. He was trying to figure out where the trail went next; there didn't seem to be any obvious signs. Suddenly, out of nowhere, a man on a bike zipped through the little white arch into the village square and stopped beside us. Dressed in a slick red and white cycling outfit, he was equipped with a mobile phone, tachometer, digital camera, and recorder. Wanting to practice my Italian, I asked him if one of his *molti* gadgets was a GPS.

"*Si,*" he replied vigorously, adding, "I'm the organizer of the trail."

What a surprise! "Wow, how lucky we are to meet you!" I exclaimed, after trying to figure out how to say it in Italian, but giving up.

"*Grazie,*" he replied.

"You must be Alberto," Neville blurted out.

"*Si,* how do you know me?" Alberto asked.

Neville explained that he had read about him while researching the Via Francigena. Alberto had joined the Via Francigena Yahoo group, a dedicated group of people who had either previously walked or were considering walking the Via Francigena. He told us he was now working with the Italian Ministry of Culture, marking out an improved route and identifying troublesome sections where more signs were needed. He also worked closely with the Italian Association for the Via Francigena in Fidenza.

He asked how we were doing. We told him where and when we had started and about our experience so far. Neville showed him his homemade map and guidebook and Alberto was impressed.

He was kind enough to provide us with the name and phone number of the boatman we needed to call once we were ready to cross the Po River, further south. He was also kind enough to invite us to stay at his place when we got closer to Viverone.

He proudly told us that there were many improvements along the trail, including better signage, and that the Via Francigena was being re-routed away from many of the busy roads. This was good news for us.

Neville and Alberto — Saint-Rhémy

"Updated maps showing the new sections will be ready before you get to Rome," Alberto said.

"Oh darn," I said. "I don't think we'll be able to get them in time."

Maybe we were a little too early to be doing this walk, I thought, but at least we had Neville's maps and guidebooks. I was sure we would be fine.

❦

NEVILLE
We wandered out of Saint-Rhémy, delighted we had met Alberto and excited to learn the trail was undergoing significant improvements, including better signage. About 500 meters out of the village, we arrived at a junction. One path climbed a grassy hill and the other wound around the hill along a gravel road.

Not only did we need better maps before we got to Rome; we

also needed better signs just to get out of the village. No signs for the Via Francigena could be seen anywhere.

"Which path do we take?" Julie asked.

I thought about what Alberto had just said about improvements along the trail.

I tried to find our position on my crude map. I decided to go uphill while Julie walked down the road for about 500 meters. We both returned minutes later to the junction.

"Nope, no signs," we both said. "Only God knows where the route goes," I thought.

"So which path do you think Alberto took?" Julie asked impatiently.

"I don't know," I replied. "I still can't figure out where we are on these maps."

We debated which way to go. Julie thought we should take the gravel road, while I thought we should climb the grassy path up the hill. In the end, Julie decided to follow me up the hill.

We walked for an hour up the steep hill and arrived in a little village—a clump of houses called Lava.

"What kind of name is that for a village?" Julie asked.

We stopped to ask directions from a man who was working on the roof of a half-finished building.

"*Buon giorno, per favore, dov'è Saint Oyen?*" Julie asked. He looked at us, grunted, and pointed toward the direction we had just come from.

"But, this doesn't make sense," I insisted. "Saint Oyen must be the other way."

A little further, we stopped another man and asked him the same question. He pointed in the same direction we were walking, contrary to what the first man had told us.

"Okay, now what?" Julie asked.

The different answers we had received started to irritate me.

A few meters later, the village ceased at the edge of a cliff. We had no choice but to backtrack down the grassy hill. Back at the junction, we took the gravel road down the hill; the one Julie originally insisted we take.

"Okay! I just hope we arrive in Saint Oyen by nightfall," Julie said.

"I hope so too," I replied. "So much for our first day in Italy," I thought.

Thirty minutes later, we reached the small hamlet of Cerisey, which was good news since it was on my map. What was not on my map was a temporary bullpen that some farmer had erected, blocking our way forward. In front of us was an electric fence separating us from four large black bulls.

"What the hell?" I said aloud.

"Now how do we get around this?" Julie asked. "And how did Alberto get around it?"

Yeah, how did Alberto get around it? There was no obvious detour around this makeshift paddock. With a creek on one side and a steep hill on the other, it was apparent we could not go around the paddock. I clambered up a sharp incline and surveyed the state of affairs.

"We could go through it and perhaps rejoin the trail on the other side?" I yelled back to Julie.

I told Julie to wait and then trudged through the knee-high grassy field towards the fence. I dropped my backpack on the ground and slipped under the electric fence and down a small embankment, and then carefully eased toward the other side of the large enclosure. Julie stayed put, staring at the bulls while they watched me. I continued moving slowly up and around past the bulls. By now, I was out of Julie's line of vision. When I got to the other side, I saw the other exit was blocked too. Disappointed, I turned to walk back to Julie.

Moments later, I found myself face to face with two black mean-looking bulls. They had sauntered over to investigate, and worse, the other two bulls had moved over to block my only exit out. I felt like a character in a Far Side cartoon; the bulls were in charge and I was the hapless dumb human.

I swiftly realized that I had to get out fast! I spotted a small opening under the electric fence on top of an old rock wall. In a flash, I made a frantic dash and scaled the wall, slipping through the narrow opening under the fence to safety, and then clambering back up the hill.

I returned to Julie who had been standing watching the other two bulls and wondering where I had gone. Between my huffing and puffing, I told Julie, "There is no way out."

Without saying a thing, Julie turned and trudged back through the grassy field to the edge of the creek. I stood there stunned that she had just walked away.

"I'm going to see if we can cross the creek," she yelled back at me.

I didn't believe there was a place to cross the creek, but moments later, she appeared on the other side. Obviously, I had lost this argument, so I followed her and we took the little road to Saint Oyen. It was far better than trying my luck again with those bulls.

❧

JULIE

We arrived in Saint Oyen and found the Château Verdun, which was a pleasant surprise. Though it is associated with the hospice at Gran San Bernardo, the interior and décor were completely different. It looked more modern, more recently renovated and more simply, but stylistically, furnished throughout. It was also more colorfully decorated with many photographs, paintings and artifacts, and ornamental glass paintings throughout the foyer.

"But the building is 1,000 years old," one of the padres told us.

The original building dates from the 10th and 11th centuries. In 1137, Amadeus III of Savoy granted the building and farmhouses to the Canons (Congregation) of the hospice at Gran San Bernardo, who used it as a stopping station on the Via Francigena.

Today, Château Verdun accepts individuals as well as groups interested in periods of study, reflection and rest. It can sleep 65 people in rooms of two to five beds, has communal toilets and showers, and has a 10-bed shared dormitory.

We relaxed in our bedroom, wrote in our journals, and then passed the time wandering through the halls and checking out the building. The various-sized rooms included lounging areas, an old library, and some smaller rooms useful for group meetings or individual quiet work. All were simply but charmingly decorated and furnished with old wooden furniture.

Exhausted after such a long, tense day of getting lost and Neville nearly being gored by bulls, we both looked forward to a peaceful dinner. As we approached the *salle à manger*, I heard a low hum. I wondered what was making the noise, and as we got closer, it increased to a loud rumble. When I stepped through the doorway and looked in, I was flabbergasted. I thought I was dreaming: worse, I thought I was having a nightmare. Seated at five long banquet-style tables were forty hyperactive adolescents talking, screaming and yelling at one another. They had taken over the dining room and the noise was deafening.

"Oh my God, do we really have to eat here?" I asked Neville. "I can't stand the racket."

We reluctantly took seats at the table closest to the doorway, with our backs to the chaos. On the opposite side of the table was a young Italian couple. Curious to learn why they were staying here, I wanted to talk to them, but there was just no point in conversing— I couldn't hear myself think.

Beside me sat a middle-aged man. I said hello, but he didn't reply. In fact, he behaved very strangely. During the whole meal, he ate with his head down, ignoring us all. Every once in a while, he would simply get up and help himself to water, bread, or dessert from the serving cart at the front of the room. After the entrée was served, he got up, walked to the other side of Neville, grabbed the salt and pepper shakers, and returned to his seat without saying a word.

"Now why did he not just ask us?" I whispered to Neville, "rather than acting as if we were invisible."

We finished dinner quickly and made our escape from the screaming teenagers. This was not the type of Italian dining experience I had expected. I was deaf by the time we left.

"Welcome to Italy," I said again.

❦

From Saint Oyen, the Via Francigena follows an old irrigation channel called the Ru Neuf, a beautiful easy walk, most of it through woods and forest. The Ru Neuf has existed for over 600 years and is the last irrigation channel still active in the Valle d'Aosta. It opened in March 1401 when the Lord of Savoy granted a concession diverting the Artanavaz River. The 13-km irrigation channel flows through the communities of Etroubles, Echevennoz, Gignod, and Aosta and is responsible for irrigating a total area of 424 hectares. Underground pipes have replaced some sections of the main channel, but most of the sections are still exposed, thus providing some great spots for me to soak my ankle.

A couple of hours after leaving Saint Oyen, I was still looking for the perfect location to put my feet in the water, soak my ankle and have some lunch. I had decided it had to be just the right setting. To my surprise, we found five Germans eating lunch on a little wooden bridge spanning a small creek, the very spot I had imagined eating at while I hung my feet in the cold river water.

"See," I said to Neville. "I'm not the only one that likes these kinds of places to rest and eat."

So I plunked myself on the bridge and, like one of the German women, took off my boots and plunged my feet into the icy water. It felt so good.

"Please stay and sit with us. Are you hungry?" one of the women asked, speaking perfect English.

They offered us Italian bread and ham and cheese, then granola and chocolate. I remembered meeting many friendly Germans on the Camino de Santiago and it seemed that they always had fine snacks.

Excited to meet other hikers who spoke English, we asked, "Are you walking the Via Francigena?"

"No, we are just walking from St. Maurice to Aosta," the older man replied. "Every year we walk a different section of the Alps. When we get to Aosta, we plan to go to Tuscany to our favorite hot springs."

"And you?" he asked.

"We're walking all the way to Rome," we replied.

"That's incredible!" they exclaimed, as their eyes widened with surprise.

We finished lunch and left together, passing through several little villages and hamlets, more populated than I had expected. At times, we walked together as a group; other times the Germans were ahead of us, while sometimes we were ahead of them. It reminded us of our experiences on the Camino in Spain.

In Chez Li Lieu, I wanted to check out the church and ethnographic museum, but they were not open. In Gignod, there was an old chateau high up on a hill, so I climbed the stairs to the top, found a lovely, peaceful spot to have a snack, and played my recorder (a musical instrument from the family of flutes but with holes for fingers and thumb to create the sounds). I love playing my recorder in open spaces with great views.

Chez Henri was a cute little village, bursting with life and color. There were plenty of delightful vegetable, herb and flower gardens, and rows of orchard trees plump with all kinds of fruit: pears, apples, plums, quince, and others whose names I didn't know. It felt like a little oasis, tucked away all on its own. I wanted to stop and rest, to pick an apple or pear, to lie on my back and bite into the glorious fruit and let its luscious juices dribble into my mouth. But I felt as if someone were watching me, checking that I would not steal their fruit. I wished for a sign that read: "Walker—Please Help Yourself."

❧

The pain in my knees that I started to feel just after leaving

Chez Henri got increasingly worse on our descent into Aosta. In fact, I was in extreme pain, cringing with every step. I tried every possible walking stride I could, sometimes zigzagging from one side of the road to the other, and other times walking sideways, to lessen the force on my knees. It didn't seem to matter. So I continued down the path, limping and crying out each step of the way.

I hobbled down the old, narrow, steep road that ran along the six-meter-high, thick stone wall. I felt like I was entering a medieval fortress. I wondered how many other adventurers might have experienced the same mix of emotions—elation and satisfaction combined with pain and discomfort—after crossing the Alps and entering the old Roman city of Aosta.

Our accommodation was the Bed & Breakfast al Narbussion, located on one of the main streets in the old city center, but tucked away off the street itself, away from the noise and bustle of everyday Italian life. It was easy to miss if you didn't know exactly where it was.

To enter, we first passed through an iron gate. We rang the buzzer and a charming elderly woman greeted us. We gave her our name.

"Prego, prego—please, please," she replied, as she quickly turned and hurried down the narrow corridor, popping out at the other side of the house into a spacious courtyard.

"Wow, Neville look at this, it's beautiful!" It was bursting with bright light and colorful plants, and foliage cloaked the picnic chairs and tables.

She led us to the room on the far side of the courtyard, tucked into the corner of the building under a staircase leading to the second level above. It was pleasantly decorated, spacious, and airy. Full of charm with its old wood furniture, it had a large king-size bed in the center of the room with a cozy ensuite bathroom. I was elated that Neville had found this little oasis, right in the middle of the old city center.

"I must say I'm extremely pleased with my selection," Neville said proudly. We graciously thanked the elderly woman and settled in.

⌘

I was so thankful I had made it this far. It was a miracle. But now I was exhausted, my ankle and knees hurt, and I needed a short nap before dinner.

Neville woke me at 6:30 pm. "We should get going for dinner," he announced.

"Sure—no rush, I'll start getting ready," I said, thinking that if we left by 7:30 pm, we would have plenty of time. Besides, it was only a ten-minute walk to the closest restaurant. I had picked out some restaurants from our culinary guide and narrowed them down to three that were within walking distance.

We arrived at my first choice, Ristorante Vecchio Ristoro, and I scanned the menu, searching for traditional foods.

"What do you think, Nev?" I asked. "They have some interesting local dishes."

"And how are the prices?" Neville asked.

I examined the menu further. "I don't know if we can afford them."

I looked around at the servers and other guests. I caught them looking at us in our hiking boots and clothes. This was a fine-dining *ristorante*.

"I don't think this place is for us, so let's move on," I said.

We hurried to my second choice *ristorante*, just around the corner from where we were staying. We skimmed the posted menu on the wall outside. It looked good, and better still, the prices were more reasonable.

"Buona sera, per favore, avete un tavolo per due persone, questa sera?" Good evening, do you have a table for two people, this evening?

"Mi dispiace c'è posto solo alle 10:00." I am sorry there is only a place at 10:00 pm.

Disappointed, and now cursing and grumbling, I suggested to Neville we try my third choice. But when we arrived there, we found hanging on the front entrance door a sign that read: "Closed Day."

"Damn restaurants, all the ones with traditional foods are too pricey, too busy or closed." I cried.

"Welcome to Italy," Neville said.

❦

We somberly walked away, and then selected the first open restaurant we came across that had decent prices and hopefully served something local.

Ristorante Il Girasole was busy and full of locals, but they had a table for us at the back. We scanned the menu to find local food. We found enough items to make a meal and ordered *un antipasto* (hor d'oeuvres), a selection of *salame* and *prosciutto* (cured ham) and *lardo* (a cured meat made from the layer of pig fat found directly under the skin).

The *antipasto* included *bruschetta con lardo* (thin slices of bread toasted, rubbed with garlic, topped with *lardo*, then drizzled with olive oil) and *mocetta con rucola e grana* (cured meat with an Italian leafy green vegetable, topped with shaved cheese). It also included *insalatina di noci* (a green salad with walnut oil), and *zucchine in carpione* (a cold dish of zucchini marinated in vinegar, sage, onion, and garlic). Finally, it included *frittatina alle erbe con fonduta e funghi* (a mini omelet made with typical Aostan cheese and mushrooms, seasoned with herbs), *cipolle ripiene* (stuffed onion with a mixture of meat and cheese), and *peperoni con bagna cauda* (roasted pepper with garlic-anchovy sauce).

Then we shared *un primo piatto* (first course) of *Risotto alla Valdostana*, a typical Aostan rice dish cooked in broth and made with *Fontina* cheese, as well as *un secondo piatto* (second course) of *Bistecche alla Valdostana*, veal steak topped with ham and *Fontina* cheese. It wasn't gourmet, but it hit the spot, and we got a taste of Aostan cuisine.

Over dinner, I said to Neville, "What a rude awakening. I guess I had completely forgotten about the Italian lifestyle and dining hours. Next time we reserve, or we go early and wait in line," I suggested.

He just looked at me and I knew what he was thinking.

We left the restaurant thankful we had gotten a table, and satisfied with, but not excited about, our local dining experience. As compensation, we went to a bar for a good, stiff Valle d'Aostan drink, typically consumed on special occasions.

I requested *"due caffè alla valdostana, per favore."*

The woman motioned for us to take a seat. What followed was a special age-old ritual. First, she took a *grolla*, a traditional round wooden pot containing anywhere from two to eight spouts (ours had two). Into the *grolla*, she poured fresh hot black *espresso*, followed by red house wine, followed by *grappa* and then orange peel. She finished it off with a coating of sugar around the rim and lit a flame to the drink. Then she dunked two straws in it and served it to us.

We each took a sip and felt immediately warmed inside, in my case all the way down to my toes.

"Oh, this goes down well; we might want one each," I said, now smiling. It was potent and just what I needed after a long hard day.

We laughed about our first few days walking in Italy. Like most people, we appreciated the wonderful small pleasures of being in Italy: the fine wine and tasty food, the hospitality and general good nature of Italians. This is why we chose to walk through Italy. But there were also the typical nuances of Italian life: the impromptu bullpen blocking our path, the rowdy teenagers at Château Verdun, and the "closing hours" for shops and "opening hours" for restaurants that made Italy unique. Our "welcome" made us feel, more than ever, physically, socially and spiritually connected to Italy.

V

Aosta: Alpine Jewel

*"As you walk and eat and travel, be where
you are. Otherwise you will miss most of
your life." – Siddhārtha Gautama*

JULIE

We woke refreshed, ready for breakfast. The night before, we had
initially asked for breakfast at 9:00 am but then quickly changed
our minds and decided on 8:30 am. This would give us time to
linger and talk to our host, and to visit the attractions and shops
before they closed at noon.

Breakfast was in a room upstairs in the adjoining building. We
eagerly climbed the stairs and knocked on the door. The charming, friendly older woman who had showed us to our room the day
before suddenly appeared at the bottom of the stairs.

"Buon giorno, prego," she said, gesturing to us to enter the room.
We entered a large living area that looked like a museum lounging
room, elegantly decorated with modern furniture, a collection of
statues, and other interesting art pieces. We spotted the dining area
and walked over to where our breakfast was laid out.

"I guess this is it," I said. On a table was a basket of assorted
packaged *biscotti* and toast, along with a selection of packaged jams
and jellies, some butter, and a small carafe of coffee. We picked

through the packaged items and lingered over coffee, all the while wondering where our host was.

I finally asked the elderly woman, who had come inside to check on us, where our host was. She told us she would be arriving soon. About 20 minutes later, in flew a woman holding a large brown paper bag. She looked flustered.

"*Buon giorno, sono* Gabriella. I am sorry for being late. I had to bicycle to the other side of town, to the only bakery open on Sunday," our host said.

She grabbed the basket, took it to the kitchen counter, and a few minutes later brought it back overflowing with fresh bread and buns. We couldn't believe our eyes. We were already full, but we couldn't say "no thank you." Instead, we slowly ate one of each variety, while we chatted with Gabriella.

Gabriella gave us some wonderful suggestions for places to visit and eat. Thoroughly stuffed, we thanked her and went off to explore Aosta.

◦◦◦

NEVILLE

We had been walking for five days, including three lengthy days of steady climbing over the Alps, one being our infamous "Day in Hell," so it was a good time for a break. Aosta, in the heart of the Valle d'Aosta, was the perfect place to stop and indulge in some fine northern Italian cuisine and local wine and join in an annual weekend long festival.

When I first saw Aosta from the hills above, tucked neatly in a narrow valley between two mountain ranges, it looked like a typical modern Italian metropolis surrounded by sprawling suburbia. Until then, we had only passed through small mountain villages and hamlets, so Aosta appeared big and daunting. But once inside in the old city center, I quickly forgot about suburbia.

Aosta was originally a Celtic-Ligurian city, founded 2,500 years ago by the tribal people called Salassi. The Roman army, under the command of Terentius Varro, captured the city in 25 BC and settled the Roman colony of Augusta Praetoria Salassorum. The remains of the seven-meter-high walls of the Roman town surround the old center, a small quarter of about 40,000 square meters. Within this square, the streets are laid out in a grid pattern, so it was easy for us to navigate the laneways while passing by many Roman monuments such as the Teatro Romano, the Roman Forum and the Porta Praetoria. Just outside the walls are the remains of the famous l'Arco di Augusto, built as a dedication to the Emperor Augustus, who, in 25 BC, defeated the Salassi. Built in late Republican style, it included a single, semicircular arc nine meters wide, with a single pillar supporting it on each of its four corners. I found it remarkable that everyday folk continued to work and live within the walls of this living museum without giving it a second thought. In many ways, Aosta's charm was its non-touristy, working-town feeling. It felt unpretentious, and for me this made it a special place to visit.

We made our way to the south gates of the old city center to watch the annual festival, the "I Cavalieri del Conte Verde." It was a re-enactment of the journey taken by the Cavalieri, that is, Amedeo VI di Savoia Conte, (the celebrated member of the royal family of Savoy) and his entourage of 25 riders. Today, participants in the festival retrace the route, crossing through the lower Valle d'Aosta and passing medieval castles and stately homes.

As we approached the gates, we saw ahead a small procession of people riding horses and dressed in colorful green, white and red medieval costumes. Following was a larger parade of medieval characters carrying swords and spears. The entire pageant gradually made its way into the old *centro* where hundreds of local residents were waiting for them to arrive. The riders and actors paraded around, mingled with the local residents in the *piazza*, and then retraced their steps back out of town.

Afterwards, we wandered over to the grounds of the Teatro Romano, an ancient Roman theatre. The original complex had once

Teatro Romano – Aosta

occupied an area of approximately 5,200 square meters, stood 22 meters high (only the southern façade remains today), and could hold up to 4,000 spectators. Nearby was the Anfiteatro Romano, an amphitheatre able to hold 20,000 spectators, far more than the population of Aosta at the time of the Roman era, and about one-half of the total population of modern-day Aosta. To the south of the theater was La Porta Praetoria, a unique Roman port or arch entrance to the city. It consisted of a series of two arches enclosing a small square. Even today, sections of the old marble arches are visible.

In the center of the Teatro Romano, I stood looking south toward Gran San Bernardo, from where we had come. Gazing up at the tall mountains of the Alps, I imagined what medieval pilgrims and travelers must have seen and experienced as they descended the valley toward Aosta. The massive Teatro Roman, the Anfiteatro Romano, and the solid three-meter walls surrounding the city would all have been beacons guiding them toward Aosta. After what would have been a dangerous journey over the pass at Gran San Bernardo, Aosta must have been a haven, where they would find security and be able to rest before continuing their long passage to Rome.

❦

JULIE

We continued to wander around Aosta. Amongst the throngs of people coming out of the cathedral, I spotted a woman that looked familiar.

"Maria, Maria!" I yelled out.

I was so surprised to see Maria. She was the Italian woman we had met at Gran San Bernardo hospice and we hadn't seen her since.

"Giulia, Giulia!" Maria shouted with a big smile on her face. We ran toward each other like long-lost friends.

We tried to converse, her in her limited French and English, and me struggling with my limited Italian and French.

"Buon giorno. Come stai?" Maria asked me.

"Bene bene, grazie," I replied. "Where are you staying?"

"I found a bed at one of the churches. I stay a few nights. Then I continue my way to Pistoia."

"Where do you go from there?" I asked.

"I walked to Santiago de Compostela, and now I walk to Jerusalem by the Lombardy route." She said something about being a missionary.

Yet, I didn't understand if she had just finished walking to Santiago and now she was walking back and heading for Jerusalem, or if she had walked there in the past. Looking at this woman, I could not imagine her walking to Santiago from Italy and then back again and continuing to Jerusalem.

"What are you going to do when you get there, Maria?"

"Non so," Maria replied. She didn't know. Maybe she would figure it out when she got there.

"Would you write me? I would love to hear about your journey," I asked Maria.

"*Si, si, certo,*" she replied. I wrote out my address for her on a piece of scrap paper she pulled from her purse. It would be a miracle if she didn't lose it, I thought. I asked her for her address.

"*Non ho un indirizzo,*" She replied. No mailing address.

"*Un indirizzo email?*" (An email address?)

"No," she replied. It was all up to her then. I hoped she would write.

We said our goodbyes with a traditional Italian peck on either side of the cheek. We wished her well on her journey to Jerusalem, not expecting to see her again.

Meeting Maria reminded us of the Camino de Santiago in Spain when walkers would meet one another, unexpectedly, along the trail and share their stories and tall tales.

"I think she doesn't have a lot of money to spend on Aosta's finer culinary offerings," Neville said to me after Maria had left us. "She's at the mercy of the various church officials for both a room and food."

"Yeah, you're probably right. She's a real pilgrim."

We retraced our steps back to the central *piazza*. Down Via Sant'Anselmo was Enoteca Vineria, recommended by Gabriella as a good place for lunch. Laura, the owner, was knowledgeable about her products and patient with me as I asked many questions.

The Swiss and French have heavily influenced the cuisine in this region. That said, many of the meats and cheeses produced here, and how they are prepared, are unique to the Valle d'Aosta. For example, cheese is used in most meals, including *polenta* (cooked corn meal), *risotto* (creamy rice dish), and *fonduta* (cheese fondue), and with *gnocchi* (potato dumplings). It is also added to many soups.

Laura recommended a plate of assorted local meats and cheeses so we could sample as many as possible. Our selection of meats included: *boudin* (a traditional sausage prepared from an old recipe that includes hand-peeled boiled potatoes, beetroot, and spices) and *Jambon du Cru*, an Italian cured ham. My favorites were *Jambon de Bosses DOP* (traditional type of *prosciutto*, seasoned with herbs and produced only in the mountains near Gran San Bernardo), and *mocetta* (a tender and tasty dried meat made with aromatic mountain herbs local to the region). I loved the herby flavor of the *Jambon de Bosses*, which is more flavorful and less salty than the prosciutto. *Mocetta* is made with beef, venison, chamois, deer or ibex. Expecting I had eaten beef, I was surprised to learn I had eaten the chamois version. It was lean and tender, with a dark texture and medium-strong flavor.

The cheese platter included a selection typical of Valle d'Aosta; *Fontina*, *Fromadzo*, and *Robiola*, the latter two made nearby in a little village in the mountains, close to where we had passed through when we descended into Aosta.

Originating in ancient times, *Fontina* is a commonly used full-fat, semi-hard cheese with a distinctly sweet taste. I neglected to ask how long it had been aged, but I figured it must have been three to six months because it was still a little soft with a mild and buttery flavor.

Fromadzo dates from the 15th Century, and its flavor and texture changes with aging. When fresh, it has a unique, semi-sweet, fragrant and milky taste, and when aged it has a stronger, slightly salty taste with a sharp tang.

I liked them all, but *Robiola* made with a varying mix of cow's milk and goat's or sheep's milk was my favorite. There are two types: the fresh version is tangy, creamy, delicate, and sweet and usually eaten within one week, while the other is aged about a month and is more pungent and salty. There are also different varieties of *Robiola* but since I neglected to ask, I assumed it was *Robiola di Roccaverano*, (a DOP cheese). It had a strong aroma and it was sharp and firm with a buttery flavor.

To accompany our meat and cheese feast, we each ordered a different glass of wine. From a selection of 13 different wines specific to Valle d'Aosta, I ordered a glass of Torrette DOC, a harmonious, well-balanced red wine with a crisp, dry flavor, and the most commonly produced wine in the valley. Neville selected Morgex et La Salle DOC, a white wine made from grapes grown in the highest vineyards of

Europe, with an aroma of mountain herbs and a dry, delicate flavor.

As it turned out, Enoteca Vineria was a great place to sample the local meats, cheeses, and wines while we watched the goings-on in the streets.

⸎

NEVILLE

Aosta, like most Italian cities, has a certain rhythm. Church bells ring out at seven o'clock in the morning, signaling the start of the day, and again at seven o'clock in the evening, marking the end of the day. Throughout the day, a parade of humanity passes by, best seen in the old historical center or *centro storico*.

In Aosta, the *centro storico* is where people gather, pass through on their way to somewhere else, or stop to talk. Old men pass the morning sipping coffee in local bars surrounding the *centro* and old women stop one another to gossip. Fashionable young women with designer sunglasses slip into clothing shops while business executives stride to their next meeting. If you stay in an Italian city and spend a day in the *centro storico*, you will get a peek into the soul of Italy. Some say people define their city, but in Italy, I think the *centro storico* defines its people.

Later that afternoon we took part in an age-old tradition. In Aosta, as with most other Italian cities, as the day's shadows grow long, an evening ritual, sometimes called the *passeggiata* or "little walk," begins. The *passeggiata* is a slow evening stroll taken before dinner, usually in the pedestrian zones of the centro storico. We watched people arrive at 5:00 pm, and for the next two hours, they strolled *fare bella figura*—to see and be seen—in their Sunday best clothes.

This evening the *passeggiata* was a combination of lively conversation and window-shopping, with everybody checking out everybody else, bumping into friends and acquaintances, and perhaps making impromptu plans to head off to dinner together.

I saw men and women young and old, babies and children, and weathered "grannies," all dressed for the *passeggiata*.

Men stood shoulder-to-shoulder, swapping secrets and rumors, and wearing jeans and a jacket or sweater draped over their shoulders. Women wore designer jeans and fancy tops or light summer evening dresses. Groups of pre-adolescent girls squeezed into hip hugging jeans, low-cut T-shirts and one-size-too-small push-up bras, giggled and sang, and danced their way through the streets. Young boys, Italian versions of James Dean with slicked-back jet-black hair, stood by wearing aviator style sunglasses and hoping to catch the attention of a fair maiden.

Seniors, in groups of two or three, sat on benches along the route, watching and gossiping. Young families lined the cobblestoned streets and laneways, the children wandering about under the watchful eye of not only their parents but also their parent's parents. Couples of all ages walked hand and hand. It was an event, free entertainment, and a great example of community spirit.

～

JULIE

The gorgeous autumn weather made it that much more enjoyable; it had been such a superb sunny day. As we wandered the streets, taking in the local activity, I suggested to Neville that we have a picnic dinner that night.

"Sure, that's fine with me. I'll go get the wine and meet you later at the deli," Neville replied.

He was a pro at selecting the wine, and I was good at picking out the food—we made a great team—so we parted, agreeing to meet in half an hour.

I didn't have far to go. There were plenty of *alimentari* (grocery shops), *fruttivendoli* (vegetable shops), and *panifici* (bread shops) close to our bed and breakfast. Using what I had learned from reading about local traditional foods in our culinary guidebook, I selected an assortment of meats and cheeses and bread.

I started my rounds at a nearby *panificio*, scanning the shelves for my first choice, *pane nero* or black bread. This hearty traditional bread is made using ingredients like walnuts, raisins, and fennel seeds. In days gone by, village locals banded together to use the village's only oven, because they didn't have their own. Making this traditional bread was a time-consuming process, usually reserved for Christmas. Today, *pane nero* is available throughout the year, and, lucky for me, they had some. I was ecstatic.

Around the corner was the deli. I surveyed the cheese case, trying to choose something we hadn't tried yet. This time I bought some *Gressoney toma* (a highly regarded cow's cheese made with traditional methods), some *reblec* (a soft and creamy fresh cheese, commonly served as a dessert topped with sugar, cinnamon or cocoa powder, and some young *Fontina*. I figured the latter two would spread well on the black bread. To round it off, I ordered some *Jambon du Cru* and *Prosciutto di San Marcel,* cured ham made with 18 alpine herbs. Finally, I grabbed some local *Millefiori* honey made from a thousand mountain flowers, to go with our cheese.

Neville met me at the deli. He had bought a bottle of Donnas, a typical red wine named after a small town further along the Valle d'Aosta. He asked about dessert.

"We don't want anything too heavy after all this cheese, meat, and bread," I added. "Let's select something typical."

Neville found a box of *Tegole*—thin, light, almond biscuits. "These should go well with the *Genepy*," he said, smiling.

I had one more place to stop. Neville knew I couldn't go without some *verdura* (vegetables) or *frutta* (fruit). On the way back to our room, I dashed into a small produce shop and picked out some fresh *pomodori* (tomatoes) and fresh crisp butter lettuce.

We dug out our camping utensils and Neville's Swiss army knife and assembled our picnic dinner on the courtyard table. Feasting

Picnic Dinner – Aosta

happily, we enjoyed the remaining warm solar rays of the day while trying our best to shoo away the owner's cats.

The *Gressoney toma* cheese was well aged and firm, but not as strong as the *Robiola* we had eaten at the *enoteca*. The *reblec* cheese was light, soft, and creamy, with a mellow flavor, similar to a soft fresh *ricotta*. It made an excellent dessert cheese, with the distinct flavor of the flower honey as an excellent accompaniment. The *Fontina* was mild, soft and buttery, and went well with the heaviness of the black bread. Our version, with walnuts and figs, was delicious.

The Donnas, known as the "mountain equivalent of Barolo," had a dry, smooth, velvety taste that went well with the meat and cheese. We had little troubling finishing the entire bottle.

We finished the meal with *Tegole* (biscuits, made with almonds, sugar, egg white, flour, and vanilla that are crispy, crumbly and great with custard, ice cream or dark chocolate). Neville's *Genepy* served as a great nightcap, warming our insides and giving us a nice buzz.

Genepy, a mountain herb *digestivo* and after-dinner strong alcoholic drink, is made using the ancient tradition of adding Alpine herb blossoms with a unique essence of Artemisia.

"That was a fine way to end our perfect time in Aosta," Neville declared.

We both wanted to stay another day to take in more of the fascinating history and the fine food and wine but felt we needed to keep moving on down the road. We knew there would be plenty more history and Italian cuisine to enjoy on our way to Rome.

VI

Initiation

"By three methods we may learn wisdom:
First, by reflection, which is noblest;
Second, by imitation, which is easiest.
And third by experience,
which is the bitterest."
— Confucius

JULIE

If our hike from Gran San Bernardo to Aosta was our "welcome to Italy," then the march through the lower Valle d'Aosta was our "initiation to walking the Via Francigena." You could call the next section from Aosta to Ivrea, an experiment to find out how we would handle the journey through Italy.

Our initiation included testing our navigation skills. Some days—most days—this was challenging; we were using homemade guidebooks, poorly translated into English from Italian, and interpreting directional trail signs that changed by the day or even by the hour. We did not appreciate what "no signs along this section" meant, or what the impact was, until we experienced it firsthand. Becoming lost became a common—way too common—occurrence.

Communicating in Italian and sometimes French (few people spoke English in this region), and then deciphering their responses and directions, was another ordeal. Asking people to talk more slowly usually meant they would talk faster and louder. More often than not, it left us more confused.

Other challenges included trying to find local foods in the various types of eateries and sleeping in various types of accommodation, many of which we had never experienced before, including *conventi* (convents) *monasteri* (monasteries), and *ostelli* (hostels). Contacting and then finding these places was often difficult. Sleeping in them was sometimes another experience altogether.

Valle d'Aosta on paper seemed like a wonderfully charming place to amble through. Medieval castles and forts, and old Roman roads, bridges, and houses lined the valley. I was looking forward to an easy trek down through the valley. Yet when I reread our guidebook, I was suddenly pulled back to reality. It was not going to be that easy.

Our guidebook stated that, on the first day, we had a 540 m ascent, a stage described as "demanding," and that it would take an estimated eight hours to complete this section, from Aosta to Chambave. The next section, from Chambave to Verres, included an ascent of 425 m, again described as demanding, but it would take only seven hours. The third day would be an ascent of 760 m, also demanding. And worse, there were missing trail markings for all of these sections.

Neville assumed we would take longer than indicated for a variety of reasons. In addition to the diverse terrain and lack of signs, there was the heat and humidity. And there was my chronic desire to stop and explore things as I came upon them. This I called "savoring the moment" or appreciating the scenery along the way, as I knew I might never see it again. Neville called it "dragging my feet." Finally, there was my obsession with food; Neville believed I would have to stop every hour to eat.

But neither of us wanted to walk longer than six hours a day. Therefore, we decided to divide the three original sections into four smaller sections, with stops at Verrayes, Arnad, and Pont-Saint-Martin.

We left Aosta, passing through the *centro storico* and under the Porta Praetoria and continuing along the main road to the famous Augustus Arch. Beyond the arch, we crossed a small Roman stone footbridge, the Buthier Bridge, that today spans a little park area surrounded by several buildings and a hotel, making the bridge almost inconspicuous. We lingered for a while taking photos, the last real evidence of anything Roman we would see for a while.

We felt excited and looked forward to our first day of walking and to reaching the *agriturismo* that Gabriella had so kindly booked for us. We cautiously kept our eyes open for the "little Via Francigena pilgrim"—posted signs that we expected would guide us to the next village of Saint-Christophe. We crossed the bridge and made our way down a few side streets looking for the "little pilgrim," but there was nothing.

We knew from our Camino experience that there were rarely trail signs in the cities. I still wondered why that was. Was it because the local residents do not like the streets or sidewalks marked, or was it because organizers believe walkers should use their instinct or rely on locals for directions? So we followed our intuition, asked some locals for directions, and finally came upon a grassy track that led through the woods. Emerging from the woods, we encountered a busy road, the ring road that encircled the city. We quickly darted across the road, between the speeding cars, hoping not to be the latest victim or traffic statistic.

Then we spotted our first official Via Francigena sign! It was at an intersection, at the beginning of one road that went left up a hill and another road that continued to the right. It seemed clear to us the sign was directing us uphill, so upward we went.

After walking for about two kilometers, Neville stopped to look at his map and questioned if we were on the right road. "According to my map book, the road should not wind back and forth like this," he said.

"Oh great," I mumbled, "We're off to a great start!"

There was no one around and we wondered what to do. We rechecked our map and guidebook. I found it impossible to make sense of the map; it had numerous lines, patches, and blotches that I couldn't figure out. We stood there—Neville trying to decipher his maps and me trying to read the step-by-step instructions of our guidebook to figure out where we were.

"This is not the right road," Neville stated again.

"Are you sure?" I replied.

Also troubling was the fact that the road had narrowed. While the surroundings were beautiful and quiet, much like walking down an old country road that connects small remote villages spaced kilometers apart, it lacked a shoulder where we could walk safely. Each time a car raced up toward us, we had seconds to jump to safety.

Finally, I spotted a postal worker who had stopped his postal truck.

"Quick," I said as we ran toward him, "let's go ask him before he disappears."

I asked in simple Italian the directions to Saint-Christophe, while Neville showed him the map, hoping he would know where we were. I wondered if the guy understood us or could read the map, but he directed us back down the road from where we had come and told us to take the first street on the left.

"We're backtracking again! Oh, man!" I stammered. I hated this. "Why can't they put up proper signs?" I complained.

We arrived back at the original intersection and looked at the sign again.

"It still looks like it's pointing up," I said in disgust.

In a huff, I turned quickly and stomped off down the other road, keeping my eyes peeled for the little "Via Francigena pilgrim." I prayed the trail would soon turn off the narrow shoulder-less road and turn into a nice green walking track that went all the way to Verrayes.

It was along this section that we crossed paths with many curious, friendly, and helpful Italians. A friendly *buon giorno* to people we encountered would spark a barrage of questions, and their curiosity was aroused further when they found out we were walking to Rome.

Walking along the road toward Saint-Christophe, we saw three women waiting at a bus stop in front of a hospital. The two older women were dressed in long dark skirts and dark long-sleeved shirts, and the third woman, a nun, wore a long, dark blue dress and habit.

As we got closer, the nun suddenly jumped up, as if she had received an instant message from God, and ran across the street toward us. Thank God, there was no traffic.

We stopped, startled. The nun introduced herself, speaking quickly in Italian. *"Buon giorno, sono Nicolosa de Valle d'Aosta. Come vi chiamate?*—what is your name? *Da dove venite?*—where are you from? *Dove andate?*—where do you go?"

She told us there was a church or something of importance up ahead. But the name she told us didn't mean anything; it was not in our guidebook. We asked about the town of Saint-Christophe and how far it was and she suggested we ask someone further down the road to direct us. A wise answer, I thought.

After welcoming us to Aosta, she said *buon giorno*, and ran back across the street returning to the bus stop.

We were bewildered but honored. Feeling very special and appreciative, we continued, wishing we could have communicated more with her. I knew it would be one of the many lasting memories of Italians we would meet.

A little further on, an elderly gentleman, who had been standing on the sidewalk in front of his house, approached us and asked curiously, *"Da dove venite oggi?*—where do you come from today?"

We told him we started in Martigny. Still curious he asked, "Why do you take ten days to reach this place from Martigny?"

"We stayed three days in Aosta." Then I added, "We're walking to Rome."

He gave us a big smile, and said, *"mamma mia!"* and wished us *buon viaggio!*

Later, we surprised a man on his moped when he arrived to attend to his vineyard. We had stopped for a break and we shouted *buon giorno* to him as he stood about 100 meters away. He waved his arm up and down, and he too shouted, *"mamma mia!"* when we told him we were walking to Rome. *"Bene, bene, buon viaggio,"* he called back.

Later that afternoon, we arrived at La Vrille, an *agriturismo* near Chambave owned by Luciana and Hervé. Their marketing literature stated:

> A warm welcome awaits you at La Vrille, a rural farm holiday and farm stay in the heart of the Valdostan vineyards. It is located right along the Via Francigena in the center of the Valle d'Aosta, on the *adret* or northern and sunny left slopes of the Dora Baltea at a height of 650 m above sea level. It has magnificent views of the surrounding mountain peaks of Mont Avic and Mont Emilius, all situated in an excellent sunny location throughout the year.

La Vrille had opened in 2002, but only started serving traditional Valle d'Aostan dinners three years later. Luciana had walked the mountains of Valle d'Aosta from village to village to talk to the people and learn about the traditional recipes of the region. We had no idea how lucky we were that they had space until we got there.

Our room was a little bit of heaven. On the top floor, with its own little patio, it was spacious, bright, and fresh. We showered, washed our dirty clothes, and changed into clean ones. Then we sat on the outside patio soaking up the last rays of the sun, absorbing the sights and sounds of the valley, and writing in our journals.

We were the second-to-last people to arrive in the dining room. Four other parties were patiently waiting, having been told that a Canadian couple walking the Via Francigena would be joining them for dinner. Hervé sat us beside a young Italian couple who spoke

English and lived in Vercelli. They were here for a few nights to celebrate their postponed honeymoon. Luckily for us, they helped translate the names of the dishes and explained each course. Luciana was in the kitchen cooking the meals.

With all Italian meals, the wine is just as important as the food, and sharing it is even better. The men chose the first bottle of wine—Gamay—a perfect choice to accompany the courses that would follow.

The *antipasti* was a mélange of four items: *frittelle di menta* (a lightly fried dough ball made with milk, their farm fresh eggs and their garden fresh mint); a rice pumpkin ball; a green salad (made with garden fresh lettuce and tomatoes tossed with homemade *olio di noci*, or walnut oil); and a small delicious *patate bollite* (a boiled potato prepared in a typical Verrayes fashion).

The *primo piatto* was *sosa*, a dish made with a finely chopped mixture of beans, zucchini, potato, peppers, carrots, and celery, all freshly gathered in the morning and allowed to set for a few hours before dinner. The amount and combination of vegetables is important to ensure there is enough moisture and flavor. *Toma* cheese is then added to the mixture before it is baked. The important ingredients for making excellent *sosa* include plenty of preparation time and the herb *timo*, or thyme, picked in May to ensure a strong flavor and aroma.

The *secondo piatto, torta gran mère*, was a hearty, nutritious fusion of French and Italian cooking. It is a traditional recipe passed down from the nearby local villagers. In the old days, melted butter was poured slowly over layers of rice, pumpkin, sausage, and *Fontina* cheese, and the entire mixture was baked in an oven for one hour. Historically, *torta gran mère* was baked in the village oven each November and December. While the remaining coals were still hot, *pane nero* was baked in the same oven.

We finished the bottle of Gamay, and considering the host's and the Italian couple's suggestions, selected a bottle of *Chambave Muscat DOC*, a *Moscato*. It was a bright, light, full-bodied dry wine, with a slightly bitter after-taste but with good depth, and a great accompaniment to the *torta gran mère* and the next course.

We were served a palate cleanser: a selection of *reblec* cheese (made from sour milk) and fresh *Fontina* and *Toma* cheese, a sprinkle of rock salt and three different types of pepper. Hervé told us to dip each piece of cheese first into the rock salt and then into one of three different kinds of pepper. Luciana had collected at least a dozen different types of pepper from around the world, and she selected two or three types for each meal; her choice dependent on the foods and flavors of the dinner, the type of cheese she chose to serve, and whatever her personal preference was that day. It was amazing how each piece of cheese took on a different flavor—more zing, more spice, more creamy or salty—depending on the choice of pepper.

For dessert, we were served *rochette dure*, or "golden rock," a mixture of bread, egg, and milk, fried in a skillet and served with a strawberry sauce. It certainly lived up to its name, a hearty, deliciously sweet, solid hunk of a dessert.

We finished off dinner with a hot dark *espresso* and rolled away from the table. This was the first full gourmet-like meal we had eaten so far. We felt like a king and queen. I could taste the passion Luciana had put into the food and the freshness that had come from her bountiful garden. We were the last ones to leave after our Vercelli tablemates said goodnight. I was awed by a culinary experience that came from a long tradition of making and sharing good food.

The next morning, breakfast was another eating pleasure. Typically, breakfast in Italy is nothing more than coffee and a biscuit or toast. Instead, we were presented with a wonderful assortment of breads, baked goods, tortes, cakes, meats, cheeses, cereals, and fruit.

"They all look so good, I have to sample everything," I said to Neville as I returned to our table with a heaping plate.

He looked at my full plate, his eyes widening. "Are you going to eat all that?"

"Sure," I said. "It's going to be a long walking day; I need energy."

Before leaving, I spoke to Hervé (Luciana had already left on an errand). He told us that they grow most of the foods they serve, including vegetables, herbs, and potatoes. They also raise goats and chickens and make their own award-winning wines that they sell and serve with dinner.

I asked if they had many guests walking the Via Francigena. "No," he replied, but he was hoping to have more walking guests in the future. That was one reason they had opened the *agriturismo*.

"I'm sure you will," I said with conviction.

I wanted to express how appreciative we were of the wonderful experience we had just enjoyed, our gratitude for their gift of sharing their lives and food for our pleasure. I imagined saying something like "Good food, wine, atmosphere, comfort, location, and hosts. What more could anyone want, especially walkers?" Instead, in my limited Italian, all I could say was: *"Grazie mille per tutto. La cena e stata deliziosa. Grazie per la vostra ospitalità. La Vrille è un bel posto dove fermarsi."* (Thank you very much for everything. Dinner was delicious. Thank you for your hospitality; it's a great place to stay.)

We left with tantalized taste buds, heaviness in our bellies, gratitude in our hearts, and plenty of energy and enthusiasm for our full day's walk ahead.

◦◦◦

After La Vrille, our plan was simple. We would catch the bus from Chambave to Chatillon. As far as we knew, from the most recent information available to us, it was impossible to walk the trail between these two towns because of damaged footbridges. The only alternative was the busy state road, but this was dangerous for walking. The *Associazione Europea delle Vie Francigene* had recommended that walkers take the bus from Chambave to Chatillon.

Taking the bus would give us a break from the constant change in elevation, and we could get ahead of schedule and have more time to sightsee along the way. Once in Chatillon, we would walk to the little town of Arnad.

To catch the 9:00 am bus, we had to leave the *agriturismo* by 8:30 am and walk to Chambave. However, we left later than planned. We had a steep descent from the *agriturismo* through sloping, grassy hills and pastures, until we arrived at an asphalt road that continued into Chambave.

We didn't think we would make it for the 9:00 am bus but we ran for it anyway. We waited for a few minutes and then realized the bus had already passed. The next bus wasn't until 10:00 am.

Not wanting to wait around for an hour, we decided to try the walk to Chatillon. I rationalized that perhaps by now they had repaired the footbridges, making the trail passable.

The morning was already warm and humid, but the next series of events would make it "steamy."

We headed back up the street and out of town, looking for signs. We couldn't find any Via Francigena signs but there were other signs to Chatillon. We climbed the hill. It was a hot, steep climb. Neville was ahead of me. Half a kilometer up the steep hill on a clearly marked trail, Neville was mumbling to himself, obviously not happy.

I ignored him until his mumbling got louder. Then he stopped and yelled out, "This is crazy; this is not the trail."

"So what," I protested, as I got closer to him, puffing from the climb, "It's still a trail, and it says it goes to Chatillon."

He was still huffy but he continued a little further. By now, we were almost a kilometer up the hill, having taken more than half an hour to get to this point.

Hotheaded and stubborn like a Taurus bull, Neville stopped in the middle of the trail. "This is insanity; this is not the Via Francigena. I'm not walking this and getting stuck somewhere out in the middle of nowhere. I don't have any maps for this section, and if we lose the signs we won't know where we are."

"But Nev," I pleaded, "The trail is marked. Maybe it's not the Via Francigena, but it is part of another trail. I'm sure it will get us there."

We argued and the sparks flew. It was a verbal tug-of-war. I didn't want to go back; I hate going back.

With the heat, the constant up and down, the steep climbing, and the frustration of not knowing exactly where we were or where we were going, Neville was fed up.

I finally gave in. I couldn't change his mind, so there was no sense fighting about it. I watched him walk past me and head back down the hill into the town. I followed.

I wondered what we must have looked like to anyone who might be watching. Here we were, slowly climbing this steep hill, stopping every few meters and yelling at each other, continuing, then stopping again and shouting absurdities at each other high on the ridge above the village for all to see. Then turning around and going back into the village again. If nobody was watching, surely God was laughing at us.

Neville looked at his watch, "Hurry," he hollered. "We might be able to catch the 10 o'clock bus. We ran down the main road with our backpacks bopping back and forth on our backs. It was just a few minutes before 10:00.

We were within 200 meters of a bus stop on the opposite side of the road when the bus passed by. We were stunned.

I cursed. "Great, now what?"

⊙≈⊙

Neville
We waited yet another hour to catch the next bus to Montjovet and then walked to Arnad. Before leaving Montjovet, we called the *ostello* in Arnad to confirm our arrival.

"A che ora arrivate?" Julie turned to me, repeating the question: "What time do you think we'll arrive?"

'Tell her about 5 o'clock in the afternoon," I suggested.

"*Alle cinque,*" Julie replied. "*Bene arrivederci.*"

We had spent two extra hours in Chambave, getting delayed twice, so selecting a late arrival time seemed like a smart thing to do.

Using our guidebook and intuition, we figured the *ostello* was on the south side of Arnad in the tiny locality of Frazione Arnad Le Vieux. As we walked along the main road of Arnad, we saw in the distance an old church and a large building beside it, and we wondered if that was the *ostello*.

There were a few young boys playing in a courtyard in front of the church beside the community park. Julie approached them and asked if they knew where the *ostello* was. Two of the boys pointed to the building in front of us.

We rang the door but there was no response. We rang again; still nothing. We were bewildered, since we had called earlier, reserved two beds, and told them we would be there by 5:00 pm.

We wondered what to do. One of the boys in the playground yelled something. Apparently, the owner had gone into town to do an errand.

"How long do we have to wait?" we asked.

He didn't know.

We sat and waited patiently.

About half an hour later, a small car raced into the parking lot and two women jumped out and walked toward us. They had keys in their hands. I looked up at the big clock on the old church. The time was two minutes to five o'clock. Now it made perfect sense why the woman on the phone had asked Julie what time we would arrive. The two women greeted us warmly and showed us inside.

The Maison La Kia was an old "pilgrims' *ostello*" attached to the Church of San Martino di Arnad, which dated back to medieval times. Inside, we found the building cozy and warm. At the end of the long narrow hall and at the beginning of the staircase that led to the three floors of rooms, was the registration desk. Behind the desk was an old library cabinet that contained travel books, brochures,

and reading material. Our host told us there was a lot of information about the town, the surrounding area, and the Via Francigena,
and if we wanted to have a look, we could help ourselves later.

On the other side of the corridor, through a low white arch,
was a small, charmingly decorated room containing eight tables
for guests to enjoy breakfast or lounge in the evening. Outside,
in the shadow of the bell tower of the church, was a small garden
available to guests. The younger of the two women, Elisa, greeted us
in English. She escorted us up the narrow flight of stairs and showed
us to our room, explaining that upstairs there were ten double rooms
and a number of shared bathrooms.

It was a cozy and simple room, about three meters square and
much smaller than other rooms we had stayed in. There were two
single beds, a single small night table, and off to one side a large
wood wardrobe.

Elisa showed us our own private bathroom just outside the room.
It had a European open-style shower, but at least there was one and
it was clean.

Maison La Kia – Church of San Martino di Arnad

We dropped our packs on the beds. Julie threw open the window and flopped on her bed. The window was about two meters tall with a big, heavy wood shutter and no screen. The light breeze made the room feel cool and fresh, ideal for airing out our sweaty, smelly clothes.

After we each had a shower, we found some hangers in the wardrobe and hung up our clothes to air. We washed our socks, underwear and tops and hung them up to dry. Within minutes, we had decorated our tiny room, hanging our clothes wherever possible.

⁎

JULIE

I asked Elisa where we could get dinner. "Nothing is open today in Arnad," she told me, not even La Kiuva, a winery and restaurant we had picked out earlier.

"I can give you directions to another restaurant. It is good. Would you like us to drive you?" Elisa asked.

"How far is it to walk?" I asked

"About a ten minute walk," Elisa replied.

"No, *grazie*. It's not far. For us, ten minutes is nothing. After walking every day for 20 kilometers and six hours, ten minutes is *no problema*."

I thought I understood the directions as she sketched a simple map on a piece of paper and explained the route.

"You take the first right off the main road going into the old village of La Arnad Le Vieux and then follow that road past La Kiuva (the winery)," Elisa said.

So off we went, with the directions in my head and the map Elisa had drawn; easy, I thought. Neville walked ahead of me, as usual. When we arrived at the first junction, where the road to La Kiuva was located, I reminded Neville, "Elisa said to walk past that road."

"I hope you're right," Neville said.

Neville continued ahead of me, while I stopped several times to appreciate the centuries-old buildings in the little village of Arnad Le Vieux. Every few steps I took, I saw a different perspective.

"Oh, I like this view! Wow, look at that house!" I exclaimed as I stopped to take a photo. After a few more steps: "Now that's a really old house." And I stopped to take another photo. "Wait, I want a picture of that one too. I haven't seen these kinds of old buildings since La Douay."

By now, I was lagging behind Neville. He turned around and yelled at me, "Come on, I want to get to the restaurant before it gets dark." He stopped and waited for me to catch up.

"Here, give me the map," he demanded, grabbing Elisa's hand-drawn map.

"I can't understand why we haven't seen the restaurant yet. There's no bloody restaurant out here. Are you sure you got the directions right?" Neville asked accusingly.

"Yes, of course," I protested. "You know what it's like getting directions from Italians—it always ends up being longer than they say. It must be at the top of the hill."

He stormed ahead. Meanwhile, I continued admiring the scenery as I sauntered behind him. I couldn't get enough of it. I loved the setting, these ancient buildings, steeped in history. I imagined myself stopping to sit and stare at the buildings for hours while I carefully sketched every detail of what I saw—all the different lines, angles, textures, shades and colors of the roofs, and the collection of things that was crammed into one little square meter surrounding the old, rundown, slanted houses. Instead, I just snapped more photos.

By now Neville was about two or three hundred meters ahead of me, almost at the crest of the hill. He just stood there with a frown on his face. As I got closer, I could see he was hot and bothered.

"Where is this *damn* restaurant anyway?" he cursed. "It's been twenty minutes now."

"Just a little further, let's go to the top of the hill; I'm sure it will be down that street." I couldn't believe I had said this. It was something Neville would often say when I asked him how long it would be before we got to where we were going.

We arrived at the crest of the hill together. "Maybe it's just around that bend, up there, and we can't see it." I pointed in a northerly direction up another narrow country lane that disappeared into a forest.

"Forget it. There's no restaurant up here. We've been walking on a road looking for a restaurant that isn't here." he replied angrily.

He pulled out Elisa's map again and I repeated her instructions. "I know she specifically said to go past the road that La Kiuva was on." Defending myself, I added, "It's not *my* fault if she gave me wrong directions."

"This must be it," Neville said, pointing at the map. "I'm sure she meant this road. It's the road I would have expected," he added. "It's easy to figure out on the map, just by looking at it."

I said under my breath, "Of course, you Martian, it's easy for you to say."

We walked back to the junction, turned left and continued down the road for a few minutes before Neville said, "There's still no sign of a restaurant. I *can't* believe this." We saw nothing ahead of us except a road that disappeared into a forest.

"If we don't see it soon, I'm going back," Neville added. "I am not walking all night up and down roads to find a restaurant that may or may not be there."

I spotted a car parked in La Kiuva's parking lot. We approached the driver sitting in his car.

"*Per favore dov'è il ristorante L'Arcanda?*"

"*Sempre diritto,*" was his reply (straight ahead).

"*Quanti chilometri?*" (How many kilometers?)

"*Circa settecento metri.*" (About 700 meters.)

"*Grazie, molte grazie, signore.*"

"*Prego. Buon appetito.*"

We looked at each other. I waited for Neville to respond. Would he want to continue? It was getting dark. I was expecting him to say that he was turning around. Instead, he marched quickly ahead of me, like a bull on a mission, yelling, "Come on, let's go, it should only be another ten minutes now."

It took another thirty minutes before we finally arrived at Osteria L'Arcaden. "You're lucky they had a free table," Neville commented sarcastically as we sat down. He was upset because we hadn't made a reservation, and he assumed it would be busy, being the only restaurant open.

We didn't need to think about what to order for dinner, as it was a set menu. We received a plate of *antipasti*, a selection of cold cuts and cheeses from the Aosta valley, followed by chestnut soup and a hot meat and potato dish.

A few tables over, Neville spied some Swiss women who were staying at the *ostello*. The older woman approached our table and chatted for a few minutes, mentioning that they had received a ride to the restaurant.

"Are we stupid or what?" Neville said after she left.

"Well, I'm not walking back in the dark," I said. I'm going to ask the server to call someone from the *ostello* to pick us up. If she offered to drive us to the restaurant, I'm sure she won't mind picking us up.

Later, Elisa's father picked us up and drove us back to the *ostello*. On the way back, I figured why Elisa thought it would take only ten minutes to walk. Then it made sense.

If we were driving, it would.

We left Frazione Arnad Le Vieux the following morning, crossed the River Dora, and walked through rich green meadows. As we got closer to the next village of Hône, we could see in the distance, high up on an outcrop at the narrowest part of the valley, a large imposing structure.

We crossed over the river and entered the small village of Bard, strategically tucked into the narrow gorge where the Forte di Bard, or Fortress of Bard, loomed above it. The fortress, nestled between two mountain ranges, blocks the way between Arnad and

Pont-Saint-Martin. One has no choice but to pass by the fort to exit or enter the valley.

The Fortress of Bard represents one of the best examples of early 1800s military strongholds. It includes three defense stations positioned at different levels on a high imposing rock spur, the lowest at 400 meters and the highest at 467 meters. The Ferdinando Opera is on the bottom, the Vittorio Opera is in the middle, and the Carlo Alberto Opera is on the top. There is a total of 283 rooms in the fortress.

The fortress was massive and daunting. We discovered an entrance through the underground parking area and found our way to the main office, where we inquired about viewing it. We took a series of elevators, each one going only a few stories, to arrive eventually at the top level. With each elevator stop, we got a different view of the fortress and the surrounding countryside. But when we got to the top, the views were even more spectacular. I could see north all the way up the valley to Aosta, from where we had come.

"We walked all that distance, I can't believe it," I said to Neville as I looked back over the distance we had covered. Suddenly, recalling all the towns and villages we had visited and the people we had met left a lump in my throat.

We made our rounds to all the lookout points, stopping at various interpretive signs to learn as much as we could about the fort. At one point, I noticed several doorways and hallways across the central *piazza* and, curious, I stopped to talk to one of the friendly women staffing the doorway into an exhibit area.

I introduced myself.

Then she replied, "I am Cinzia… Cinzia Chiara." I liked how her name rolled off her tongue—it had that Italian rhythm. She asked me where I was from, speaking perfect English.

I told her we were from Canada.

"Oh, I have always dreamed about visiting Saskatchewan," she said. "Why?"

"I just like the sound of the name. And the pictures I have seen, it looks so different from Valle d'Aosta. I thought it would be a neat place to visit," she replied.

"Yes, very different from here. It's extremely flat. So flat, in fact, you can see for miles," said Neville. "There's an old Canadian saying about places in the prairies, like Saskatchewan: You can stand on a shoebox and see for miles."

"I like that. Being able to see for miles would be a different experience."

We told her we hoped she would get to Saskatchewan one day, and said our goodbyes. We made our way down a windy, paved pathway that lined the outside of the fortress. Along the way, I took in more views, imagining what it must have been like in days past.

Leaving the village of Bard, we followed the path south of the fortress. Neville was up and gone before I got my pack on, but he stopped further down. As I got closer to him, he was standing in front of a gate that blocked the path.

"We can't go through," Neville said. "We have to find another way."

"What on earth are you talking about?" I asked. "That can't be. Are you sure?" Smugly, I said, "Let me have a look," thinking I might be able to interpret some of the Italian. I walked up to the gate and read the paper sign.

"Shit, it's closed until later in September."

"We can't go this way. We'll have to find another way, but I don't think there is any other way out of here, except the *strada nazionale*," Neville explained.

"Well, *I'm not walking on the national road.* I'm going to ask if there's another route," I said bluntly, stomping off to a nearby picnic area to ask the two men who were eating their lunch.

"There's no other way," they told me. "The busy *strada* is the only other way to walk out of here."

"Non ci sono altre strade per Donnas o Pont-Saint-Martin?" I asked again.

"No," the men replied flatly.

I returned to Neville. "Well, we will just have to climb the fence."
I calmly said.

"No, we're not, we can't do that," he stated flatly.

"Well, I am, because I am not walking on that busy road; it's
dangerous, so this is the only way. We just have to find a way to
climb the fence."

"No, I'm not going to do that," he kept repeating.

"Well I am; let's go. There has to be a way."

We both removed our packs. Neville boosted me up onto the old
rock wall and I cautiously slipped myself over the gate to the rock
wall on the other side. Neville then passed our backpacks to me one
at a time and I lowered them to the ground. Then Neville followed.
Once on the other side, he helped me down off the wall. I felt so
smug and proud for having made it over.

"See, that wasn't so bad," I said.

Neville just mumbled.

In front of us were the remains of the ancient *Via delle Gallie* or
"Roman Road of Gaul," a two-kilometer section of oval-shaped,
flat, cobbled stone road. As we continued along, I felt so ecstatic
that we were walking this ancient route, in solitude, just the two
of us. It was remarkably beautiful and quiet. It felt as if we were in
another world, another time. Remnants and ruins of bygone days
were everywhere. I just wanted to sit there forever and envision what
it might have been like in those days. I wanted to feel the energy
that hung in the air and in the trees and on the old rock walls and
arches and boulders. I wanted the history of the old Roman road to
seep into my mind and bones.

◦◦◦◦

NEVILLE

We didn't have beds booked when we arrived in Pont-Saint-Martin.
We made the big mistake of going to the tourist office, waiting an

Via delle Gallie Consular Road & Forte di Bard

hour for the office to open, and then asking them to find something for us. The first place they suggested required dodging our way along the busy, dangerous *strada statale* for a couple of kilometers. We quickly realized the stupidity of this and returned to the office, hoping to find another place. Then we had to wait another twenty minutes before the same woman served us. This time she suggested a small *agriturismo* at the edge of town.

I remembered that this place was in my accommodation guide, but I had incorrectly assumed, given the photos on the web, that it was an extremely basic cabin somewhere in the countryside. Instead, we found it was ideally located at the edge of town in a small industrial area, near a "Conad" store (Italian grocery store chain) and within walking distance of the famous old bridge, Pont-Saint-Martin.

An elderly woman and her husband greeted us. The woman, who had one arm in a sling, showed us to a large, two-bedroom, self-contained apartment attached to the back of the main house.

She explained to us, as she held a set of clean sheets, that she had broken her arm and could not make the bed.

"*Nessun problema,*" Julie told her, "*Va bene, prepariamo noi il letto* —we will make the bed."

The apartment was simple, much like the photos had suggested, but surprisingly comfortable and relatively well equipped. We had a separate bedroom, a separate bathroom with a real shower, and a small kitchen to cook our own meals. From our apartment window, we had a south-facing view of nearby farms. It was not extravagant like the *agriturismo* outside of Chambave, but we were delighted to have discovered this little gem of a place so close to the town center—and for only 40 euro.

The town of Pont-Saint-Martin officially marks the end of the autonomous region of Valle d'Aosta. In the past, travelers and pilgrims would cross the famous Roman stone bridge of Pont-Saint-Martin before making their way to the big city of Ivrea and the beginning of the flat rice fields of the Po River valley. We spent the late afternoon exploring the city and visiting a small museum that described its history and that of its famous bridge. It was here we learned about the legend of a pilgrim named Martin who was travelling to Rome.

Martin stopped in a small village near the River Lys to spend the night. During the night, the overflowing river destroyed the bridge, forcing Martin to stay in the village. The village elders met and decided that they wanted a huge, new solid bridge but they did not have any money to pay for it. Martin decided to help by asking the Devil to build the bridge for them, but the Devil demanded to have the first 'being' that crossed the bridge as compensation. Martin accepted the Devil's offer.

When the bridge was finished, all the inhabitants could do was gaze at the Devil's masterwork; they would not cross it. So Martin threw a piece of bread on the bridge, attracting an old hungry dog that ran up and crossed the bridge, thus becoming the first being to cross the bridge. In retaliation, the angry Devil tried to destroy the bridge, but Martin put a holy cross on the top of the bridge, forcing the Devil to flee.

On that day, the pilgrim was renamed Saint Martin, and the village was renamed Pont-Saint-Martin. And the bridge is still there, a big, spectacular stone bridge.

We returned to our apartment to enjoy a simple home-cooked meal of *antipasti*, *pasta* and *vino*. After dinner, we sat on lawn chairs outside, admiring the changes in the evening sky as dark, ominous clouds rolled in. During the night, we awoke to the sound of loud crashes and rumblings and bright flashes. The wind blew violently, knocking over the lawn chairs, and it rained hard and steadily. We were witnessing a brilliant, fierce thunderstorm, something we had not seen before in Italy. It reminded me of the tropical thunderstorms we had seen in Singapore.

We tried to return to sleep, but it was impossible. For the next couple of hours the storm rumbled and roared as if we were on a battlefield. All the time, I wondered if this was an omen. What might the Gods have in store for us?

❧

We left Pont-Saint-Martin the next morning, crossing the old bridge and heading south towards Ivrea. Almost immediately, we ran into construction on the path that forced us back onto the state road. After much mucking about, we were finally able to leave the state road, and we were looking forward to an enjoyable hike, passing through a series of small hamlets and villages. The only obstacle was that all the Via Francigena signs disappeared as soon as we left the state road.

We looked around, but there were no signs anywhere; nothing, not even a set of directional or road signs. Reluctantly I dragged out my homemade guide and maps. I did my best to find our location on the maps and then chart a route through a maze of villages and small country roads. My maps were, at best, pitiful black-and-white reproductions of once colorful maps. It was difficult to tell if the black lines were roads, fences or contour lines, or something else altogether.

We knew we had to navigate through this section by using my maps and compass, a healthy dose of basic instinct, good luck, and a lot of direction from various locals. My strategy was simple. I would find the next village on the map and then we would make our way slowly there, stopping to ask the occasional person for directions, and checking and rechecking my compass to ensure that we were still heading south. It was a time-consuming, clumsy process, but we slowly made our way towards Ivrea.

All around us were the last remnants of the Valle d'Aosta; gentle sloping hills lined with old vineyards that dated back to the days of the Romans. We wandered along narrow stone-lined laneways, small paved country roads, and farm tracks through a number of "no-name" villages. The storm from the previous night had passed and the sun was shining, meaning it was hot and humid by mid-morning. Yet, it was oddly exciting, as if we were real adventurers—or real wanderers like the pilgrims of days past.

❧

JULIE

Somewhere between Settimo Vittone and San Germano, we stopped in one of the small villages to rest. Across the street were a few houses and a large complex of buildings.

It was bloody hot, humid, and time to eat again, so I plunked myself down on the old rock wall with a sigh of relief. I took a swig of water and pulled out a piece of fruit, noticing no one was around—it was siesta time.

Then out of nowhere, from behind us down the road, an older woman appeared with her big brown German shepherd.

"Buon giorno," we both greeted her, and she returned the greeting.

She had short whitish-gray hair and wore a blue dress with a multicolored apron on top and a necklace with a locket. Like many of the Italians we met, she was curious about us and asked in Italian:

"Where are you from? Where do you go? When did you start? How long do you walk? When do you arrive in Rome?"

She thought we were crazy to walk all the way to Rome. "I have seen other pilgrims but not from Canada," she said.

She began to tell us about herself and then was distracted by her dog. While her dog ran after a stray dog and cat that had been loitering nearby, she ran after her dog, trying to prevent it from scrapping with the other animals. It was like a scene in a movie, a typical Italian chaotic moment, and we were the characters watching.

I think she told us that she had lived in this village for many years, and that she had lost her husband three years ago when he died in a work accident in the vineyards. Her son worked at Mont Rosa, a ski resort 100 kilometers away. She was alone except for her dog.

She showed us the locket that hung around her neck and opened it to reveal a picture of her late husband, a handsome man. As she talked, her voice became soft and quiet, and I felt sad for her. I wanted to tell her how sorry I was to hear this. I wanted to keep her company and continue our conversation. But I couldn't find the words to tell her any of this.

Then I told her we had to go. She asked if we were coming back this way. I wished I could have said yes, but instead I told her, "No, we fly home from Rome."

"Molto male—too bad," she said, and shrugged her shoulders. She seemed saddened to hear this and I felt a lump in my throat. It appeared that she was not only curious but also lonely. We were strangers passing through, but for her, we were a diversion, a

welcome relief from her lonely life and an opportunity to be taken away briefly to another world.

She wished us a good, safe trip. I wanted to hug her as we said our goodbyes, and I felt the pull to stay. As we walked away, I kept looking back, wondering if there was some special reason for meeting her. Was I supposed to stay here and get to know her? Maybe she was a good cook and I could learn something from her. I wanted to go back. I just kept thinking, if only I could stay here and visit with her some more, even if only for a few more hours.

But that didn't happen. It was one of those moments where I regret not following what I felt in my heart. That memory is still crystal clear in my mind. I cherish the memory and I am grateful for the opportunity to have shared a conversation with her. I wish I could hop on a plane and fly back to Italy, and walk through her little village just to see and talk to her again. I wonder what she's doing today.

❧

"Coming down" the Valle d'Aosta was a lot more like "going up"—more than I had expected. The hilly terrain, with its steep ascents and rugged descents, as well as sliding down slippery meadows and walking on too many busy roads, to say nothing of the long distance, had worn me out. Above all, hiking in hot, humid, thirty-degree (Celsius) weather had exhausted me. So when I collapsed on the bed at the Ostello Salesiano Eporediese in Ivrea, I couldn't imagine getting up to walk again the next day. I slept for hours while Neville went out and perused the town.

When Neville returned, he roused me to search out a restaurant for dinner near the *ostello*. Inside the old city walls, we found a quiet, quaint *ristorante* called Monferrato that offered some local cuisine.

Over dinner, we talked about our walk over the past few days, recalling the events and challenges. While we had been through some tough sections, we had survived our "initiation."

Signage was still a problem and we gathered it might be an even bigger problem later. Getting lost had been more challenging than we expected. Now we appreciated what "no signs" really meant.

We both had mixed feelings about our guidebook and maps. They hadn't been as easy to use as we had expected, but as many times as I had cursed them, they had several times saved us from walking way off course.

Overall, the accommodation was better than expected. Our stays in *ostelli* had been unique and interesting. And the food at the various *ristoranti* had been excellent and often a highlight of the day.

Communication was still a struggle. Trying to ask for directions and then deciphering the directions was at times easy but at other times very difficult. Some people talked slowly and clearly when they realized I was struggling, but others talked faster and louder even when I asked them to speak slowly.

And then there were our challenges of communicating with each other. When things didn't go as expected, or when we were tired and frustrated, the least little annoyance could exacerbate the situation and cause disagreements and bickering.

We talked about how many wonderful, helpful people we had met along the way. Many of the Italians were curious and friendly, keenly interested in what we were doing and where we were going. And it was interesting for us to learn about their lives and their interests.

We were also surprised by our accomplishments and how well we both did with our body ailments. My ankle was holding up quite well and my plan was working—when I didn't give it enough rest or ice, I soon knew. I was proud of myself, and I actually thought it was quite amazing that I had managed to walk all this distance with an ankle that was still recovering. Neville's sore back had also worked itself out. He figured the humidity and the heat and the continuous movement had helped.

So we had been tested, but we realized this initiation was a necessary preparation. We had discovered that sometimes it was necessary to modify our expectations and adapt to whatever confronted us. But this was easier said than done. We realized that, however cumbersome and frustrating the walk may have been at times, it had its own rhythm. And we were starting to understand the rhythm of Italian life. At least we thought so.

That night before we went to sleep, another thunderstorm, much like the one we had experienced in Pont-Saint-Martin, rolled in and let loose. We watched the lightning show from our room, front row seats from our top floor balcony.

"Wow, two storms in a row! What do the Gods have in store for us next?" we asked each other. Was it an omen of what lay ahead?

Part 2

Bittersweet Encounters on Paths Unknown

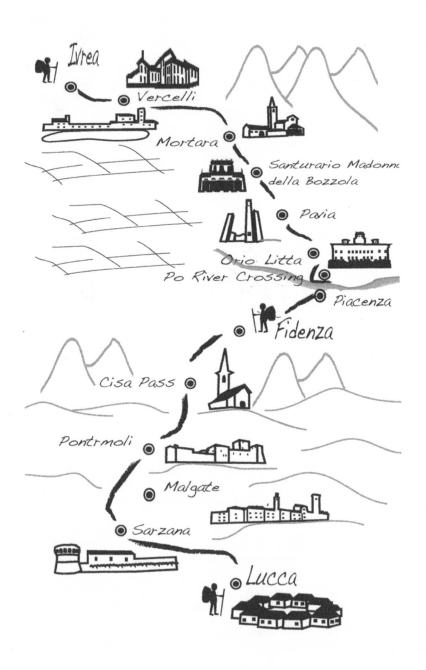

VII

The Vercellese

"Every path has its puddle."
– An English proverb

NEVILLE

"Where is everybody?" I wondered aloud. "This place is deserted."

The town was still. The streets were bare except for one lone old man who came out of a nearby bar. It was Sunday and siesta time, but even so, Vercelli was much quieter than other Italian towns we had visited.

It had rained the day before and the dampness and humidity hung in the air, making the medieval buildings look drab and lifeless. After being in the Valle d'Aosta, surrounded by colorful vineyards and lush green mountains with snow-capped peaks, Vercelli seemed strangely different, as if we had been transported to another planet.

We had decided to go to Vercelli because it is one of two major centers of rice production in Italy. The city is on the *Fiume* (River) *Sesia* in the Po River plain, a city of 50,000 people and one of the oldest urban centers in northern Italy. It was the first town in Piedmont to have the physical and political arrangement called a *città-stato*, or city-state, an early example of urbanization in the 5th century BC.

The young couple from Vercelli, whom we had met at the *agriturismo* in the Valle d'Aosta told us: "It's a stunning, beautiful city. Come to Vercelli and try the wines."

"Why not?" I thought. Besides, we might be lucky and get to visit a working rice farm, something I was sure would please Julie.

We had called the Convento di Biliemme, asking for a bed for the night. The good news—they had beds. The bad news—the *convento* was three kilometers somewhere south of us. Julie had trouble understanding the directions from the person on the phone; all she had understood was something about bus number three.

We wandered along the main street into the town center, looking for a tourist office or even a town map. While Julie went across an intersection to look for bus number three, a woman approached me.

"Do you need help?" the woman asked.

"I'm looking for the Convento di Biliemme," I replied, surprised that she spoke English.

She slowly shook her head. "The *convento* is far, far, far away and all the good accommodation in Vercelli is outside the town center," she explained. I asked her about a hotel in my accommodation guide.

"No, *that* one is an *uccellatoio*—a whorehouse. You don't want to stay there," she whispered.

I nodded in agreement. I told her my wife had gone to check out the bus schedule.

She shook her head. "It is Sunday. The local buses are not running today."

When Julie returned, the woman told us to wait. A few minutes later, she returned in a small car. She directed us to get in. Julie and I looked at each other, a little bewildered.

"*Prego prego.* I drive you. *No problema,*" she said.

We stuffed our gear and ourselves into her little car, and she drove us to the Convento di Biliemme. Julie offered a token of appreciation, but she wanted nothing for helping us out. Before we could thank her again, she drove off.

We rang the doorbell and a gruff voice answered. I pushed open the small metal door and we squeezed through it. After climbing a set of stairs to the second floor, we inched our way down a dark hallway, passing numerous cardboard boxes, bags stuffed with clothing, and all kinds of junk—probably collected since the day it had opened.

We were greeted by an aging hippy, with long white hair, wearing a white robe. He did not speak much of either Italian or English, but grunted, smiled and waved his hands as he gestured us to follow him down the hallway to a plain room with eight bunk beds. Further along was a communal washroom that included a couple of old sinks and a toilet, but no shower.

I leaned over to Julie and said, "This, I gather, will be our home for tonight."

"I guess we should be grateful we have a place to sleep," Julie replied.

We spent the remaining afternoon exploring the old city center. Under Roman rule, Vercelli was a Roman *Municipium*, with new houses, temples, markets, theaters, amphitheaters, a fluvial harbor, and an aqueduct, surrounded by massive walls. There were 20,000 people living in the city by 100 AD.

During the 13th and 15th centuries, the Visconti and Savoia families transformed the town into a military stronghold, building a new castle and a citadel. This included expanding the existing walls. After the French conquest in 1704, the Roman walls of the city were demolished and the bricks were recovered and reused to build new houses. Today, avenues surround the center of the town where the old walls once stood.

By the Middle Ages, Vercelli was an important center for the pilgrims traveling to Rome, a crossroad for the two primary routes of the Via Francigena that crossed the Alps and continued south to Rome. The first route, the path we had been travelling on, originated from the Gran San Bernardo, passing through the Valle d'Aosta to Ivrea. From there, it passed by Lake Viverone and the towns of Cavaglià and Santhià to arrive at Vercelli. Sigeric, the Archbishop of Canterbury, took this route on his journey to Rome.

A second, lesser-known route crossed the Alps and entered Italy from France via Moncenisio, where it followed the Cenischia Stream, arriving in the town of Susa. From Susa, it crossed through the Susa Valley, past Turin, before reaching Vercelli. By the 12th century, sixteen places of hospitality for pilgrims existed in the city and throughout the surrounding region.

✿

Roman and medieval history aside, what attracted us to Vercelli was the rice. The area that surrounds Vercelli is some-times known as the *Vercellese*, a district of roughly fifty towns and villages covering an area of 1,200 square kilometers and dominated by rice cultivation. Italians in this area have a saying: "Rice is born in water but dies in wine."

In the spring, water is the foremost feature of the Vercellese. From Vercelli, you see a landscape of rice paddies and lagoons, criss-crossed by dark tongues of earth lined with rows of poplar trees. It stretches as far as the eye can see.

In the past, rice was a rare essence, a medicine, even a miraculous panacea. In fact, it was easier to find seeds of *Oryza Sativa*, which is its botanical name, at the apothecary or pharmacist than in the stalls of food markets. Some scholars believe rice came to Europe in the 8th century; others claim that the Byzantines were growing rice in the southeast region of the Iberian Peninsula as early as the 7th century. Still others state that it was not grown until the late 10th century, about the time that the Arabs established rice farming in Spain.

However, the majority agree that rice production in Italy dates from the 15th century. Legend has it that in 1468, someone in the Po River valley had the idea of planting some rice seeds.

Documentation from the Council of Ten, dated July 7, 1533 in Venice, exempted rice from an excise tax because it took the place of vegetables.

In the medieval era, the Vercellese was a land of *grange*, large agricultural farms of the Benedictine and Cistercian monks. During this period, rice production continued to spread, adapting to the distinctly poor and infertile Vercellese terrain. Despite strong opposition, especially in the 15th and 16th centuries, rice cultivation expanded further with the growth of natural and man-made canals.

Today, more than sixty percent of the rice consumed by Europeans comes from this region.

ༀ

JULIE
When I discovered we would be passing through rice country on the Via Francigena, I researched information in books and on the Internet and discovered that there were a number of rice farms and estates in the region. I found several on the map that would be close to the trail and suggested to Neville that perhaps we should stay in Vercelli a couple nights and see if we could visit one of the farms.

He reminded me that we wouldn't have time for that. "And I doubt we'll walk through there, because the trail is mostly on the road. I was thinking we should bus through it," he added.

Even so, I was sure there was a way we could visit a farm. "We could always take the train or bus there, visit the farm and then train or bus to our next walking point," I pointed out.

"Yeah, we'll see," he replied, non-committal.

I consulted our homemade culinary guidebook before leaving Ivrea and selected three rice farms, hoping we would be able to visit at least one. On my third call, I struck it lucky. I was surprised but elated when a woman came on the phone and spoke English. I explained why I was calling and immediately she responded with,

"Yes, you can come for a tour. We would be happy to show you around our farm."

Proud of myself, I ran excitedly to Neville, who was coming out of the Ivrea train station, having checked out the timetable.

"Guess what? We have a date with a rice farm."

"Wow, that's great!" he said, surprised but pleased.

The Azienda Agricola F.lli Gasparotto (family farm) is located in the little hamlet of Frazione di Brarola, just east of Vercelli and close to the Via Francigena. For over fifty years, the Gasparotto family has cultivated rice. In 1968, Bortolo Gasparotto moved his wife and family of five sons and two daughters from Breganze to Brarola in search of a better life. Initially it was a typical family rice farm where horses were used to harvest the rice.

Today it is still family run, but it now has 145 hectares of land and uses modern technology and mechanical harvesters to cultivate more than nine thousand quintals (a quintal is equal to one hundred kilograms) of rice each year. Three of the brothers are mostly responsible for the overall operations of the farm. Over the past ten years, the brothers have focused on producing high-quality rice using modern methods combined with the best cultural traditions.

We had arranged to meet them at the Vercelli train station. At 9:00 am, a four-wheel drive truck drove up. A young woman, Alessandra, stepped out to greet us and introduced us to Roberto and Pietro Paolo, two of the three brothers.

We stuffed our packs into the back of the truck, eagerly jumped into the back seat and left the rush hour chaos for the country-side of Vercelli. Roberto and Pietro Paolo didn't speak English so Alessandra did the translating. She told us they were taking us first to see their rice fields.

Roberto turned off the main road, drove down several narrow dirt roads that ran between their expansive rice fields, and eventually stopped in the middle of the track.

When we stepped outside the truck, I looked around and could not believe the vastness of the landscape—miles and miles of rice fields. It was stunningly beautiful with the bright sun reflecting off the rice sprigs—shades of gold and golden-brown shone everywhere. Monte Rosa, with its snow-covered top, loomed in the background.

Roberto reached over and picked a small sprig of *Carnaroli* rice. From the other side of the track, Pietro Paolo picked a sprig of *Baldo* rice, and then handed us a third sprig of rice called *Vialone Nano*. These three types represented the traditional and most precious varieties they cultivate.

After the field tour, we arrived at the farm estate, in the hamlet of Brarola, where there is only a small collection of homes besides those of the family. We were introduced to the oldest brother, Giovanni, and other farm helpers.

Roberto and Pietro Paolo guided us to one of the buildings that was full of equipment and big sacks of the different rice varieties. Roberto pulled out a handful of rice from six different sacks that were all marked with *Riso di Qualità Superiore*. He put the rice on

Pietro Paolo & Roberto Gasparotto, Julie and Alessandra

the table, identifying each type, including the three we had seen growing in the fields.

I placed each type in my hand, examining the smell and the texture and slowly rolling the grains between my fingers as Giovanni, Roberto and Pietro Paolo explained the differences. They told us that *Carnaroli* is one of the great super-fine varieties, preferred by haute cuisine chefs for its supreme quality, perfect for non-sticky risottos, rice salads and the fine rice dishes. *Baldo* is a young variety derived from the more common rice called *Arborio*. It is a fine, starchy rice, able to withstand all forms of cooking and great for all types of risottos and oven-baked dishes. *Sant'Andrea* is typical of the Baraggia region north of Vercelli. It has compact, elongated grains, making it perfect for soups, rice pudding, croquettes, fritters and rice cakes.

Another variety was *Venere Nero Aromatico*, or Black Venus rice, the result of crossbreeding Italian and Chinese rice varieties, and often called "emperor's rice," a reference to the black-colored rice eaten by the emperors of China. Another type, a hybrid, was *Riso Rosso Ermes*, or Ermes Red Rice—a long, narrow-grained aromatic rice that was the result of crossbreeding Black Venus rice with other varieties. Finally, there was the rare *Riso Ostigliano*, a pink whole meal rice, full of iron, but today it has almost disappeared from the markets.

Roberto then guided us outside to another set of buildings, where he explained each stage of the production: harvesting, sorting, separating, and drying. Normally they harvest in mid-September, though this can vary from year to year.

"We'll start to harvest the *Carnaroli* in about one week from now, and if it rains, we must wait at least one day later until we can harvest," he explained. Lucky for us, we were here to see the rice growing in the fields before it was harvested.

The raw grains are stored in a very tall storage silo until a certain humidity level is reached. The kernels are then separated from the husk, sent through a series of grates into a processing area, and fed into another machine to further dry and remove the balance of humidity. Once ready, the rice is sent to a local community processor.

In a large garage, there was a massive harvester, a Laverda 2760IX, purchased in 2002. Roberto explained that it takes three or four hours to harvest a single 10 to 20-hectare field of rice. The harvester separates the grain from the stems, and once the round is finished, the grain is poured into a large truck and brought back to the farm.

Roberto showed how he uses modern technology to decide when the rice is ready. He took a few grains of rice, ground them, and then put the contents into a special container that measures the humidity.

"The best level is about 13%," he explained.

I saw a piece of equipment on a table and asked what it was.

"That's the old rice mill," explained Roberto. "That's the way my parents would grind the rice in the old days." I imagined them painstakingly grinding rice for weeks—the same amount that could now be ground in a day.

He took us to one more building and showed us the doorway to the upper level where the *contadini*, or farm workers, used to live up to the 1960s.

Roberto ended his tour in the showroom. Inside were many of their products such as ground rice flour and bran, pasta, biscuits and cookies, soups mixed with legumes, and rice cereals. I walked around the showroom examining all the products they sold, wondering how I could get them home. Obviously, I couldn't carry them to Rome. It was a tough decision; I wanted them all.

When the tour ended, they surprised us and said in Italian, "We invite you to stay and eat lunch with us."

"Oh, no, that's not necessary."

"No, no, we insist," Alessandra replied.

"Va bene, grazie, grazie mille. Then can I help?"

"No, no, you relax in here."

Alessandra led us into the farmhouse living room and suggested we wait there. We talked more about the farm and our walk in Italy.

She popped in and out of the room, periodically helping Roberto who was cooking in the kitchen.

What were they making? In this region, there is a specialty rice dish, known as *Panissa di Vercelli*, enriched with vegetables and lard. The preparation includes chopping lard or bacon and onion, and frying them gently in a saucepan until the onion starts to turn brown. Peeled, chopped, deseeded tomatoes are added to the mixture, which is then seasoned with salt and left to cook. Beans that have been soaked for 12 hours and then boiled are added and left to simmer for another 30 minutes. It's a time-consuming meal to make, and I certainly didn't expect anything like that today. I imagined they would be preparing a simple meal of pasta accompanied with some cured meats and cheeses.

My curiosity got the best of me and I asked Alessandra if I could watch Roberto cook. I was surprised when I entered the kitchen and saw him dressed in his special apron. He was cooking *risotto* but it wasn't just an ordinary *risotto*.

He told me, *"E la ricetta speciale di mia madre...la mia preferita*– It's my mother's special recipe; it's my favorite."

"Veramente? Perché? Is that true? Why?"

"Ci metto delle spezie."

Wow, I learnt something! I had never thought of adding spices to risotto. I watched him add the last bit of broth and finish with *Parmigiano-Reggiano* cheese.

He called to Alessandra and Pietro Paolo that the *risotto* was ready. We were summoned to the table outside on the patio. The warm, sunny afternoon was perfect for sitting outside and enjoying Roberto's fine cooking and the warm hospitality. Pietro Paolo's dog sat nearby, watching us and waiting.

We eagerly dug into the large bowl of *risotto*. *"Il risotto è buono, molto buono,"* I said after my first bite. It was creamy and delicious, just the right al dente texture, with a wonderful combination of flavors. After a second helping of *risotto*, chunks of *Parmigiano-Reggiano cheese*, sliced *cotto* (thinly sliced cooked ham), and plenty of bread appeared (Italians love their bread). We lingered over an *espresso* and chatted more about our walk and the farm, while the dog waited for scraps.

After lunch, I told Roberto that I wanted to buy some rice biscuits and rice to take with us. He escorted us to the showroom and offered us anything we wanted. I picked out two packages of rice cookies; they would make good snacks along the route. I also selected some of the special Ermes Red Rice that I figured we could cook for ourselves somewhere along the way. He encouraged us to take something else, but we told him it would be too much weight for us to carry.

Roberto and Alessandra returned us to Vercelli, following the Via Francigena route that snaked along the river. Now, in the mid-afternoon sun, the city was transformed to a colorful and attractive center buzzing with activity. Our first impression of Vercelli had changed.

We thanked our hosts profusely for their kindness, generous hospitality, and Roberto's delicious cooking. I felt sad to say goodbye to such beautiful people, and we hoped we would see them again soon.

Was it a coincidence that the Gasparotto family was the first to accept my request, or was it fate? In any case, I felt honored and grateful for their genuine acts of kindness. They were some of the most sincere and hospitable people that we had met in Italy. Not only did they go out of their way to accommodate complete strangers and give us a tour of their farm, on one day's notice, but they spent hours with us and then fed us. The best part: we were served a meal that couldn't get more local, cooked by the same person who produced the rice. What touched me most was that he chose to cook his favourite rice, with passion, honoring his mother— a memorable experience that left me with a lump in my throat.

VIII

At the Mercy of Strangers

"Unyawo alunampumulo
— The foot has no nose."

A Zulu proverb emphasizing the need to be
hospitable and treat strangers well. Since our
foot has no nose, we do not know where our
foot might take us one day.

NEVILLE

After Ivrea, through the Po River valley to Fidenza, we had not pre-booked any accommodation. There weren't many inexpensive places to stay, and I was uncertain of what was available at any cost. My accommodation guide for this region was thin.

We knew the routing through the valley would be difficult and tedious at times. There were signage issues, long stretches, and sections that required walking on dangerous, busy roads. "Boring, flat landscape; hot and humid with mosquitoes most days," were among the descriptions offered by others that had journeyed through this region. Thus, some simply chose to bypass it altogether.

This section was unlike the Valle d'Aosta, where there was an abundance of places to stay for the night, and where the surroundings included tiny valley hamlets and quiet country dirt paths, generally well marked. And even if you did lose your way, there were always people nearby from whom you could ask directions. But here in the Po River valley, in the middle of rice and maize fields, I could not imagine finding somebody to ask for help.

In short, we did not have a plan, other than to suggest that we would just wing it, hope for the best and take each day as it came.

So when we arrived in Mortara late, about 5:30 pm, I asked Julie to make a call from the train station phone booth to the abbey we had selected from our list.

I watched Julie struggle to comprehend what the man on the other end of the phone was saying.

"Please talk more slowly," she asked in Italian, but apparently, the man only talked faster.

Julie hung up the phone, turned to me and said, "His dialect was impossible to understand, and his directions are confusing. The more I asked him to repeat himself, the more difficult it was to understand him. It's going to be a challenge finding this place."

On the far southern outskirts of Mortara is the abbey, or Abbazia di Sant'Albino. It is one of the most important churches of the region of Lomellina, dating back to the 5th century.

In the past, passage through this region of swamps and marshes and wild animals was dangerous for travelers. During the Middle Ages, Sant'Albino was a resting-place for wary pilgrims traveling to Rome. Scrawled on the bricks are inscriptions from pilgrims, and one dates back to 1100.

Mortara is the rice capital of Lombardy, but it had a very different ambiance from Vercelli. There was something oddly unnatural about Mortara. Missing were old, colorful, charming buildings, and there wasn't even a wonderful pedestrian avenue for the evening *passeggiata*. A legend suggests the town changed its name from Pulchra Silva, meaning "beautiful forest," to Mortis Ara, or "altar of death," after the large number of casualties in the infamous bloody battle between Charlemagne and the Lombards on October 12, 773. The abbey became the burial ground for fallen soldiers, and among the casualties were two of Charlemagne's paladins, Amelius of Alvernia and Amicus from Beyre. The Paladins, sometimes known as the Twelve Peers, were a group of twelve powerful warriors that commanded Charlemagne's troops.

⊱⊰

As far as we could determine, there wasn't a tourist information center, so we looked for a town map. We found a defaced old metallic plaque with a crude diagram of the town. Staring at the map, I guessed that the abbey was on the far side of town.

Thus, our plan was to walk along the main road leading away from the train station, in the direction of the town center and towards the abbey. Just to ensure that we were going the right way, we stopped various people, asking for directions. The good news was that everybody knew about the abbey; the bad news was that everybody gave us a different answer regarding how to reach it.

Therefore, our pursuit of the abbey became a series of comic encounters that left us ever more confused and lost. The first person, an old man pushing a bike, suggested that we needed to walk down a nearby small side road, then cross one or perhaps two major roads, and then hike another two kilometers or so south.

"It is in the middle of a field," he claimed.

His information left me dubious that he knew where it was, so we asked a second man, dressed in a suit. He told us to continue down the same main road.

"Just as you cross the highway you will see it," he claimed.

We stopped a woman wearing big dark sunglasses, in a tight short skirt and high heels. She shook her head, and said, "It is far, far away, too far to walk. You need to drive there."

We figured she probably didn't walk much.

After endless wandering through the narrow streets of Mortara, we eventually arrived at the outskirts of town at a roundabout. By now, it was 6:30 pm and getting dark. We had been walking around in circles for an hour, but we had not seen an abbey or any building that could pass for one.

We called the abbey again. The same man who liked to talk quickly answered the phone, and again Julie could not understand a word he said. We still did not know where it was.

I became frustrated and impatient. "I'm not in the mood to wander around in the dark, looking for a mysterious abbey. Even if we did find it, we'd have to walk all the way back into town just to find some place to eat," I told Julie.

In my accommodation guide, Mortara had a lone one-star hotel. That would have to do, I figured.

"*Please* call the *albergo*," I asked Julie impatiently.

"We should go on a bit more, just a little further," Julie insisted.

"I don't want to walk another three kilometers and then have to walk back into town in the dark."

We argued. Both of us were tired and in an ugly mood, especially me. Julie finally gave in and called the *albergo*.

"*Buona sera. Avete una camera doppia, per favore?*" she asked. Yes, he had a double room.

We retraced our steps back into town and found it in the old center, down a narrow, dark laneway. But as we approached the *albergo*, I knew I would regret this.

It was an old hotel and there was only one room available. The owner directed us upstairs to the back, along a balcony of sorts, and then opened a sticky metal door to the room. What should have been a standard hotel room looked more like a prison cell: a small concrete square room with two single beds and a tiny cramped washroom—the old European style with a shower head on the wall and no curtains. The hotel room door had a narrow window opening at the top that reminded me of some of the rooms we had slept in while traveling in Asia.

The room itself faced directly into the neighboring buildings; it was as if we shared a communal courtyard one floor up. I wondered if this place was one of those *alberghi*, an *uccellatoio* like the one Dorella had mentioned in Vercelli. I tried not to think about it.

We sat on the bed, looked around, and wondered how we got ourselves into this predicament.

"It could be worse," Julie reasoned.

"It feels like a flophouse," I said dispiritedly.

"It's only one night," Julie reminded me, but I wondered if it could get any worse.

We quickly showered, changed, and hurried outside to search for something to eat.

It was dark and the streets were quiet and empty. The air was motionless; it felt eerie. We walked almost all the way back to the train station.

"There's something weird about this town," I said. "There's nobody around. And there are no restaurants open, not even a *pizzeria* or a bar." I had never experienced staying in a town or village in Italy where not a single bar was open.

"I guess we'll just have to go back to the *albergo*," I suggested glumly.

"No!" Julie protested, "There has to be some place open."

After we wandered around some more, I spied a nondescript restaurant and *albergo* almost directly across from the train station. It looked like an average business traveler's hotel. I didn't remember seeing it when we had first arrived in Mortara, but I had been so fixated on finding the abbey I had simply missed it.

We asked about dinner.

"*Si, no problema,*" the man at the door said. "*Prego.*"

We walked into a bright dining room, the size of a large banquet room. A combination of loud, hard rock and rap music echoed through the room. Five people, each sitting at a table alone, made for an odd sight.

"It reminds me of my days working for that software company, when I traveled a lot and had to stay in one of those "budget no-frills" hotels, eating dinner alone," I said sadly.

As we perused the menu, the waiter approached us and suggested the special *primo piatto* of the day, which was some kind of *gnocchi*. We politely thanked him for his suggestion but told him we had not decided yet and were not ready to order.

We quickly decided on a *pasta* dish, but then sat and waited for our server to return to take our order. As we started to wonder if he would ever reappear, he returned to our table with two plates of the *gnocchi*.

"Oh, this is great," Julie whispered sarcastically to me.

We tried to explain to him that we did not order the *gnocchi* and we wanted a different pasta.

The waiter stood there, saying nothing, looking confused.

"I am sure the *gnocchi* is fine, Neville, let's just take it; let's just eat it and go," Julie finally said.

"*Si, prego,*" Julie told the waiter. He set the plates down in front of us and left.

The music by now was getting insanely loud, forcing Julie finally to ask the waiter, "*Mi scusi, signore, può abbassare il volume?*" She made the motion of turning down the volume.

"*Si, signora,*" he replied, and he immediately walked over to the amplifier and turned down the volume. There was an audible sigh of relief from us and the other five diners.

❦

JULIE

Eager to get out of Mortara, we were up early the next morning and gone by 7:30 am.

Not much further, less than a kilometer from where we had turned around the night before, sat the abbey, Abbazia di Sant'Albino.

"Wow, look at that! I really wished we had stayed here. It looks like a neat place. It's one of the most beautiful settings I've seen so far," I said.

Surrounded by colorful fields of rice, the abbey looked magical. The mist was slowly lifting and the sun's rays beamed off the rice fields, casting golden brown and yellow hues in the morning light.

"Let's go see if we can look inside anyway," I suggested.

I walked up to the door, rang and waited. "Someone must be around, but then again, if there aren't any visitors, the keeper might not be here." I rang again, but there was still no answer.

I was disappointed we couldn't see the inside. It would remain a mystery, just one of the many places along the way that would be left to our imaginations.

After the abbey, most of the walk to Tromello was through an eternal expanse of rice and maize fields. Previous walkers had suggested skipping this section because it was flat and boring. I remembered those same words from people who had walked through the *meseta* on the Camino de Santiago. However, we had decided to walk through the *meseta* anyway, because it was such an unusual landscape and because not many people were walking it. With this in mind, I suggested to Neville we walk through sections of the Po River valley anyway. And I am glad we did. While I love mountains, the green forests, and the ocean, I also love the solitude of walking through wide-open spaces. There's something special about it.

"Here we are alone, just you and I, out in the middle of nowhere, in beautiful shimmering golden rice fields, unlike on the Camino de Santiago where there was pilgrim after pilgrim. This is exactly what I wanted then, and had expected from the Camino, but never got," I reminded Neville.

There are things to consider when walking through endless rice fields and farmland when it is hot and sunny. For one, there may be little shelter or fresh water along the way. So when we passed a farmer's home and the owner and his barking dog greeted us, Neville reminded me we were running low on water and had another eight kilometers to go before the next town.

"*Buon giorno,*" we said. "*Per favore, abbiamo bisogno di acqua da bere,*" I asked the farmer.

The farmer didn't hesitate to guide us toward his water tap. "*Prego, prego,*" he beckoned. Oh, the cold, refreshing water felt and tasted great! I wet my bandana and wrapped it around my hot and sweaty head and neck.

The farmer sent us on our way after we told him we were walking the Via Francigena. *"Sempre diritto,"* he said, pointing toward the south.

We continued our walk through more rice fields, then along a dirt track through a grove of trees, and then turned south to follow another dirt road through more fields.

When it was time for a break, I plunked my pack down on the grassy shoulder of the track and breathed in the warm, humid, morning air. This was a perfect spot. I scanned the scenery: nothing but rice fields forever. I loved being out there in the middle of nowhere.

"Wow, I can't believe how warm it is, Nev," I said, impulsively tearing off my sopping wet top. I dug into my pack and pulled out my recorder and stood there playing it among the bright golden rice fields. It was truly heaven.

Lost in reflection – golden rice paddies – Mortara

⟨❦⟩

NEVILLE

Between Mortara and Tromello, we briefly lost the trail several times, and finally it just vanished. We arrived at an intersection between two farm tracks and there were no more signs. We wandered up and down looking for something, anything, but there was nothing to tell us which way to go. I looked around, and for as far as I could see, there were only endless fields of rice and maize. My nightmare of getting lost in the rice fields had begun.

If we had any hope of arriving in Tromello, or anywhere for that matter, it was apparent we required a local farmer or two to help us navigate through this labyrinth of rice paddies and maize, if we could find one.

Fortunately, a farmer did drive by and we stopped him, asking for directions. He suggested we continue past his house and there we would find the road to Tromello. We marched on, and at the intersection, we got further directions from another farmer who told us to walk along the small provincial road for about three kilometers. We spent the next hour walking along a quiet, almost traffic-free, provincial paved road.

As we approached the center of Tromello, it felt as if we were making a slow-motion entrance onto some grand theater stage. Tall, leafy poplar trees, spaced ten meters apart, lined each side of the road. A church loomed in the distance and got bigger with every step we took. There was a sense of welcome, friendliness and warmth as we passed town citizens, all of them smiling and waving us on.

As we arrived in the center of the town, Julie announced she was hungry, and we stepped inside the first open place, a small *trattoria* where a few locals were eating lunch.

"*Prego!*" The bartender greeted us warmly, pointing the way to the nearly empty dining room where only three men were eating together. All eyes were on us as we made our way to a table.

We were *stranieri*, strangers to town. In a town of this size, a stranger would not walk through town unnoticed.

Julie slipped off to the bathroom. After walking through the heat, sweat dripped down her face and her shirt was drenched. While she was gone, I struck up a conversation with a couple of the men.

"We're walking the Via Francigena," I said.

"The Via Francigena?" one of them asked.

"Yes. We're walking to Rome. We started from Switzerland a couple of weeks ago," I replied.

This triggered a quick round of questions and excited chatter, mostly in Italian, between the two men. The conversation quickly spread like wildfire throughout the *trattoria* and into the bar. By the time Julie returned, our server had returned with our food. She was smiling, laughing and talking to the men too, about the Via Francigena and us. Obviously, we were the hot topic of discussion for the day.

We ordered two plates of hot duck, a local specialty, and a salad, as well as a bottle of water and some bread. The duck was moist and delicious, and the salad was hearty, just what we needed to feel renewed and ready to tackle another ten kilometers.

Before leaving, the owner gave us a couple of stiff coffees to send us on our way. Then he presented us with the bill. The entire bill came to only 10 euro for both of us.

◦❧◦

JULIE

As we stepped out of the *trattoria,* an older man on a bicycle stopped in front of us. He was short and dressed in pants and a shirt covered with flecks of white paint. He was talking so fast I couldn't understand everything he was saying, but he motioned us to follow him while he rode his bicycle.

"My name is Signore Bindolini. Where do you come from? Where do you go?" he asked—the usual questions we heard from everybody we met along the Via Francigena.

Signore Bindolini stopped at the end of the main street, got off his bike, and walked over to a little compound of buildings behind a wall.

"*Venite, prego, prego,*" He said enthusiastically, unlocking a gate and motioning us inside. Beyond was a tiny courtyard full of stuff piled against the wall of the building. He unlocked another door that was tucked into a corner of the building and ushered us in. Inside was what looked like a bar, only big enough to seat four people. I wondered if it was part of his home; it was an odd place for a bar.

I thought I heard him say something about a drink, so I expected he was about to offer us a *digestivo* to follow our meal at the *trattoria*. He picked up a bottle of wine and offered us some, but we politely said, "*no, grazie,*" and explained we still had ten kilometers to walk that afternoon.

He pointed to the wall behind the bar, saying something about "other pilgrims." He showed us postcards he had received from other pilgrims who had passed through the town. These same pilgrims had sent him postcards from Rome or other cities along the Via Francigena.

Signore Bindolini then gave me two small white cards with an image of the town of Tromello. He wrote his name and address on the back of one of the cards. He asked me to send him a postcard from Rome and another one from home.

Next Signore Bindolini went to the refrigerator. When he opened it, I saw the refrigerator was stocked full of water bottles. He handed us each a bottle. Then he opened another door and pulled out two ice cream bars from the freezer. Bless his heart, I thought, he is so kind.

"*Grazie, molte grazie,*" we said. We could not thank him enough.

"We must go now," I said. Taking us under his wing, Signore Bindolini proudly escorted us to the outskirts of town, ensuring we safely rejoined the Via Francigena, a dirt trail through the farmlands towards Garlasco.

"*Grazie ancora,* Signore Bindolini," I said as we shook his hand and said goodbye.

"*Buon viaggio. Ricordate cartolina di Roma,*" he replied, sending us on our way. "*Sempre diritto,*" he called out again.

Julie and Signore Bindolini – Tromello

Minutes later, I looked back. Signore Bindolini was still standing there. We waved goodbye once more. As he walked away, fading into the distance, I felt humbled to think that an ordinary place like Tromello offered such generosity and kindness to *stranieri* and pilgrims alike.

One day I wish to return to Tromello and again visit Signore Bindolini and tell him that he touched my heart and that I will forever remember his hospitality.

❧

We walked through more fields of rice and corn, following the Cavour Canal and crossing it twice. The Cavour Canal, built in honor of Count Camillo Benso di Cavour, Prime Minister of Piedmont at the time and the chief architect of modern Italy, carries water from the River Po. It irrigates the land to the north, particularly the Vercellese region where dry summers hamper the cultivation of rice.

About three kilometers before reaching Garlasco, we turned right and went south away from the canal. We stopped to talk to a farmer who was standing in the middle of the dirt path supervising two workers, one operating a combine harvester and the other driving a truck.

"*Buon giorno,*" I called out as we approached.

"*Buon giorno,*" he replied.

"*C'è molto riso,*" I said. There is much rice.

"*Si, certo,*" he added. Yes certainly!

Trying to engage in conversation, we watched one man maneuver the truck underneath the arm of the combine. The man driving the combine flipped a switch and the rice poured into the truck.

"*Dove andate oggi?*" the farmer asked.

"*Andiamo al Santuario*—We go to Santuario Madonna della Bozzola," I replied.

"Ah, but this is not the way. You must return to the canal, turn right and go east. Continue for another couple of kilometers, cross the *strada statale* and then head though the forest for one kilometer." He pointed in an easterly direction.

"*Grazie, molte grazie. Buona giornata,*" I said, and we retraced our steps back to the canal.

For Neville, this was all too confusing. He thought Garlasco was further south in the direction we had been heading. "We are going the wrong way," he claimed.

"Nev, I am *sure* the farmer knows what he is talking about. Maybe this route is another way to Garlasco," I replied.

Irritated, Neville reluctantly followed me. When we reached the *strada statale*, there were no Via Francigena signs or even signs to Garlasco.

"According to my map, Garlasco is over *that* way," Neville said, pointing down the busy *strada statale* in the direction we had been heading before we met the farmer. "I think we should be going in *that* direction," he argued.

"But the farmer pointed over *this* way and said it was through the forest. I think we should go this way," I protested.

"Maybe you misunderstood what he said," Neville suggested.

"*No!* I know what he said," I protested.

So there we were, standing on the side of the road, arguing about which way to go. We could have drawn an audience any time; if we did, I didn't notice.

Finally, Neville gave in and we crossed over the busy *strada statale* and followed a path through some deep grass into the forest. Neville was grumbling the whole way, and it didn't help that, after arriving at the edge of the clearing, there was nothing before us except more trees.

"It's not this way," argued Neville. "I'm going back to the road; this is crazy. There is no bloody sanctuary around here! But it might be that small, old building we saw earlier when we crossed the road and entered the forest. I'm going back to check it out."

I started to question myself too. I was sure we were going the right way according to the farmer, but I also thought that we should have arrived there by now. Maybe we hadn't gone a kilometer; he might have been a little off in his distances—it would not be the first time we had experienced that. I was definitely in doubt, so I grudgingly turned around and followed Neville back towards the road.

A high fence surrounded the building. Neville walked up to the gate and called out, but we couldn't see or hear anyone.

I thought it was an odd-looking sanctuary and an odd location, but what did I know. You never know what to expect on the Via Francigena. In fact, we had no idea what the supposed sanctuary looked like, but my intuition told me this place looked more like a cottage with a few spiritual decorations. A variety of small religious artifacts hung in the middle of the courtyard between two old buildings.

The longer we stood there, the more convinced I was that this was not the place.

"Well, there's no answer anyway, so let's go. I'm going on into the forest. We probably haven't gone far enough," I told Neville.

Being stubborn as a bull, Neville countered with, *"Well I'm taking the road!* I don't care what the farmer said, Garlasco is *that* way, and I'm going *that* way!"

"And I'm going *this* way; I don't care about Garlasco. The sanctuary is this way, and I'm going this way," I yelled, turning and stomping off into the forest. Minutes later, I heard Neville behind me.

We continued through the forest, past the same clearing where we had stopped before. Ahead we heard sounds we could not initially identify.

"We must be getting closer to civilization," I said encouragingly. Up ahead was a young man dressed in black pants and jacket, sitting on his motorbike and talking on his mobile phone.

When he finished, I asked him, *"Mi scusi, per favore, dov'è il Santuario Madonna della Bozzola?"*

"Diritto," he replied, *"Sempre diritto."*

We heard church bells in the distance and twenty minutes later we stumbled into the small hamlet of Bozzola. In front of us was an enormous building decorated with ornate sculptures and looming over the hamlet—the sanctuary. It was massive; you simply could not miss it.

We approached the sanctuary and looked inside but saw nobody. I went into a little gift shop in an adjoining building. When I asked the elderly woman inside about beds, she told me the man with the keys would be back at 5:30 pm. It was now 4:30 pm.

We ordered cold tonics at the nearby bar and then walked back to the gift shop at 5:30 pm, expecting to meet the "key man." He had not yet arrived. The woman quickly made a phone call.

"He is tied up in traffic," she claimed.

We went back outside and sat on the cement benches in front of the sanctuary, waiting. Becoming impatient, I went back inside a couple more times. They still had not heard from the key man.

By now, Neville was convinced nobody was coming and we were not going to get a room.

It was getting late for us. We were tired, grumpy, and cold. My body was cooling down and my damp sweaty clothes were giving me a chill. I lay on the bench leaning against my backpack, thinking how silly this was. I just wanted to take a shower and change into some clean, dry clothes. Surely, we don't have to wait this long, I thought; either they have a room or they don't.

We waited some more. By now, there were fewer and fewer people around. I returned to the gift shop, and this time there was only one person in the shop, a younger woman.

She made a call. When she hung up, she said to me, "The man was at the doctor's office; he's coming soon."

About ten minutes later a car zoomed into the parking lot. A man leapt out and hurried over to us. His belt was loaded with keys that clanged as he walked toward us. *"Ah, pellegrini—sono Cesar,"* said the man with the keys. It was now 6:40 pm.

He led us through the gate (that was already ajar) into a large courtyard and introduced us to a young man. "Do you want to shower?" he asked. *"Si, si,"* we replied.

Cesar directed the young man to take us upstairs to our room, and we followed him up a set of steep stairs and entered a tiny room with four bunk beds, a short dresser, and chest of drawers. The young man pointed to where we would be sleeping. We quickly realized that our room served as the front entrance and a bedroom for guests. Behind our room, there was a long hallway and more rooms.

There was some confusion as the young man walked back and forth between some showers down the hall and into the room next to ours. Finally, he directed me into the next room and told me I could shower there. He sent Neville to shower down the hallway.

I fought with the bathroom door, which was made of tin. It was difficult to open and close. I carefully stepped into the small tight shower, struggling with the sliding shower door. "Oh, well, at least I can have a hot shower."

When I finished my shower and opened the bathroom door, I was startled to find a woman standing in the middle of the bedroom and talking on her mobile phone. She was the young woman who had been in the gift shop. But what was she doing in here? She finished her call and started talking to me in Italian as though I understood everything she said, which I did not. She pointed to the bed, saying, *la mattina,* something about "the morning."

I thought she wanted me to sleep in her bed, or the other bed next to hers, but why? What about Neville, I thought. Maybe she doesn't want us sleeping in the same room.

"Ma, mio marito dove dorme?" And my husband, where does he sleep?

"Si, va bene," she pointed at the bed again. I was still confused. Then she said something about seven o'clock in the morning.

Finally, I figured out what she was telling me. She would be leaving at 7:00 am and did not want to disturb us.

"No problema, we are also up at 6 or 7," I told her.

I think she understood. *"Grazie*–we sleep there," I said pointing to the next room. She seemed to accept that. I thanked her for the shower and left.

The young man reappeared later and instructed us to go with the same woman for something to eat. A few minutes later, she appeared from her room and signaled to us to follow her. She led us down the stairs, through the courtyard, past a large stage with many chairs, and through a parking area decorated with banners. We followed her through another door, a back entrance to the cathedral, and down another corridor into a large open area that looked like the inside of an old barn or factory. We crossed an open area, passed through another set of doors, down another corridor, and finally arrived in a room that looked like a mess hall, where about twenty people, mostly men, were seated at a long table and chanting.

The young woman showed us to our seats and we sat down. I glanced around and saw two dogs lying quietly on the floor. The chanting and praying continued, interspersed with short hymns. I noticed a couple of women at the front of the table joined in the chanting.

Shortly afterward, there was some commotion towards the front of the room. While the women continued chanting, they got up from the table and went into the room next door. I heard pots and pans clanging. Minutes later, the women reappeared and started assembling pots and pans on the table, while they continued to chant with the men. It was amusing to watch.

After what felt like an eternity, the chanting stopped and the women served dinner. Many bowls and platters were passed down the table, heaped with pasta, meat loaf stuffed with bread and topped with tomato sauce, as well as a green tomato salad. Plates of pizza and sandwiches followed. For dessert, we were served cups of yogurt and fresh pears.

The man beside me, Riccardo, introduced himself, speaking perfect English. He asked the usual questions: "Where do you come from, where do you start, and where do you go next?"

He asked if we knew about the legend of the sanctuary. "No," I replied. "Please tell us."

"In September 1465, a deaf and dumb 13-year old girl named Maria was leading her flock of sheep to the pasture. Suddenly the sky turned dark because of an approaching storm. Maria took shelter under the small roof of a small building. On the wall was a fresco depicting the Virgin Mary, and then suddenly there was a bright light and the Virgin Mary appeared. She gave Maria a mission—to tell the people of Garlasco to build a Sanctuary here as a protection for the whole region of Lomellina.

Maria returned to Garlasco, no longer deaf and dumb, and she quickly went about telling everybody about her vision. The citizens of Garlasco immediately believed her and carried out her request. From that point on, the girl was known as Maria Benedetta, for the miracle the Virgin Mary had bestowed upon her."

"It is the anniversary of this historic event. There is a big celebration this week," Riccardo added.

Ah, that makes sense, I thought. It explained why the courtyard and stage were decorated.

Preoccupied with Riccardo's story, I didn't notice that everybody had rushed through dinner until the tablecloth was pulled away from underneath my plate, before I was finished eating.

Riccardo then offered us a tour of the sanctuary. We graciously accepted, and I asked him about his role in the sanctuary.

"Well, I am a sales person during the day," he replied, "but I come here often at night to help out and to go to mass."

Riccardo explained that the four young guys at dinner were recovering drug addicts. He told us, "that ten of them live here and work in the church. It is a special rehabilitative program, and if they have the money, they hope to renovate more of the sanctuary to house more people."

The sanctuary is a huge complex, bursting with farm animals—ducks, hens, rabbits, and rows of caged guinea pigs. Outside, there are more ducks, and sheep and goats. At the end of the tour, Riccardo led us through the secret passageway to the café-bar, and told us to come through here in the morning so we could have *caffé* and *brioche* before heading out. Cesar, the key man and now bartender, served us a couple of *espressi* to finish off the heavy meal.

Riccardo turned and told us he had to go to mass. We thanked him for the tour and said our good-byes. We then gulped down our *espressi,* said *buona notte* to Cesar, and left through the main bar entrance.

"I'm tired now, Neville, but I want to see the night sky before I head in," I said.

We walked to the end of the little village on the edge of the forest and reflected on the past few days. They had been challenging. We had walked long, hard days and got lost too many times, resulting

Santuario Madonna della Bozzola

in nasty arguments where we blamed each other or others for our misfortunes. On the other hand, we had rambled through some stunning countryside and had met some wonderful people who graciously welcomed us and took care of us.

When we had arrived at the sanctuary, we were at the mercy of strangers. Although we waited two hours for someone with keys to open the door for us, the hospitality and kindness of everybody more than made up for it. They had provided us a simple bed, a hot shower, a full hearty meal, and a good night's sleep—all free. We felt honored and grateful. What more could a pilgrim ask for?

We stood there in the dark looking up at the sanctuary. A full moon rose behind it, illuminating the black sky and casting its soft white glow over the building and us. It felt magical, spiritual, as if something or someone was watching over us.

"It really is a sanctuary—our sanctuary. I feel blessed. And the best part is we have it all to ourselves."

IX

The Mystery of Maria

*"An angel is a spiritual creature created
by God without a body for the service of
Christendom and the church."*
— Martin Luther

JULIE

We were standing in the middle of the village square in Orio Litta, near the communal *ostello,* talking to the man who ran the place. He was welcoming us and asking questions about our walk. As we told him our story, I heard a female voice nearby. I just figured it was one of his family members talking to another person.

I heard the voice again. I looked up at the building, the same building the caretaker had come from. It was a three-story building at the edge of the old village square, built into the walls surrounding the town.

I could not believe what I saw. A woman at the window was looking down at us. She had been trying to get our attention.

"MARIA!" I yelled excitedly. *"Buon giorno!"* Neville and I looked at each other in amazement. "I can't believe she's here," I said to Neville.

We were elated to see her. But how the heck did she get here ahead of us? And what was she doing in *that* building?

We hadn't seen or heard from Maria since Aosta, and frankly, we hadn't expected to see her again. With the large pack she carried, I never would have thought that she could keep up the pace, but here she was.

☙

After we left our sanctuary in Bozzola, we had crossed through the countryside of Lomellina before arriving in Pavia. I had never heard of the city before, nor had I seen it in any tourist guidebooks until I read about it in Neville's homemade one.

> Pavia has a rich two-thousand-year history, based on many battles, sieges and conquerors. It was founded in the 5th century BC, then conquered by the Romans in 89 BC and renamed Ticinum. In 568 AD, the Lombards, a Germanic tribe, marched into Italy and, after a siege that lasted three years, made Pavia the capital of the Lombard Kingdom of Italy. This empire lasted more than 200 years until Pavia and the Lombard Empire fell under the control of Charlemagne, King of the Franks, after the famous "Siege of Pavia." For the next eight hundred years, Pavia changed hands multiple times, becoming French, Spanish and Austrian, and again French, before finally becoming part of the Kingdom of Italy, an independent state formed in 1861.

After Pavia, we continued towards the Po River and the small hamlet of Orio Litta. Just beyond the signpost for Transitium Padi, after we had crossed over the bridge of the River Lambro on the outskirts of Frazione di Lambrinia, the landscape opened up. For two to three kilometers, we followed the *argine sopraelevato,* an elevated track with the river on the right side and fields of maize on the left. A separate smaller path went left towards Orio Litta while the main track continued on past, following the river.

Walking towards Orio Litta was one of those unique settings

along the Via Francigena that left me breathless. I will never forget it. Both on the Camino in Spain, and now on the Via Francigena, there were certain towns that looked so inviting and intriguing from a distance. Now, standing here staring at Orio Litta, I was overwhelmed by a sense of wonder, just as I had been when, on the Camino in Spain, I saw the town of Sansol from the distance. This was not because Orio Litta looked the same as Sansol, but because it evoked the same magical feeling inside me; it was a fairy tale setting. I just wanted to spend time soaking up the images and colors, and the beauty of the surrounding countryside.

I suggested to Neville that he go ahead to the *ostello*. "I won't get lost," I assured him. "I just want to take some time here to play my recorder." I sat down on the edge of the bank and watched Neville stroll down the path, surrounded by golden cornfields. Eventually he disappeared after a couple of bends in the path, swallowed up by the eight-foot-high corn stalks.

I could have sat there for hours, in my own little heaven. I love to sit out in the middle of nowhere, surrounded by natural beauty, and play my recorder. I feel the connection to the land, and the images and feelings last forever.

Sometime later, I was jerked back to reality when an older man came from behind me, walked past without saying anything, and continued toward the village. I wondered where he had come from; I had thought I was all alone. But in Italy, just when you think you're alone, someone always pops up out of nowhere. It was my signal to head into the village.

I caught up with Neville, who was sitting on a boulder and waiting for me about a kilometer before the village center. He told me that, while he was waiting, an old man had ridden by on his bike. Neville tried to ask the old man, in Italian, for directions to the *ostello comunale*. The man instead offered to take him there. Neville tried to communicate that he was waiting for me. The old man must have understood something, because Neville heard him say something about "ten." Neville took this to mean the old man would come back in ten minutes, and he anxiously waited, hoping I would show up before the old man returned.

The man came back ten minutes later, but I still had not arrived and the man went away again. Neville did not expect to see him again, but surprisingly, not more than five minutes after I arrived, the old man returned.

Riding his bike slowly, he led us through a series of quiet streets to the central square and over to a building where Pier Luigi Cappelletti, the host of the *ostello,* was waiting. Pier Luigi, a schoolteacher, for the last ten years has personally welcomed every pilgrim that has come to Orio Litta and stayed at the *ostello.* He has a special book that he calls the "Book of Honor" and he asks every pilgrim to sign his book. Over the last decade, roughly 1,000 pilgrims have passed through Orio Litta and stayed at the *ostello.*

❧

It is funny how things happen. Timing is everything, or is it synchronicity? If we hadn't met the old man with his bike, we might never have met Maria again.

Pier Luigi led us to the *ostello,* up to the second level, and showed us our room for the night. It was basic but pleasant, with one large dark old chest of drawers and a large rug separating two single beds. Every time we walked, the wooden floorboards creaked loudly.

There was no mattress on the second bed, and so Pier Luigi said he would bring down a mattress from the level above.

Maria suddenly appeared carrying several bags. She must have heard the conversation because she proceeded to tell us that she had slept in *that second bed* the night before, but got rained on. I looked up at the ceiling. What does she mean "rained on"? I had this image, that somehow the rain leaked through the roof of the second level, and then leaked through to the first level, wetting her and her bed. It still didn't make sense.

Oh boy, this was hard work; our conversation was too advanced for my limited Italian, but I tried my best to understand her story. As far as I could understand, a person in the bed above her had spilled water, or something, and it had leaked through the floor-boards and on to her and the mattress. I hoped the "something" was just water. I didn't ask if it was a man above her. I imagined something different, comical, but I couldn't begin to explain that one in my crude Italian without being vulgar.

Pier Luigi brought down the mattress from above and set it on the springs. I sat on it, checking to see if it was dry. Thank God, it was. Pier Luigi bid us well and left.

Expecting Maria to leave as well, she surprised me when she climbed up the creaky stairs with her bags to the floor above us. I asked her in Italian if she was sleeping here too! *"Sì,"* she replied. Now I was even more perplexed—what *was* she doing in the other building, and now why was she sleeping *here?*

Everything in Orio Litta seemed to be closed, except for one lone bar and a *pizzeria*. We agreed to meet Maria at the bar after we had showered and done our laundry. From there, we would walk over to the *pizzeria* together.

On the way to the *pizzeria*, we stopped to call the boatman to confirm our Po River crossing. Maria asked me to find out about the cost; she was thinking of taking the boat too. I spoke briefly to the man, asking about the crossing and time.

"He told us to meet him at ten o'clock," I told Maria and Neville. "It's five euros each," I added. Maria didn't say anything but we assumed she would come with us the next morning.

We walked into the small *pizzeria*, a tiny takeaway joint only two by three meters in size. Scanning the pizza menu on the wall, we chose from a dozen different kinds. Maria ordered the traditional *pizza napoletana* topped with tomato, mozzarella, and basil, and we ordered a large contemporary pizza, topped with chunks of tuna, olives, and *rucola*, a peppery leafy vegetable that was a staple component of the ancient Roman diet.

While we waited, Neville complained that his stomach was upset and he wasn't sure if he wanted to eat *anything*. Maria looked at us, puzzled, and I told her Neville had a bad stomach. She suggested he drink lemon juice on an empty stomach before eating the pizza. Good advice, but all the shops were closed. So where could we get a lemon? Maria suggested we try the café-bar across the street.

Neville went alone while Maria and I stayed at the *pizzeria* and chatted. I assumed he would have no problem getting some lemon. Several minutes passed by and Neville hadn't returned. I told Maria I was going to see Neville, sensing he might be having difficulty communicating to the bartender that he wanted fresh squeezed lemon juice in a glass.

I found Neville standing in front of the bar trying to explain to the bartender what he wanted, while the bartender looked perplexed. I asked the bartender *"Per mio marito solo limone in un bicchiere, per favore."*

The bartender looked at me, puzzled, holding up a lemon. *"Sì,"* I confirmed, *"in un bicchiere."*

He held up a glass, *"Sì, grazie."* He still looked perplexed, but at least he knew what we wanted.

I explained that Neville had a bad stomach, and that the lemon would be good for it. The bartender chuckled, shrugged his shoulders, and looked at us oddly, as if it was the strangest request he had ever had. Neville downed the lemon juice.

We returned to the *pizzeria* and picked up our pizzas, then walked back to the *ostello* to the large common room. It was great to see Maria again. With my limited Italian and her lack of English, we communicated as best we could and had some good laughs. We chatted about our travels, and we learned a little more about her. She told us that she had been staying here for a few days, and that she only stayed in places, like churches, where it was free. I figured she probably hadn't stayed in as many towns or villages as we had, and that was probably why we hadn't seen her earlier.

We enjoyed each other's company and each other's pilgrimage experiences. The quality time we spent with Maria in Orio Litta was one of our most memorable experiences—just as we had cherished our time with other pilgrims in the past when we walked the Camino in Spain.

⌘

NEVILLE

I awoke early the next morning with the sound of the church bells chiming just outside our window. Maria had agreed to meet Julie and me at the café-bar, and then we would make our way to the Po River.

When we arrived, the same bartender from the previous night was working. Julie asked the bartender for more lemon. *"Mi scusi signore, ancora un po' di limone per mio marito."*

The bartender stared at her strangely. We waited a minute before Julie laughed and said *"non è necessario, no grazie va bene così."*

The bartender laughed, realizing it was only a joke. Julie told him, smiling, that the lemon worked; it was a good cure.

We spied Maria talking to some older women. We ordered two coffees and croissants and found a place to sit down beside her.

Just as we were about to leave, Maria turned to Julie and told her that she had decided to walk another route, along the north side of the Po River. Further on, closer to Piacenza, there was a modern road bridge where she would cross the Po River and walk into Piacenza.

"Bellissimo—this way is nice," she told us. Besides, she wanted to stop at the little church of Corte Sant'Andrea and this meant that she would miss the boatman.

We had an hour to get to the boatman, about a five-kilometer walk from Orio Litta. So we agreed to walk together to the crossing point, where Maria would proceed by herself and we would join the boatman.

Well, that was the plan, but Maria liked to stop every few minutes

Julie and Maria – Pellegrini leaving Orio Litta

and talk to people. It surprised me that Maria ever got anywhere. At one point, she stopped to talk to some middle-aged women, and they just kept talking. By now, I was ahead of both Maria and Julie. I looked back, waiting. I could see Julie trying to inch Maria along, trying to tell her that we had to keep going.

Julie eventually caught up with me. By then I had reached the elevated dirt pathway that hugged the river. We both looked back, and we could see Maria in the distance, just rounding a bend in the path in the middle of the cornfields, about a kilometer behind us.

"What's up?" I asked. "Is Maria not coming with us to the crossing point?"

"I told Maria that we walk faster, that we must hurry to catch the boat and we will see her in Piacenza." Julie replied.

"And what did Maria say?" I asked.

"No problema."

We arrived at the crossing point and waited for the boatman. We had arrived a few minutes early, so Julie walked back to the trail and looked back, hoping to see Maria. There was no sign of her in the jungle of maize fields.

ᚱᚱᚱ

In the past, pilgrims heading to Rome from northern Europe would have to traverse the Po River. In the village of Corte Sant'Andrea, they would arrive and wait. A large raft, guided by long ropes, would carry animals, goods and people to the south shore of the river. From there, pilgrims would continue to Calendasco and then to Piacenza.

Danilo Parisi, the boatman, has ferried modern-day pilgrims across the Po River for ten years. Since 1999, he has transported over a thousand pilgrims. The numbers have steadily grown, especially since 2005, he told us, and in 2008 alone, he helped 263 pilgrims cross the river.

It was a short, enjoyable, five-minute powerboat ride, arriving five kilometers further down the river to Danilo's home on the other side.

Danilo lives in a two-hundred-year-old stone house that serves as a home for his wife Grazia and their family but also as a small hostel for pilgrims. In 2008, he provided meals for over 100 pilgrims, and 44 pilgrims stayed there.

We spent almost an hour at his home. Danilo recounted some of his history as the boatman and showed us his home and the rooms that he had set aside for pilgrims. We wrote our names in his special registry—a book he has kept since he began ferrying pilgrims. We were numbers 127 and 128 for that year.

The Via Francigena winds its way through farmers' fields and small roads, heading toward Calendasco and Piacenza and crossing the River Trebbia. Danilo told us about a detour we could take when we reached the little hamlet of Malpaga, just west of the River Trebbia, which at that time of year was normally dry. He suggested that we could cross the river, take a short cut across farm fields, and rejoin the Via Francigena closer to Piacenza.

Crossing the Po River with the boatman – Corte Sant'Andrea

We left Danilo and followed the Po River along the elevated banks, keeping a lookout for the path that led to Calendasco, but we obviously missed the cut-off (something we were good at doing), and walked too far.

A man in a pickup truck drove by, and we stopped him to ask for directions. He looked at us with our packs and no doubt realized that we were not only lost, but kilometers away from anywhere resembling a town.

"Jump into my truck and I'll give you a lift to Calendasco. I'm going that way," he told Julie in Italian.

We threw our packs into the back of the pickup truck. Julie climbed in the passenger side of the tiny truck and I, being the gentleman I am, jumped in the back, snuggling up to our packs. It was a 20-minute ride along dusty dirt tracks and small farm roads before we reached Calendasco. The journey reminded me of a similar ride we had taken in the back of a pickup truck in Thailand a few years before. I wrapped my bandana tightly around my face to keep out the dust and the occasional bug.

Arriving in Malpaga, we saw signs for the *guado* on a path heading towards some trees. Danilo had written on a little map the word *guado,* but we didn't understand what it meant. I asked a couple walking nearby about the sign. They directed us to another path, which we later realized went to the same place as the original path. *Guado,* we finally figured out, meant "a ford or shallow river crossing."

We walked across the dry riverbed and, as we did, we both had a strange feeling that something significant and unsettling had happened here. We would later learn that it was near the site of the Battle of the Trebbia (the first major battle of the Second Punic War between the forces of Hannibal and the Roman Empire in 218 BC).

Before the battle, Hannibal decided in advance that the west side of the River Trebbia was an ideal battleground. He found a gully where he placed 2,000 men, commanded by his brother Mago. The next morning, Hannibal sent his small cavalry of Numidians across the river with orders to goad the Romans into battle with a series of attacks on their outposts.

The Roman commander, Longus, reacted as expected, sending his own cavalry against the Numidians, before finally ordering his main army and his army of legionaries to cross the wet, cold river.

Longus' main army advanced slowly in the traditional, orderly Roman manner. The Roman troops were wet and tired from crossing the river and outnumbered. Hannibal's cavalry attacked the main flanks of the Roman army, while Mago's hidden cavalry of 2,000 forced the legionaries to retreat. Within hours, it was obvious the Romans had lost the battle, and Longus' army and 10,000 legionaries fled back to Piacenza.

This was the first and most important defeat that Hannibal inflicted on the Roman legions, demonstrating to the world that he was a superior commander.

Julie

We made our way along a series of small county roads before finally reaching Piacenza. The city of Piacenza pre-dates Roman times, much like many of the cities along this section that also existed before the Romans, Celtic, or Ligurian tribes had settled the area.

After arriving in town, we walked around trying to figure out how to get to the church where we planned to stay, then finally, sought directions from a padre. He guided us to a bus stop and gave us directions on how to reach the church. We took a scenic bus ride through the old *centro storico* and sprawling suburbs to the outskirts of the city.

When we arrived at the Church of San Lazzaro, a solemn padre greeted us and gave us a set of keys and some instructions. Expecting to stay at that church, I was very unhappy to hear that we would have to walk another two kilometers further east heading out of the city, to another building where the church hostel was located.

"Great, I can't believe we have to walk along this busy Via Emilia highway," I whined. "This is what I call *insanity."*

We finally reached the hostel, located right on the busy highway. It felt as if we had walked more than three kilometers. I was grumpy and tired, but I was surprised how calm Neville was, as he is usually the one to freak out about ending up at a place where it's too noisy and he's kept awake all night.

The hostel was surprisingly modern inside, but it felt cold and isolated, as we were the only pilgrims staying in the three-story building. I could not imagine how on earth Maria would find this place. There were several places to stay in Piacenza and I was sure she would not walk all the way here.

We cleaned up, wrote in our journals, and then rested a little before going out for dinner. Just as we were getting ready to leave, we heard the door of the hostel open. We rushed downstairs and there was Maria, looking tired, hot, and flushed, and carrying a bag of groceries. We hugged her, so excited and so relieved that she had made it. I wondered where she had found a grocery store along the highway; I certainly hadn't seen one.

She complained about her neck and back being sore from her long walk. No wonder! When I helped relieve her of her backpack and the extra bag she was carrying, I felt how heavy they were. And she had walked from Orio Litta? I couldn't imagine doing that. My body would not tolerate that for two kilometers, let alone twenty.

I wondered how she had found the hostel after a long day of walking. She told me she had gotten a ride from someone, and then picked up groceries along the way. I still don't know how much she actually walked, but given the way she looked, it was still too much for her.

We left Maria to eat alone while we went across the street to a nearby restaurant. Before leaving, I massaged her neck and back, and told her I would do more when we returned.

When we came back, Maria was still up. We talked about our plans for the next day. We had already decided to bus back into Piacenza and then take the train to Fiorenzuola, bypassing a busy and dangerous section of the Via Emilia. Maria agreed that walking the highway to Fiorenzuola was dangerous, and perhaps she would take the bus and train like us. We told her there was only one bus, at 9:00 am in the morning that would take us back into Piacenza to the train station. We expected she would leave with us in the morning.

❧

NEVILLE

The next morning, when we were ready to leave, Maria was just getting up. She told us she would stay in Piacenza for Sunday mass and then take a bus or train to Fiorenzuola and walk from there. We again agreed to meet in Fidenza that evening.

Our 9:00 am bus arrived on time and we rode to the train station. Soon after we got there, the train to Fiorenzuola arrived and a handful of people got off and on the train. When we arrived in Fiorenzuola and started walking toward the stairs, we happened to look ahead and there was Maria standing on the platform!

"What the hell? I don't believe it. How did she get here?" I asked in disbelief.

I wondered how she had managed to get to the train station and on the same train without us seeing her. She obviously didn't take the only bus going back into town that morning. Why did we not see her on the train platform in Piacenza?

It was all a mystery.

We stopped to buy water and sandwiches because we knew that along this stage of the route there would be no place to get food or even water. Strangely, Maria did not buy anything. Instead, she asked many questions about the path and about the places we planned to stay once we arrived in Fidenza. She asked us to write the same names down on her tattered map. I wondered how she would get to Fidenza. Our experience from walking through this region was that you needed a good map. It was obvious she did not know the way to Fidenza or where to stay when she got there.

Once again, Maria surprised us and told us that she wanted to stay in Fiorenzuola for mass at 11:00 am. We parted company again, once more agreeing to meet in Fidenza.

Our walk to Fidenza from Fiorenzuola took us first to the Cistercian monastery and the village of Chiaravalle della Colomba in the comune (municipality) of Alseno. Colomba means "dove" and legend has it that a dove marked the site of the future abbey with a wisp of straw.

It was here that the signs for the Via Francigena changed.

"This doesn't make sense," I reasoned. "The signs point north, but we want to go southeast."

Even if we decided to take this route north, we had no idea how far to go before turning south towards Fidenza. Missing signs and changing paths had become all too common along the

Po River. I thought about what pilgrims of the past must have felt as they struggled through what would have been dangerous swamp marshes infested with wild animals and malaria-carrying mosquitoes. I was sure missing signs were the least of their concerns. However, all this nonsense was wearing us thin, and we had become frustrated, short-tempered and quick to engage in nasty arguments.

We asked locals, and they all confirmed we had to travel north, even though our maps suggested otherwise. It seemed so odd—in order to reach Fidenza, we had to walk away from Fidenza.

"What are we going to do?" Julie asked.

"We're going to 'farm whack'," was my reply.

In the end, we decided to rely on our crude maps, my compass, and our basic instincts to "farm whack" (much like "bushwhack") our way across the countryside from one farmhouse to another, southeast towards Fidenza.

A couple of hours later, much to our relief, we stumbled into Fidenza, but our struggles did not end there. We had trouble finding accommodation within the old center. In fact, in the center of the old town was the official office of the Via Francigena, but the office was closed, and it was closed the following day too. If they had been open, I was sure they could have suggested a place where we could spend the night.

We stood in the *piazza* wondering what to do next. A couple of older men befriended us and made some phone calls, first to a place we thought might be open and then to a church, which was also closed. Finally, they called the Convento San Francesco, which was about three kilometers outside the old center.

One of the men told us to wait, then returned a few minutes later with his car and told us to get in. Both men then drove us out to the *convento*.

When we arrived, a grumpy Asian friar greeted us at the door. He invited us in and showed us to our separate rooms. It was our first experience on the walk sleeping separately. We settled in and went out for a pizza dinner at a nearby kiosk.

"I wonder if Maria even made it to Fidenza," I mused.

"I wonder if she knew about the *convento,* or maybe she chose another place." Julie said.

That night, as we lay in our single beds in our separate bedrooms, every time we heard a door open, we both expected Maria suddenly and magically to present herself; just like she had done in Orio Litta and in Piacenza and in Fiorenzuola. She was good at surprising us.

Maria never did show up that night, and we never saw her again.

The next morning Julie stopped me in the hallway. "I wonder if she will ever write to me."

"I hope someone—like her—will magically appear to keep her company, to share meals and stories with her as she makes her pilgrimage to Jerusalem," Julie added.

X

Trickery and Demons

"We're all pilgrims on the same journey
But some pilgrims have better road maps."
– Nelson Demille

NEVILLE

Our hike through the Po River valley had tested our fortitude. We had faced many challenges, not the least of which was getting hopelessly lost. We then spent enormous amounts of time and effort trying to find our way back to where we were supposed to be. The communication struggles and the long days did not help matters.

We were emotionally bruised and slowly being pushed to the breaking point. This little walk was not only taking a physical toll on us, but we were also becoming mentally "unhinged," perhaps slightly crazy. We tried to see the humor of our situation, whether it was due to our follies and misgivings or due to unforeseen situations. But it didn't help. Obstacles and challenges lay in our path. It was an exasperating time for both of us, and I had serious reservations about the whole adventure.

More so, I had become unusually skeptical and distrustful. That said, as often as things went wrong, people mysteriously showed up to make it right. For example, we would stumble into some odd, unpleasant, or nasty state of affairs, as if "demons" inexplicably were doing their best to make our journey more difficult. Then almost immediately, an "angel" would show up to save us. Most people were more than pleased to provide help when asked. So what was our problem? Were we the crazy ones? The circumstances left me confused, and all I knew was that I wanted it to stop.

Ahead of us was a lengthy climb up to the Cisa Pass on the medieval road La Via di Monte Bardone, a path that travelers and pilgrims took up and over the mountains into Tuscany. Once we crossed over into Tuscany, I prayed we would close a difficult chapter of our journey.

⁓⌘⌘⌘⁓

As we were about to leave the *convento* in Fidenza, another friar—a friendly one, not the grumpy one from the night before—greeted us at the door. He was surprised and disappointed that we would not be staying another night.

"When you leave the city, you must look for the signs to Santa Margherita and follow these," he said. "This is the correct route to take to Costa Mezzana." He was the only person who wrote *buon viaggio* in our pilgrim passports.

When we started walking, we saw the signs to Santa Margherita, just as the friar had told us, and we turned left to follow a smaller road towards the east, continuing until we reached another intersection at a very busy four-way crossing.

"Somehow this is not making sense," I told Julie. My crude maps suggested we should be heading out into the countryside along dirt paths.

Julie and I debated about which direction we should go.

"I'm convinced we should not have turned left so soon, but instead gone down further to the next road and turned left there," I told Julie, as we stood in the middle of the intersection staring down at the map. I pointed to the south where I figured we should be crossing.

"I believe the friar. We should continue along the road to Santa Margherita," Julie firmly replied.

A lone middle-aged man wearing a jogging outfit and aviator sunglasses approached us. He agreed with Julie and said we were going the right way.

I finally relented and we continued along the road. Even though we were in the countryside, surrounded by farms and rolling hills, the road was busy. It was rush hour and Italian workers were rushing into the town of Fidenza to work. It was a long, nasty one-hour walk to Santa Margherita.

When we finally arrived in Santa Margherita, I was upset and angry. We were now miles away from both the trail and our final destination for the day. At a grocery shop, we asked for directions to Costa Mezzana.

"Go down the road and follow the signs to Costa Mezzana," the shopkeeper suggested.

"No, pass the next intersection, go another couple of kilometers and then turn right there—it is quicker that way," his wife countered.

The shopkeeper and his wife debated about the best route to Costa Mezzana, while all the time I rechecked our maps, trying to figure out what they were saying and who was correct.

Was it that difficult to find Costa Mezzana? I thought to myself.

Finally, after what seemed like an eternity of deliberations, they agreed—compromised you might say—on what was the best way to go.

"Go up to the church, turn right and follow that road to Costa Mezzana," they both said, smiling.

We continued up the road, looking for the next intersection and a road to the right. When we arrived, there was no church, but there were signs pointing right and south towards Costa Mezzana.

Skeptical, I took off my pack, stomped over to a bar, and asked the bartender for directions. He too told us to continue down the same road. So perhaps this was the right road after all.

By now, I was livid that we wasted time walking along a busy country road that had clearly taken us away—maybe far away—

from our destination. All I wanted to do was take the shortest route to Costa Mezzana.

"If this road goes directly there, then we'll take it," I told Julie, frustrated.

To my surprise, the walk south turned out to be pleasant and mostly free of traffic. Only a few farm trucks and harvesters passed us. We were obviously not walking on the Via Francigena; it was somewhere to the south and west of us, crisscrossing the rolling hills in front of us, a landscape that reminded us of Tuscany.

At some point later, we reached a small T intersection where we saw Via Francigena signs pointing towards Costa Mezzana. The road was adjacent to a small dirt track heading back up the hills in the direction of Fidenza. I was still upset when we finally approached Costa Mezzana.

"Clearly I was correct," I told Julie. "We *should not* have turned left so soon after leaving Fidenza, and we *should not* have gone towards Santa Margherita. Instead, we should have used my directions, which would have taken us on a trail across the countryside, probably on quiet dirt tracks away from the busy roads and traffic!"

Demons, I figured, had tricked us.

⸎

Upon reaching the outskirts of Costa Mezzana, we climbed a steep hill to enter the village. We were on the lookout for something to buy for lunch later in the day. The only bar in town was closed, but fortunately we found a tiny grocery store, so we bought some water and food, then sat down and ate a cup of yogurt for a late morning snack.

As we sat there, an Italian man arrived, carrying a pack with an umbrella strapped to the side. He asked about food and we directed him to the tiny grocery shop. Curious, we asked him if he was walking the Via Francigena and he introduced himself, "*Si, sono* Giuseppe."

Like us, Giuseppe had started in Fidenza that morning. Clearly in a rush, he bought some food and left, even before we finished eating.

The trail went up the hill away from the village, along a dirt path, past a castle and through fields of vineyards. Further along the path, we intersected a small, secondary country road and saw a brand new Via Francigena sign pointing to the right. We went right and sauntered along the quiet country road. Along the way, there were wonderful bird's eye views of the surrounding countryside, so we stopped often to take photographs and enjoy the scenery.

As enjoyable as it was, everything appeared wrong. For one, we were walking further west and even north, away from where we should have been going. My maps suggested we should be going down the hill but now we were actually climbing up the hill! A lone car approached us, and I stopped the driver and asked him for directions.

"You are walking to Costa Mezzana," he told us.

"We are walking in a big circle back to where we came from. *Damn!*" I yelled.

We backtracked to the little intersection and rechecked the sign. It was loose, so I figured somebody or something had tampered with the sign and pointed it in the wrong direction. We concluded that we should have gone further past the first sign and then turned right. We had lost an hour walking in the wrong direction and then backtracking to this little intersection. I made a mental note to recheck all the signposts in future.

A trickster had fooled us again!

We stumbled into Medesano late in the afternoon and found the communal *ostello*. Giuseppe, whom we had met briefly in Costa Mezzana, was standing outside talking to an elderly couple and waiting for somebody to arrive and open the place. Two women finally arrived, unlocked the front door, let us in, registered our names, and directed us upstairs to the bedrooms.

That night we had dinner with Giuseppe. Julie and Giuseppe did most of the talking since Giuseppe spoke little English. Giuseppe and I compared our maps and guidebooks, and discussed routes and all the things modern-day pilgrims like to talk about.

Giuseppe told us, "I am only walking to Sarzana, maybe Aulla. Then I take a train to Monte Carlo to visit some friends."

For Giuseppe, this was not a pilgrimage, but a recreational hike through the Apennine Mountains. Afterwards, he was planning to spend some relaxation time lying on the beach or gambling.

Nevertheless, we did learn that he had walked the Camino de Santiago five times and had plans to walk it again next spring.

In true high-class fashion, we shared a bottle of champagne as an aperitif. Later we shared a bottle of red wine and ordered the set menu for dinner, which turned out to be an excellent meal. We agreed to meet early the next morning for coffee at the corner café-bar.

The next morning I knocked on Giuseppe's bedroom door. He was already up, dressed and ready. As he had been the day before, he was in a rush to get going. "Meet me at the café-bar," he said, but when we got there, he had finished his coffee and was ready to start walking. We said goodbye, telling him we would catch up with him along the way.

When we left the café-bar, we climbed a small paved road up the hill. It was still early. The morning light was breaking through the mist and clouds, and to the north, the Cisa Pass looked strangely eerie, like something out of a dark 1950s comic book.

As we descended the hill, about half way down there was a small new Via Francigena sign pointing the way further down the hill. I put my hand on the sign; it was obviously loose, suggesting that, as before, somebody or something had tampered with it.

To my left was a wide-open farmer's field, and to my right, only trees. Therefore, it made sense for the path to continue down the hill. I asked Julie to wait and I descended further down, but the trail simply disappeared into the underbrush. It was all very odd.

Returning to Julie, I spotted way off to my left, across a large expanse of fields and grass, a small brown sign. When we trudged over, we discovered that it was a small Via Francigena sign that this time pointed back up the same hill.

Obviously, a trickster or demon had been here before us and turned the signs around. We started to wonder if the trickster was Giuseppe himself.

❧

It was market day in Fornovo di Taro and every square meter of the streets was crammed with trucks, vans, food stands, and tables of clothing and other wares, including some simply hanging from the awnings. Finding the signs for the Via Francigena or any directional or street sign was impossible.

We finally found a phone booth squeezed between two vendor stands. Julie pushed herself into the booth, and called the *agriturismo* in Sivizzano to check if they had a room for us and to find out the exact location.

Market Day – Fornovo di Taro

I heard a woman with a very loud and strange accent answer the phone. She talked so quickly that Julie had a tough time understanding her. Each time Julie asked her to repeat what she had said more slowly, the woman talked faster.

Julie got off the phone and turned to me, "I think she has a room but I still don't know where it is."

As we left Fornovo di Taro, our guidebook indicated that the trail passed the church and then went along Via Punica, or maybe it was Via dei Collegati—I was not sure. However, if we could find the Piazza Liberta, we would be in luck. We found the church and, by getting directions from various townspeople, we finally arrived at the Piazza Liberta. A woman waved us on and told us the Via Francigena continued up the hill towards Caselle. We climbed steadily as the road switched back and forth, taking forever to reach the top. Along the way, not once did I see a sign for the Via Francigena, which made me a little skeptical that this was the correct way. I was not sure if we ever reached or passed through the village of Caselle.

We continued until we finally reached a paved provincial road.

"Do we go left or right?" we both asked.

We decided on left and started walking up the paved road. There was nothing to suggest we were going in the right direction but there were some buildings up ahead. So perhaps this was Sivizzano, I thought.

A black BMW SUV suddenly drove up and screeched to a halt beside us—right in the middle of the bend in the road, blocking cars as they drove up. A woman poked her head out of the driver's window and started babbling at us, in what we believed was Italian. Well, it sounded Italian, but her dialect was very different. I started to wonder if everybody here spoke a different dialect. Julie tried to talk to her, but the woman just waved her arms around, pointing up and down the road, shouting at us.

We stood there, bewildered. Was she upset with us for walking along the road? Did she have trouble with backpacking pilgrims from foreign countries?

Suddenly it dawned on us that she was the woman from the *agriturismo*. She had obviously come looking for us. We would not be hard to spot—two silly Canadian pilgrims walking along a *strada statale* in the middle of the day.

We told her, "Yes! We are the people that called earlier."

She became even more excited. Talking quickly, she gave us directions to her place—something about "a little further up about one kilometer away at the bottom of the hill." Then she sped off and left us standing there dumbfounded.

‹❦›

JULIE

We continued along the provincial road in the same direction that the woman had driven. After walking nearly two kilometers, we saw no *agriturismo,* nothing.

We soldiered on. When we passed by the last set of houses, we saw nothing but wide-open space and green fields on either side. I told Neville I was going back to the last house we had just passed to ask for directions. I rang the buzzer, and a young woman hesitantly answered the door.

"Do you know where the *agriturismo* is?" I asked.

She didn't know the place. I showed her the address. She suggested that we return in the direction we had come, back down the hill.

"This is crazy," I said to Neville. "Did we miss it? How *could* we have missed it?"

Again, we retraced our steps, determined to find the place. We looked around continuously while descending the hill. Still nothing to suggest an *agriturismo* was nearby.

"This is getting crazy," I repeated. "I'm going to stop the next person I see."

I decided I couldn't wait for the next person, so I rang the buzzer at a nearby house. A woman, preceded by her dog, wandered up to the metal gate that enclosed the large modern house and expansive yard. I repeated the question.

"Yes, but you have to continue on this road, up the hill, about a kilometer or two," the woman replied, pointing in the direction we had come from.

"This is *pure insanity,*" I shouted to Neville. "I hope she's right." After walking back and forth along a section of road for a couple of kilometers—for the third time—I had had enough of this foolishness. "If we don't see it up here, then we forget about it, and we just continue until we get to the next village."

About twenty-five minutes later, I saw in the distance a large white house, set back off the road, with a row of cypress trees lining the front of the property. As we got closer, I saw a small sign hanging in the trees. I squinted to make it out.

"Oh, *my God,* here it is!"

"And there's her black SUV," Neville said, pointing down the driveway. It didn't look like an *agriturismo,* but more like a roadside *albergo* in the middle of farm country.

We walked up, and a man came out from the house and told us to wait. Then the woman with the odd dialect poked her head outside the door and said, *"Prego."*

She led us through to the other end of the house and showed us the room. It was more like a self-contained apartment, with a little kitchen, a dining and lounging area with a fireplace, and a separate bedroom facing the backyard. The woman nattered away while she took us on a whirlwind tour of the unit. I asked her to speak slowly, but she just smiled and talked faster.

We didn't want a large room, only a small one, and only for one night. We expected this room would be expensive.

"Quanto costa una camera?–How much for the room?" I asked.

"Ottanta euro," she replied.

"La colazione è inclusa?–Is breakfast included?"

She motioned that we could help ourselves. She showed us the coffee, some items in the fridge, and some fruit in a bowl.

I asked her about lunch. She offered to take us into Sivizzano, which was three kilometers away, to the local café-bar where we could perhaps buy something to eat. Or she could make some lunch for us.

"And dinner?" I asked. She told us that she could do the same.

"Ottanta euro per tutto–Eighty euro for everything," she repeated.

We agreed to stay and she agreed to prepare lunch and dinner for us. About half an hour later, she reappeared with some deli meats, a selection of cheeses, plenty of sliced bread, and cold cannellini beans. We could help ourselves to the wine, water, oil and vinegar, and some fruit. We thanked her and felt relieved we could relax in peace.

That afternoon we lounged in the late autumn sun and took the opportunity to wash some clothes that were long overdue for a good cleaning. We kept the bedroom windows wide open, enjoying the cool air and the hot rays of the sun.

Later in the evening, about eight o'clock, there was a knock on the door. The woman flew into the room and set about cleaning the table and preparing the room for dinner. An Indian or Pakistani man wearing a turban followed her, carrying our dinner. She nattered at him, giving him directions, and together they tried to start a fire. Neither of them seemed to know what they were doing. It was comical to watch. After several attempts to get the fire going, they suddenly vanished, leaving the fire to smolder. What could have been a romantic dinner was now marred by thick smoke. We were forced to open all the windows to air out the place, but the outside air was so cold that we couldn't sit comfortably at the dining room table. So we quickly ate and returned to the bedroom to escape the smoke.

Thankfully, dinner was good and there was plenty of it. A gigantic bowl of spaghetti with a light tomato sauce, a selection of cold deli meats, a large bowl of green salad, and a bottle of ordinary, but cold, red wine, which Neville had no problem getting down. We chuckled about the weirdness of it all and wondered if we were her first guests ever.

❧❦❧

Neville

We left the next morning, without seeing either the woman or the man, and continued along the main road until we reached a path that slipped into the little hamlet of Sivizzano. There was nothing much to it and there was no one around. It was good we hadn't come there for dinner the night before.

Our route took us through groves of forest and country farms, until we reached the little hamlet of Terenzo. The trail climbed steeply and soon became an overgrown track that almost disappeared into the forest. We climbed constantly, and as we went higher, the temperature dropped, forcing us to don gloves and hats to keep warm. At the top of a hill, the trail broke out onto a small road. It was definitely much colder now. The clouds had moved in and it was becoming windy.

When we arrived in Cassio, we found a closed *ostello* and nobody around to ask about accommodation.

Julie walked up the lonely little village road in search of a phone booth. The only phone in the village was out of order, so she walked further down the road to the only open bar, and the owner offered to call the *ostello* for her. Lucky for us, he reached the person in charge and told Julie that someone would come in fifteen minutes to open the *ostello* and let us in.

The man in charge of the *ostello* arrived just as Julie got back. He showed us to an empty room on the second floor with five bunk beds. There was no place to wash our clothes and it was cold and damp inside. Even taking a shower was impossible.

The man in charge told us the café-bar would be the only place serving food that evening. When we walked in, we saw a tiny bar with a handful of small round tables. It was empty except for a man eating alone at one table. There was no menu; just a set meal of the day that included an antipasto, a pasta dish for the first course and a meat dish for the second course.

The bartender took our order; his assistant went into the back to get the food, put it in a microwave, and then served it to us. It was nothing special, but we were grateful that we could at least eat something.

By the time we finished dinner, the place was slowly filling up with some of the local town folk: an elderly woman and her son, a middle-aged couple, and another man. This might be the entire town for all we knew, and it looked like everybody was here to watch the football game and play cards.

The next morning we were up early. "It's damn chilly, actually freezing cold," I said to Julie. There was no heat in the hostel.

We dressed quickly and rushed about, wanting to warm up as quickly as possible. Then we sauntered back to the same bar where we had eaten dinner the night before. The streets of the little village were deserted.

The route today was short, only 16 km that initially went along the *strada statale* n. 62, but later went along some dirt tracks that hugged the road, before arriving in Berceto.

There was little traffic on the road. The air was cool and fresh and the early morning light was perfect for photos. In the distance, through the morning mist, we could see mountains as well as clouds that lingered and then drifted away as the morning sun broke out. I could feel the warm rays of sun on my face and for the first time in many days, I felt more relaxed.

After about four kilometers, we veered off the *strada statale* and followed a dirt track towards the village of Castellonchio.

"Boom, Boom." The dull crack of gunshots rang out in the valley below us. Seconds later, we heard more gunshots and dogs baying in the distance. Soon after, a couple of dogs raced up the hill and stopped in front of us, frozen in their tracks.

The dogs had a confused, disappointed look on their faces. They must have thought we were wild boar, but instead we were tired, lost and confused pilgrims.

We continued along the dirt track, following blue and white signs. The official Via Francigena red and white signs from yesterday had disappeared. I wondered why we had not reached Castellonchio by now.

"BOOM, BOOM!" More gunshots—this time they were closer and louder, down in the valley to our left.

"What day is this?" I wondered aloud. "It's not Sunday is it?" Sunday was the day devoted to wild boar hunting in Italy.

Julie turned and gave me a look. Like me, she was fearful of accidentally being shot by a hunter. All we wanted to do was move along quickly, get out of the woods, and find the village of Castellonchio.

⸉⸙⸊

Just before lunch, the town of Berceto came into view. The trail descended towards the town along what had been part of the medieval Monte Bardone Road. Ancient stone walls lined both sides of the path and we passed the remains of the Conti Rossi castle.

One source suggests there is a legend that in the year 718, Moderanno, the Bishop of Rennes, traveled this road to visit Rome. A miracle happened at the highest point of the route—where Berceto sits today—causing Moderanno to ask King Liutprand to build a monastery there. By the 12th century, Berceto had become an important stopping point along the Via Francigena. Even today, as we walked into the little town, it had a medieval but odd feeling about it.

From Berceto, we called the hostel at the Cisa Pass, only to learn the place was completely booked for the night. I found it impossible to understand why a hostel with 24 bunk beds, at the top of a remote mountain pass, was full; we had seen only a handful of other pilgrims on the Via Francigena. We tried phoning another place, but nobody answered. We then tried finding the *ostello* in town, only to discover a closed, derelict building. At that point, we wondered if it made sense to continue up to the pass anyway and try our luck with accommodation, but we decided it was now getting too late to chance it.

Thwarted, we enquired about rooms at the *locanda* where we had eaten lunch. Fortunately, they had a double room available.

⁓

JULIE

As night fell, our room became extremely damp and cold. We just wanted to stay inside, all bundled up, and forget about going out into the night. However, we had to eat, so we reluctantly donned our warmest clothes, layering up with shirt, fleece, heavy long pants and jacket.

Berceto is a small town, so thankfully we did not have to wander far to find the only open restaurant in an *albergo* at the other end of the main street. But an odd feeling of gloom hung in the damp evening air.

When we entered the restaurant, there was nobody around to greet us, so we walked further into the building looking for the dining room and came to a doorway blocked by a hanging curtain. Curious, I peeked behind the curtain and saw an empty dining room and one man, shabbily dressed in what looked like an official server's uniform that he might have slept in. He looked to be in his 60s, chubby and partly bald, with an odd-looking eye and crooked, dark-framed glasses. His longish, dirty, gray hair was desperately in need of a trim. He still had his shirt hanging outside of his pants and his belt undone. I presumed he was still preparing himself as he straightened his tie in front of a mirror.

I must have startled him, because he stopped, hesitated, then said *"Buona sera, prego,"* and ushered us in. I assumed he was the host.

He escorted us to the table in the far corner of the dining room. As he moved across the floor, he had a strange walk; it seemed that one half of his body moved ahead faster than the other half. His arms dangled loosely, swinging on their own, as if they were not part of him.

With his odd-looking face and appearance, he could have been a retired Mafia character who had been through one too many fights. He gave me the creeps.

He wasn't the only thing odd about the restaurant. A group of men came in and sat on the opposite side of the room. More people entered, and all were seated around the perimeter of the dining room; no one sat in the middle of the room.

Not long after we had ordered our dinner, a single older man, dressed in a suit, arrived and chose a table against the opposite wall, facing into the room towards us. This man also looked like he was Mafia. He stared at us and everyone else in the room the whole time while he drank a bottle of wine all by himself.

From then on, a strange scene repeated itself throughout the evening. The host would enter the dining room to greet the guests. Shortly after, a couple of young servers would come into the room to tend to the guests and then they would stare at the host and laugh and giggle before walking out of the room, still laughing. I wondered what this was all about and why the host seemed unfazed by it all. Periodically, the host would return to our table, saying nothing and just grunting when we requested something. Otherwise, he stood alone in front of the fireplace at the back of the room, first staring at us, and then slowly shifting his eyes around from one table to the next, staring at each person, as if he was a panther studying his prey. The young servers repeated their laughing episodes.

I felt chilled and unnerved the whole time. It felt like we were characters in a bad play. We ate our dinner quickly and headed back to our room.

Returning to the *locanda,* we found the family huddled in the corner of the dining room, watching TV in the dark. The scene looked like something out of a suspense movie.

"There's something weird about this place Julie," Neville said.

"It seemed like a nice little town when we first arrived, but there's something strange about it—the empty streets, the restaurant; and the people seem distant and mysterious. It's all too weird. And it feels odd to be the only ones staying in this dark, empty hotel. I can't wait until morning comes."

We hurried upstairs and locked our door, hoping that no evil spirits or demons would get us during the night.

❦

Centuries ago, pilgrims traveling from northern Italy faced the perilous challenge of crossing a series of mountains south of the Po River valley to continue their journey to Rome. The Apennine Mountains stretch 1000 km from the north to the south of Italy, traversing the entire peninsula and forming the backbone of the country. Within this range lie the Ligurian Apennines that follow the curve of the Gulf of Genoa, parallel to the coast, and extend as far south as the Cisa Pass in the upper valley of the Magra River.

For Romans, the principal crossing of the Apennine Mountains originated from the town of Rimini using the Roman road, the Via Flaminia. Centuries later, the Byzantines controlled this region, and then the Lombards built an alternative route further west that started in Fidenza and traveled southwest to Berceto, over the so-called Lombard Pass or Monte Bardone, close to the present-day Cisa Pass.

Today, following the Via Francigena route, it would be a long hike to the Cisa Pass and on to Pontremoli, a long strenuous day with much up and down. So Neville had purchased a local map with enough detail to plan what he hoped would be a shortcut over the pass, lessening the estimated distance of 30 km. I hoped the short cut would mean we would arrive in Pontremoli at a decent hour, so we could find a place to sleep and enjoy the culture and history of the place.

We left the town of Berceto and quickly found the main Via Francigena route. The first part ran along the small *strada statale* that led to the pass. Thankfully, it was a quiet, peaceful walk on the road with little traffic to worry about. Berceto and the other smaller villages disappeared as we got higher. In the distance, mountain ranges stretched for miles in all directions.

Within an hour, we had arrived at the *ostello* and learned why the entire place had been booked the night before. A large group of Italian cyclists had taken over the place, and there were no more beds or even space on the floor to sleep. They were just leaving as we arrived.

"See, that's why I wanted you to call," Neville explained.

"But what if we didn't call and we just showed up? They would have had to put us up somewhere," I rationalized.

We continued our walk to the pass; it was pleasant, easy walking, with thick green forests on either side of the narrow mountain road. It felt great being up there alone and having the space all to ourselves.

At the pass itself, there were a couple of café-bars. A little gift shop sold fresh local cheese and bread and the woman behind the counter made each of us a take-away sandwich with a mixture of local cow and goat cheese. I had not expected to find any food here, but in Italy, it's always surprising where you can get food.

We made a quick detour into the little church that stood at the top of a flight of concrete stairs, so we could stand even higher than the pass. It was the cutest church I had ever seen. As we looked across the horizon and down towards Tuscany, we could see the same Italian cyclists descending a narrow, winding country road, the same road we would walk.

I felt on top of the world. It was a divine walk. It wasn't as high as the Alps, but it was the second highest part of our walk since we had left Martigny.

Taking the alternate route, we descended into the valley on a little narrow country road that switched back and forth. We figured we were making good time, descending more quickly than we had expected. Neville assumed that if we could be in the village of Groppoli by noon, we would be in Pontremoli by 3:00 pm. We would both be happy about that.

We arrived at a little hamlet that we thought was Groppoli and stopped an elderly man to ask for directions to Pontremoli. The old man mumbled something we didn't understand. He waved his hands up in the direction we were going, and then he waved them down, showing us a little path near where we were standing.

"I don't know what he's telling us about that path; it looks like it goes to someone's house. Do you think he's playing games with us?" I asked Neville.

Neville decided the old man didn't know what he was talking about. He figured we should keep going, so we marched on, climbing the switchback road above the village.

But minutes later Neville stopped and shouted, "This is *not right*—this road is *not* on my map. Let's go back."

"Oh *man*! I am *not* going back, you know I hate that!" I snapped back.

Neville marched on again, stopping every few minutes and saying, "It's not the right road."

"Oh, come on, how do you know, maybe the map is wrong," I insisted. Neville was getting more irritated. "Julie, this is stupid, this can't be the right road, it doesn't zigzag like this on my map."

"Oh, for God's sake! Alright then, let's go. I can't believe we're doing this yet again."

We retraced our steps to the village and asked another man for directions.

"Should we believe this guy instead?" I asked Neville.

"We don't have much choice."

Somewhere further back we had missed the correct road. There was nothing at the intersection suggesting we should turn down that road; in fact, it looked like someone's driveway, so we had walked past it. To add insult to injury, we learnt we had not gone as far as we had expected; it was nearly 1:00 pm and we had just left the little hamlet of Gravagna, which was only halfway to Groppoli. Neville was clearly frustrated, and I hoped we were now on the right road and that the directions we had received were correct.

Leaving Gravagna, we descended a windy, narrow mountain road. I felt like I was in another world; it was so serene. Towering trees lined the road and I imagined I was walking through a densely wooded Sherwood Forest. If it was going to be like this all the way to Pontremoli, I didn't care what time we arrived.

Unexpectedly, we heard a horn in the distance. It sounded like the bus horn we had heard when we first entered Italy at the Colle del Gran San Bernardo. Then we saw the bus climbing slowly up the steep hill toward us, heading in the direction from which we had come.

"It must be going to the little hamlet we just left. I wonder if it is coming back," said Neville.

A few minutes later, we heard the horn again, this time from behind us.

"It's probably going to Pontremoli," Neville said. I just ignored him; I was enjoying my peaceful walk.

But Neville stopped the bus and talked to the driver.

"*Oh no!* I don't want to," I said to myself.

Then Neville yelled to me, "The driver says this is the last bus for the day."

I walked over. Neville looked at me, I looked at him, and the bus driver looked at both of us. Neville repeated himself, but I thought, "Yeah, sure, how do you know? Maybe the bus driver is tricking us, or maybe Neville doesn't understand what he's saying." But it was clear Neville wanted to get on. I hesitated, but then I realized that we probably had a very long way to go.

I reluctantly climbed aboard. My soulful walk had ended abruptly.

I sat down numbly, wondering why I had agreed to get on the bus. With my backpack still on, I sunk into the seat, turned around to look through the back window, and forlornly watched the beautiful scenery zip by. The only other passenger, an older woman, nattered away in Italian to the bus driver.

The bus ride down the valley was dizzying, as the road switched sharply back and forth. It was another 20 minutes before we arrived in Groppoli, the town we had expected to arrive at by noon.

I knew Neville wasn't happy either, but he justified the decision: "It's almost two o'clock, and if we hadn't got on this bus we would still be walking. We probably wouldn't have arrived until 6:00 pm or even later. And you wouldn't have gotten to see anything."

Maybe he was right. The idea of walking through forest and switchback roads in the dark didn't thrill me, especially considering the strange spirits that seemed to have been lurking around us for the past few days.

⚬᪲᪲᪲⚬

NEVILLE

Arriving in Pontremoli seemed anticlimactic. It was a strange place. There was a food fair in progress in the main *piazza,* but all the food was from other places in Tuscany and Italy. I found this odd, given the rich culinary background of Lunigiana. I figured there would be *torta d'erbe*—delicious herb tortes, similar to a pie—or roasted chestnuts on sale, but there was nothing like that at all. There were tables of sliced meats and cheese from Parma, and oddly enough, buckets of candies.

High up on a hill overlooking the town was the castle of Piagnaro. The original castle dates back to the 9th and 10th centuries, but it was later destroyed, then rebuilt, and then destroyed again. What remains today dates back mostly to the 14th century. Since 1975, the castle has been home of The Museum Statue Stele Lunigianesi, strange space-creature-like stone figures of prehistoric men and women, dating back to the third millennium BC.

We walked up to the castle through a maze of narrow laneways. Julie had phoned the night before and had been told that there were no beds for us, but we agreed that we had nothing to lose by going there and asking again. But when we got there, we found the castle closed. According to the sign on the door, it might reopen at three o'clock.

As we stood there waiting for the castle to open, we met an Aussie couple, John and Ingrid. They told us they had just finished walking the Camino de Santiago that spring, something neither of them had every imagined doing in their lifetime. They were now on a whirlwind tour of parts of Europe, including Italy. Having just arrived in Pontremoli, they were trying to decide if they would stay the night. We joked about traveling, tourists, and all the silly things that can happen, and we promised to meet again that night if they decided to stay.

After we parted, Julie suggested, "Let's try the tourist office and see if they can check the castle."

"I don't know if they have beds; I don't know much about the castle," the tourist office woman said. "But I'll call them for you."

She quickly called and just as quickly hung up. "It is not possible to stay there. The castle is booked."

Disappointed, we sauntered over to a *convento* near the train station. We asked about staying two nights, and the Padre said that would be fine.

Later that evening on the way to dinner, we ran into another walker who had stayed at the same *ostello* as we had in Cassio. He told us that the castle in Pontremoli was open and that they had plenty of beds.

"Only I and a couple of Italians and another Australian couple are staying there tonight," he said. "The view from the castle is wonderful."

Hearing this just upset us more.

Annoyed by this, I asked Julie, "Why did we not just stay at the castle until it opened?"

"Why did you agree to my suggestion that we go to the tourist office?" Julie countered.

"We screwed up—again," Julie snapped back at me.

Julie was angry and so was I. Yet again, days of frustration boiled over like a witch's brew. All the way up the Cisa Pass, since leaving Fidenza, it was as if we were being tricked or cursed. It seemed that nothing was going right.

The sun was setting, casting a strange reddish orange glow against the ominous black clouds that swirled above the old town. It made for an eerie sight.

By now, we were in no mood to meet up with John and Ingrid, so we dragged ourselves to the Ristorante da Giorgione for dinner, a small place at the south end of the old center that had been there for more than thirty years. A somber woman greeted us and took us to our table. We were the only people in the restaurant.

I ordered a bottle of Tuscan Chianti Classico from 2003, hoping the wine might help patch up our differences. We each ordered a plate of *testaroli*, typical pasta crêpe served with rich, green *pesto* and cheese, and it was supremely tasty. We then ordered two plates

Sun setting & ominous black clouds – Pontremoli

of *Agnello di Zeri,* the famous lamb from nearby Zeri (a region northwest of Pontremoli, known for its special lamb and potatoes). We were told this was the only place to get Zeri lamb in Pontremoli.

Traditionally, the lamb is cooked in a cast-iron oven over a bed of twigs and burning embers, flavored with chopped bacon, garlic, parsley, rosemary and sage, and served with succulent Zeri mountain potatoes. We expected it to be delicious, but the lamb impressed neither Julie nor me. I think it was because of how it was prepared, or perhaps it was the cut of lamb, but it was lacking in flavor. On the other hand, perhaps it was just our foul mood that evening.

After dinner, we walked through the narrow, dark, almost empty laneways of Pontremoli, back to the *convento.* As we navigated through the streets under a full moon, I thought of one of the many legends of this region—the Werewolf of Pontremoli.

> There is a legend about a werewolf; an ordinary man that would change into a wild beast. Villagers were terrified of him. The beast would bay and bark like a dog and cry like a human, filling the village with bizarre noises. Villagers who met the beast, even those that were armed, ran away in fear of dying of fright.
>
> On humid, hot nights under a full moon, between the hours of midnight and three o'clock in the morning, the werewolf would appear. He ran with local dogs that followed him along the deserted village roads, barking and growling with him. The villagers only felt safe in their houses and thus rarely ventured out in the evenings.

That night, we went to bed feeling uncertain about this place. We thought we had escaped the demons and tricksters when we crossed over the Cisa Pass, but it seemed they had made their way to Pontremoli with us.

XI

Valley of the Moon

"Travelers, it is late.
Life's sun is going to set.
During these brief days that you
have strength, be quick and spare
no effort of your wings."
— Rumi

NEVILLE

We left Pontremoli Saturday morning, planning to spend the week-end in the small hamlet of Malgrate, near the town of Villafranca in the heart of Lunigiana (a small, remote region of northern Tuscany sandwiched between Emilia–Romagna and Liguria).

Historically, Lunigiana was both a border and a link between the wide-open, northern expanse of the Po River valley and the rolling hills of Italy's southern peninsula. Because the valley (and the Via Francigena that ran through it) was the passageway linking northern Europe to Rome, it had great strategic importance for adventurers, pilgrims, merchants, and armies. Over the centuries, various empires conquered the area, and numerous old castles are scattered throughout the narrow valley.

Lunigiana is a land known as the "Valley of the Moon," (*luni* comes from the Latin word *luna* meaning moon), and is steeped in countless legends and myths. Its pagan history dates back to the prehistoric civilizations of the Ligui-Apuani peoples that lived in the region some 3,000 years ago. The Ligui-Apuani, cattle herders that worshipped the moon, left behind stone statues, sometimes known as "statue menhirs," that focused on rural traditions, culture, the environment and hospitality as a way of life. You can still see grotesque faces engraved in stone on the walls and above the entrance arches of houses; their sole purpose is to keep away evil spirits and demons—and we were all for that.

～◦∞◦～

When we arrived in Villafranca, we wanted to get directions to the B&B Casa Dolce Casa in Malgrate. We walked into a grocery store to ask for directions and buy some food for lunch. The woman kindly called the B&B and got directions, and then painstakingly drew a map on a piece of paper.

According to the directions, we had to walk down the *strada statale* toward Pontremoli to the third roundabout, and then turn right and walk one kilometer toward Malgrate. We started walking down the busy road, and after 20 minutes and three roundabouts we found ourselves heading back towards Pontremoli. We never did see a sign for Malgrate.

Did we get the wrong directions again?

At the third and final intersection, there was a single house but nobody around to ask for further directions. Fortunately, a local police car appeared and we flagged it down. We asked the officers in the car for directions, but they did not know where the place was; they looked perplexed. Julie asked one of the officers if he could call the B&B.

He agreed and after talking for a few minutes, he turned to us and said, "The woman will be here in 10 minutes to pick you up."

Then the police drove off. To our surprise, a woman arrived five minutes later, which was very quick by Italian standards. We apologized and tried to tell her the clerk had given us the wrong directions.

The woman, Vittoria, drove us back along the same *strada statale* that we had been walking on, returning to the same spot where we had left the grocery store. She drove up a small road and passed three roundabouts, before turning left and traveling along a smaller road for another kilometer to Malgrate.

Vittoria showed us to a large room on the second floor, with a king-sized bed, a separate lounging area, and a south-facing balcony. It was pure heaven and a welcome retreat after what we had faced over the past few days.

We used the balance of the warm, sunny Saturday afternoon to catch up on our long overdue laundry and then relax and write. Vittoria told us about a little restaurant near the castle on the nearby hill. She suggested that if we left early, we could explore some of the castle and then go to dinner. She kindly called the restaurant and booked us a table.

⁕

The original role of the castle of Malgrate was defensive, controlling the valley of the River Bagnone, including the roads coming from the Cisa Pass, the Apennines and the Garfagnana. The Malaspina family of Filattiera built the castle, with its distinctive round tower, in the 8th century. In 1351, the castle expanded to include extra fortifications and trenches. In 1641, the settlement surrounding the castle was transferred to the Marquises Ariberti of Cremona, and the castle was converted into a fortified town.

We had the castle to ourselves. When we arrived, it was near closing time, so we had just a few minutes for a tour. We climbed the staircase to the top of the outside walls and admired the surrounding valley. As the sun slowly set, it lit up the entire landscape in hues of yellow, orange and red.

The restaurant La Torre di Malgrate is located a hundred meters from the castle, up a hill that leads into the surrounding country-side. When the restaurant finally opened, we were shown to our table. Large groups of people started to arrive, and the place soon became crammed with adults, kids and grandparents, along with a few couples like us.

We were served a set menu, for 15 euro each, that included *gnocchi di farina di castagne* (gnocchi made with chestnut flour) and *involtini con funghi* (veal with mushrooms), as well as wine and dessert. It was a tasty and memorable dinner.

ॐ

Filetto, a little hamlet located two kilometers from our B&B, was unlike the other villages and hamlets of Lunigiana. Originally a Roman *castrum,* or army camp, it was designed in a simple walled square. Over the centuries, the town expanded, adding three additional walled squares. Its corner towers are still standing and its tiny original main square hosts many summer events. In old times, the nearby forest of chestnut trees was a holy place where pagan gods were worshipped and where chestnuts were collected, a staple used to make many foods.

Castagne Arrostite (Roasted Chestnuts) – Filetto

Sunday afternoon we walked to Filetto to attend a chestnut festival. It was a hub of activity, with men roasting chestnuts in large cast iron pans over open fires, while other people lined up to buy and sample the various foods made from chestnuts, chestnut flour, and other traditional foods. We joined one of the lines of people and started with a *torta d'erbe,* which was so good that we had to go back for seconds. We eventually tried almost everything. The line-up for fresh roasted chestnuts was the longest. It took two men a full 15 minutes each to roast a large pan full of fresh chestnuts and only a dozen people to purchase and consume the same amount. Therefore, in minutes, the entire batch sold out and everybody had to wait another 15 minutes for the next batch to be roasted and ready.

Finally, after four batches, Julie got her order. She was in heaven. We found a nearby bench and consumed the entire order of roasted chestnuts in a matter of minutes. By the time we finished, we were full from eating almost every imaginable item made with chestnuts. Afterward, we wandered the narrow streets of Filetto and browsed through a pottery workshop on the main street, where courses on pottery, ceramic art and decorations are held throughout the year.

We learned later, that every year in August, Filetto hosts the "Mediaeval Market." The narrow alleys and the secluded squares of the village fill up with merchants in medieval costumes, the shops sell all sorts of handicrafts, and the restaurants serve traditional foods.

⸙

I wished we could have stayed longer in Lunigiana. Our time in Malgrate had been brief, but in those two days, we felt we had washed away the evil demons and tricksters that had plagued us since we had left Fidenza. We hoped and prayed that Lunigiana was the closing of one chapter and the opening of another, a fresh start for our journey and our relationship.

When Monday came, we knew we had to move on if we wanted to reach the coast by midweek and Lucca by the weekend. This meant we would have to skip through some sections to reach our next destination, Sarzana. This would include walking back to Villafranca and following the west side of the river Magra. The route would continue along a small, secondary road, passing through old forests and a few small hamlets, before reaching Terrarossa, five kilometers from Aulla. From Aulla we would take a bus or train to Sarzana to make up some time since we wanted to be in Marina di Massa the next day. From Sarzana we would continue to the coast to the seaside village of Marina di Massa, follow the beach to a spot where we would simply head inland and away from the beach towards Pietrasanta, and eventually to Lucca. Along the way, we would pass through Luni.

I read about a legend about Luni, of naked virgin mermaids and water nymphs that would linger on the beaches of Luni, eventually causing the decline of the city. The thought of stripping down and spending some time at the beach, (even though it was early October) was so tempting. It might be just the thing to recharge our batteries and help us regain our energy and enthusiasm to continue to Rome. I might even find some naked mermaids and sea nymphs frolicking in the ocean.

XII

Road to Damnation

"Life is short and death is certain."
– A Buddhist saying

NEVILLE

We were off to a bad start. It was a foreshadowing of trouble, an indication that the day would not turn out well. It all began when we arrived in Aulla.

Aulla is a modern city with big shopping centers and little charm. In front of us lay a sprawling metropolitan landscape of buildings and busy roads, making it difficult to get to the town center.

Over the centuries, Aulla has occupied a strategic position. It is at the base of three important passes—Cisa, Cerreto and Lagastrello—as well as being located on the Via Francigena to Casola and on the road to the Garfagnana. Situated on a vast plain surrounded by hills, at the confluence of the Aulla and Magra Rivers, it was a principal trading destination between the interior and the sea. Unfortunately, bombing during the Second World War destroyed much of the old medieval city.

We agreed to take either a train or bus to Sarzana from Aulla. I preferred taking the train, but Julie thought the bus made more sense. Once in Aulla we set out to find either a bus or train and choose whichever one came first.

Perched on top of a hill all by itself we found what looked like a new, ultramodern train station. There was no ticket office and no staff—just printed schedules, and a single TV monitor showing train numbers and destinations and times—and a single machine where one could buy tickets. We quickly realized there was no way to take the train directly to Sarzana.

There was a small handwritten sign indicating that if you needed more information, you should check with the people at the station café-bar. We went into the bar and asked about buying tickets to Sarzana.

"You need go to La Spezia. From there you can figure out how to get to Sarzana," the woman behind the counter suggested. She also told us we could take a local bus into the town center and possibly catch a bus to Sarzana.

After heated deliberations, we decided to take our chances with the train. With only five minutes left before the next train to La Spezia was due to arrive; I tried to buy two tickets. The ticket machine only accepted the exact change, so Julie rushed into the bar, got some change, and rushed back. I quickly threw the coins into the machine, while Julie checked the track number. We ran upstairs to the tracks, saw the train on the platform, and jumped on. It was busy, but we were able to find two seats. I breathed a sigh of relief. It was just about then that I looked across the platform and spied another train. On the side of the train were the words "La Spezia."

"What the…!"

We asked the woman beside us where our train was going.

"Parma."

"*Shit!* This is the *wrong* train!"

While Julie struggled with her walking sticks, I grabbed my pack and Julie's pack and we tumbled off the train, ran across the platform, and jumped on the other train. We learned later that the track number had changed, but this critical information had not been posted on the digital TV monitor. Lucky for us, the train to

La Spezia was running late. And lucky for us, once in La Spezia, we found a train going to Sarzana.

⌘

Local historians in the 15th century wrote about a place called Serrazzana, and about Sergianum, a Roman settler from the family Sergia. The name Sarzana appeared for the first time in a diploma signed by Emperor Otto I, and dated 19th of May, 963. It assigned the "Castrum Sarzanae" to the bishop of Luni. A *castrum*, or stronghold, was located in the spot now occupied by the Sarzanello Fortress, also known as the Castracani Castle. The first documents that referenced Sarzana as an actual town date back to the year 1000.

That evening we walked through the old part of Sarzana past the citadel. Ancient stone walls, typical of so many medieval Italian cities, surrounded the old center. The town was full of people walking the narrow, cobbled laneways. It was a working town, not touristy, but there were plenty of shops and café-bars and even an antique alley to amuse the locals and the few tourists.

I selected a restaurant near the Porta Romana, as it appeared to have an interesting menu with local foods. Besides, I had learned that a trio of gorgeous, well-endowed women managed the eatery.

The interior décor was out of the ordinary, funky with eclectic pieces of artwork hanging on the walls. We ordered half a bottle of red house wine, *un tagliere di salumi* (mixed meats such as *coppa, speck, prosciutto,* and *salame*) and a plate of *testaroli al pesto* (a pasta crêpe made with Lunigiana *pesto*). Disappointingly, the *testaroli* arrived cold. When we complained to our pretty but somewhat aloof server, she took them away and reheated them in a microwave. When she returned, the food was still cold. When we complained again, she offered neither apologies nor suggestions. We decided to cut our losses, skip dessert and leave as quickly as possible.

"So much for first appearances," Julie pronounced. She was as upset as I was about the experience, even more so because I had picked a place run by buxom blonds.

Our experience at the restaurant left me in a foul mood. Adding to my grumpiness was the fact that the next day we would enter a section of the route that passed through some busy industrial and residential areas of northern Tuscany, before arriving in Lucca. I described it as "standard Italian suburbia," which meant more roads and more congestion. The most problematic section was from Sarzana to Pietrasanta, an industrial suburban melting pot of Italian humanity that included the towns of Massa and Carrara, the latter home to Italy's famous quarry mines. Some describe Carrara as a dusty and noisy hell of a place that operates 24 hours a day, seven days a week. Therefore, it was important to avoid this section and find the other route that ran along the seaside village of Marina di Massa.

Getting out of Sarzana became a challenge. We followed the Via Francigena signs out of town, past the Porta Roma, under the arch, and then looked for an alternative route to go north around the town walls. We saw a trail marking, so that was a good start, and quickly walked up the left side of a busy residential road in rush hour, doing our best to avoid the traffic. All the time we kept a lookout for more Via Francigena signs. We knew that somewhere the route would veer off to the right and then climb the hills and pass the old fortress ruins that overlooked the town of Sarzana.

Yet within minutes, we had arrived at the communal *ostello;* we had almost gone in a complete circle.

"Per favore, dov'è la Via Francigena?" we asked a priest waiting for the bus. He looked dumbfounded and said, "I know nothing about the Via Francigena."

We continued further to a busy roundabout. We stopped a young woman and she told us we should go back a few streets.

We turned, walked back, and met another priest standing

outside the *ostello*. He grabbed my arm, pulled me down the street a few hundred meters, and pointed down a little road.

"That should lead you to the fortress on the hill," he claimed.

We followed the road for a short while, but I was convinced we were nowhere near the right path.

"The fortress is over there on the hill, behind us. We should have walked right past it," I yelled to Julie. Obviously, it was becoming one of those days. We retraced our steps to the busy road, turned left and followed it until we reached another intersection with a small road to the left. We looked up the street in search of a sign. Then Julie spotted a faint, small Via Francigena logo painted on the rock wall. We had found the path—finally!

⟡

JULIE

Neville was grumpy, because it had taken us an hour to leave Sarzana. It was now ten o'clock and he had wanted to be further along. I just ignored him. We continued up the pathway and after 30 minutes reached the old fortress.

As we approached the fortress I told Neville, "I want to go check it out, do you want to come?"

"*No,* I'm not coming," he said grumpily.

"Ah, come on, just a few minutes. I want to ramble around the grounds and see inside the ruins and take in the views."

It looked mystical, standing on the hilltop alone. In its ruined untouched state, I felt as if I was the first person who had discovered it. I just wanted to romp around, take in the views and let my imagination run wild while I played my recorder.

"I'm not interested. We're already behind. It already took us an extra hour to get out of the city and we have a long walk today. The weather doesn't look great either. I'm not stopping to look at some stupid ruins. I want to get going to Massa so we can get there before dinner," Neville said angrily as he stormed off.

His voice trailed off as he got further ahead of me. "You can go by yourself; I'll meet you in Massa."

"But we'll never get back here again. What's wrong with a few more minutes?" He ignored me, and carried on.

I thought about going up alone and catching up with him later. But the Via Francigena was not like the Camino in Spain. I couldn't read the maps very well and the signage was poor or nonexistent. I didn't feel confident that I could find the way on my own.

So reluctantly, I gave up and plodded down the track, leaving lots of space between Neville and me, and periodically looking back at the fortress. I took photos every time I stopped. At least I would have something to remember it by. I fought back the tears as I descended the trail and looked back until the fortress disappeared behind the trees.

We descended the other side of the hill and followed the trail, mostly through more suburban populated areas, all the way to Luni. It was not enjoyable. We passed by large, modern homes strung along busy residential roads. At every house, hyperactive dogs of all sizes would race up to the gates close to the road and bark loudly, and incessantly, jumping like they had been cursed or hit with a bolt of lightning. I felt utterly unnerved and wondered if it was a warning of some impending doom. As if the fortress episode wasn't enough, I had to be tormented by dogs. Infuriated, I yelled back at them.

"Man, I hate this walk. I don't want to go on if it's going to be like this," I mumbled under my breath.

For the next couple of hours I sulked, as we walked toward Luni in a light rain shower. I had looked forward to visiting Luni. From what I had read, and from what Neville had told me, it was a significant historical site. The Romans founded Luni in 177 BC at the mouth of the Magra River. Originally, the city was at the sea, though today the ruins of Luni are almost two kilometers away from the ocean. It was a military stronghold for the campaigns against the tribal Ligurians, after which it flourished as a major Roman port

Crazed barking dog on the Road to Damnation

when the exploitation of white marble quarries in the nearby Alpi Apuane (Apuane Mountains) began in the 1st century BC.

But once there, I wasn't the least bit interested in spending time touring the ruins and the outdoor museum in the cool, damp weather. I needed to move along quickly to keep warm.

Leaving Luni, we followed a series of small yellow and white stickers posted here and there along the route, until we arrived at an intersection that led to a local paved road with signs pointing right and left. We decided to go left along a quiet residential road. From then on, we never saw another sign.

We followed the road, walking through small neighborhoods with a railroad on one side and houses on the other, until we finally reached Avenza.

This section of the route was more built up than the previous section with plenty of houses, buildings, shops and cafes on both sides of the road, which stretched forever.

It looked like it was going to rain, so I asked Neville, "How long before we reach Marina di Massa?"

He replied, "I estimate it will be another four kilometers." By now, it was only sprinkling, so I suggested stopping for a break and having a quick coffee.

We entered a café-bar and from the moment we walked inside, I knew it was one of those places. I said *"Buon giorno,"* but nobody responded. The bartender and the two men sitting at the bar simply turned their heads and looked at us as if we were aliens from outer space. They said nothing.

Feeling cocky, I said *"Buon giorno,"* again, this time even louder. The people in the bar just smirked and looked at one another, and then turned away, ignoring us. These people did not seem friendly.

We ordered our coffee and sat at a tiny table near the front window, surveying our maps and guidebook. Neville thought he knew the way and assumed it would take us less than an hour before we reached our destination for the day.

"Oh, that's not bad. Thank God it's not raining much anymore; if we're lucky, it may stop," I said.

We left the unfriendly bar and continued down the same road, expecting to walk out of Avenza and cross into Marina di Massa. We crossed over a canal and, checking again, stopped a man to ask for directions. He directed us straight ahead, but Neville decided to take the first right, being sure that was the way, according to his map book. We continued along the side road, passing another intersection. I saw a lot of traffic ahead, especially big trucks, and I became concerned.

The drizzle returned and I was getting upset. "This doesn't feel right. We're walking towards a busy highway. We must be going the wrong way; why would they make us go through this busy industrial section? This is craziness!"

"Do you want to go back?" Neville asked with biting sarcasm.

"No, you know *I hate to backtrack.*"

"All right then, let's just keep going."

We arrived at the next intersection. It was busy, with big, noisy, long trucks that zoomed by, splashing water everywhere.

"There's *no way* I'm walking on a road like *this!*" I yelled.

Neville asked, "What do you want to *do?*"

"I don't know!" I cried. "I just don't want to be on this busy industrial road."

We saw no signs. We stood there, two lost souls in the rain, bickering about what to do.

Neville suggested, "Let's just go a little further up this road and see what it's like, and maybe we'll see some signs."

After ten minutes along the road, we saw nothing more promising, just more of the busy highway. I stopped and yelled to him, "I don't want to go on. This is insane!"

"Then what do you suggest we do?" His patience had reached its limit.

"I don't know. I just know I *don't want to walk on this road.* There's no good choice here." I felt lost, angry, and helpless. I couldn't make a decision. We were stuck having to decide between two bad choices.

Finally, Neville suggested that we go back to the intersection we had passed a little further back.

So we retraced our steps to the first intersection, looked up the road and saw on the other side a Via Francigena sign. I yelled, "Oh, my God, there it is! I can't believe it! Thank God!"

By now, it was raining more heavily. "I want to stop and put on my poncho, Nev." He looked at me with annoyance, as he often does when I stop to attend to some need or other. He just wanted to keep moving.

Looking ahead, about a kilometer down the road, I saw another busy road in the distance. I hoped we would find the trail before we reached it. But, when we arrived at the intersection, I stared up and down the road in disbelief.

"Neville, this is *insanity*! We have just gone around in a *bloody circle*!" It was the same road we had been on earlier, the one that connected with the busy industrial highway. I was beside myself; I felt like dropping to my knees and staying there.

"Now what?" I was sure this was the wrong way, but Neville assured me that, according to his maps, this was the right way. Yet we couldn't see any other roads, except the one we were standing on.

"Come on, let's just go on, the trail must be up further," Neville rationalized. I took a big breath, cursed, and continued ahead. What else were we to do? For some reason I believed him. It was raining hard now; large puddles had formed on the road, especially on the shoulder, forcing us to walk nearly into the middle of the lane. To protect myself, I held out my walking stick to keep the cars away from me. I was going crazy, yelling, "This is *pure insanity*! I don't want to be here. This doesn't make sense." But Neville just ignored me and tromped on.

Every step I took I got angrier. I couldn't believe we had gotten ourselves into this predicament. Now I felt like a truly lost, lonely, afraid, helpless pilgrim.

In despair, I sobbed, *"God help us. I can't stand it any more. Please get me outta here."*

Further down the road, we saw another intersection. Cars were turning right onto the highway and heading in our direction. A high terracotta wall ran parallel to the road for several hundred meters. At first, we both thought it was an entrance to a factory and everyone was leaving work.

When we arrived at the intersecting road, I almost collapsed. "It looks like it goes into oblivion. Not only that, we can't even walk on the road; there's absolutely no shoulder. It would be insane to even think about it with all those cars." My despair turned to rage. I sobbed and yelled and started going hysterical, like I did at the Gran San Bernardo, *"I can't go on, Neville! This is super insanity! What the hell are we going to do?"* We stood there on the side of the road in the pouring rain, surrounded by miniature ponds, while the continuous stream of never-ending traffic hummed along all around us.

After a few minutes, Neville took the lead. "We have no choice but to walk back to where we started." He made his way over to a set of train tracks that ran parallel to the road. "It's easier, we can avoid the huge puddles of water and be further away from the traffic," he rationalized.

I was at first hesitant, thinking a train might come along any time, but then I decided it was worth the risk.

Not far down the road, we came upon a driveway that we hadn't noticed when we passed it earlier. It was an entrance to a large complex hidden behind high cement walls. We both thought the same thing; it was if we were being directed by a supreme being: without saying anything, we both turned right and walked up the driveway. But Neville said it first, "Maybe we can stop here and call for a taxi."

We walked up the driveway, which led to the composting and recycling company, Cermeco, and knocked on the security guardhouse. I wondered what the guard was thinking when he saw us. I imagined him working in his office and hearing a knock on the window, expecting a transport truck driver, but instead looking out to see two human beings, both saturated, dressed like green aliens, speaking a foreign language, and looking lost and frightened.

Thankfully he came up to the window, although hesitantly.

"Buon giorno," I cried out. *"Per favore, possiamo chiamare un taxi, vorremmo andare a Marina di Massa!"*

"Si, un momento," he replied, again hesitantly.

He seemed bewildered, but he pulled out a telephone book and searched through the Yellow Pages. He tried one place, but there was no answer. He tried another and again there was no answer. I wondered why it took so long to find and dial a taxi number. Obviously, it was not as easy as I had expected.

He called a third number and this time someone answered. He gave directions to the plant and told the person on the line we wanted to go to Marina di Massa.

"Circa dieci minuti," He told us when he hung up the phone. Ten minutes.

"Grazie mille." I was so relieved.

He invited us to wait inside the gatehouse. Dripping wet, we took off our ponchos and jackets, so as not to soak his chairs and the inside of the gatehouse. I felt awkward having disturbed him, so I tried to explain to him that we had walked from Switzerland and planned to walk to Roma. He had that look on his face, as if he thought we were crazy. He must have thought it was an interesting piece of news—*notizia*—because he told all the truck drivers that stopped at his gatehouse window on their way into the plant.

The taxi arrived in 10 minutes. We thanked the gateman and the taxi driver drove off, past the same intersection where we had turned around, then zigzagged down a series of smaller roads. We saw no Via Francigena signs. There was no way we would ever have found the route to Marina di Massa.

❦

NEVILLE

We arrived at the Ostello Turimar. It was a strange place.

"Why did I pick this place? It looks like an institution," I told Julie.

"So why did we come here?" Julie asked sarcastically, obviously upset.

Ostello Turimar reminded me of the big, cold, concrete complex just before Santiago in Spain—large white cement block cells spread over a large expanse of asphalt-paved property. The size of the sprawling grounds and the never-ending buildings shocked me.

"Are there showers and hot water?" Julie asked the woman behind the counter.

"Yes," she said, "but you may have to run it for a few minutes."

She gave us the key for our room. The good news—the only good news, it would seem—was that our room was at the end of a hallway, away from all the noise of others staying there.

I told Julie to have the first shower, and I would straighten up our wet clothes and gear.

A defunct shower! I heard her cry out from the bathroom.

I stuck my head into the bathroom and saw the broken showerhead.

"I've been walking for hours in the pouring rain on the busy industrial road and I'm tired and cold. All I want is a hot shower," she cried.

While Julie waited in the room, naked and cold with the towel wrapped around her body, I went back to the office to get a key for another room.

We moved over one room into a large corner suite. Julie, with the towel wrapped around her, ran over to the next room. While she ran the shower and waited for the hot water, I moved our gear from one room to the other.

"No hot water! It's only lukewarm!" Julie yelled out.

Once more, I went back to the office to tell the woman there was no hot water.

Along the way, I thought about the British comedy show, Fawlty Towers, the mad TV sitcom about the fictional hotel on the English Riviera.

"Maybe this is the Italian version of the same show," I thought.

I ran into an Englishman and his Swedish girlfriend. "Are you staying *here*?" I asked the Englishman, wondering why anybody would want to stay here.

"Yes. I've been stuck here for the past two weeks wanting to escape." He said he'd been told this was the cheapest place and maybe the only accommodation around. He was on a marble-carving course and now trapped in this "concrete hell-hole" as he described it.

He reminded me of the English character, Max, from the controversial movie, The Midnight Express. It is a film about a young American man, Billy Hayes, who was thrown into a Turkish prison, a dirty dungeon from hell, from which he spent years trying to escape.

Like a good prisoner, the Englishman leaned over to me and whispered in my ear, "I have discovered a source of hot water. It's in the Rosa building, just across from the office. It's the only place in the entire complex you can get a hot shower."

We never did get any hot water that night and Julie gave up on the shower. We spent the rest of the night feeling cold, incredibly tired and miserable.

⁕

Why did we charge on to Marina di Massa? Why didn't we just stop and think about what we were doing?

It seemed as if we were on a mission, driven to keep forging on, even when faced with constant setbacks. It was like we had become possessed.

Today finally broke us, with the endless road walking, busy traffic, barking dogs, and finally getting lost in the middle of rush hour during a blazing torrential rainstorm, in the center of the industrial complex of Marina di Carrara.

We had hit rock bottom. We were numb and bewildered. We were barely talking to each other and irritated at almost everything around us. I, for one, could not imagine continuing. It did not make sense. What was the point?

Our dreams of an adventurous cultural and culinary walk through Italy were shattered. After almost 30 days on the road, every little difficulty had become a crisis, and now it felt like our whole trip had exploded.

Part 3

Enchanting Discoveries on the Road to Rome

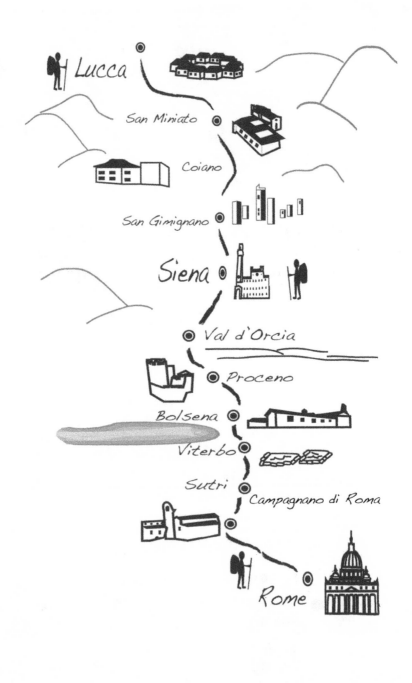

Lucca

San Miniato

Coiano

San Gimignano

Siena

Val d'Orcia

Proceno

Bolsena

Viterbo

Sutri

Campagnano di Roma

Rome

XIII

Lingering in Lucca

"May God give you, for every storm
a rainbow, for every tear a smile,
for every problem life sends,
a faithful friend to share, for every sigh
a sweet song and an answer for each prayer."
— Irish Proverb

JULIE

We escaped to Lucca. It was exactly what we needed.

When we arrived at the B&B San Frediano Guest House late in the afternoon, a pleasant, helpful German woman greeted us. Hilde escorted us to our room on the second floor, and I felt hugely relieved. I dropped my pack, flopped on the bed, and let out a sigh. "Now, I can imagine staying here!"

The room was spacious, pleasantly decorated, and softly lit. The window faced into a narrow, open courtyard the full height of the building, so we expected it would be quiet. It was perfect. Well, almost. Having separate rooms would probably have been more perfect, but it was what I needed to rest and recuperate. It was my safe haven.

❧

NEVILLE

This walled city of 85,000 people has attracted tourists, travelers, and pilgrims for hundreds of years. As with many towns in Tuscany, the Etruscans had founded Lucca, but the Romans, as reflected in its urban layout, had built and developed it. Evidence of its Roman origins included the oval-shaped Piazza del Mercato, once an early Roman forum. Positioned at the junction of three important roads, the Via Cassia, Via Clodia and Via Francigena, Lucca flourished during the Roman period.

The Via Francigena played a significant role in the continuing development of Lucca. The Lombards, during the years 568 to 774 AD, exploited and maintained the network of roads, then known as the Via Lombarda, to allow safe and easy passage of goods and military personnel to Rome.

At the end of the first millennium, pilgrimage was all the rage, as people "from all walks of life" traveled to Rome. Depending on one's status in society and more often, as penance, some would travel as far as Rome while others continued to Jerusalem. But Lucca was also an important holy sanctum. Pilgrims came to Lucca to view the *Volto Santo di Lucca,* or Holy Face of Lucca, a venerated wood corpus of a crucifix on display in the Duomo di San Martino.

By the 13th century, the Via Francigena and Lucca reached their respective zeniths. By then Lucca was an important center for the sale of silk. It was also a center of finance, whereby pilgrims exchanged their local currencies before continuing south to Rome. During this period, many of Lucca's 100 churches were built, the most famous being the Duomo di San Martino, the Chiesa (church) di San Frediano and the beautiful Chiesa di San Michele.

JULIE

We knew what to expect from Lucca. We had visited the city a few years earlier so we were familiar with the layout and character of the town. Many locals spoke English and it would be easy to communicate with people. Here, I would have less of the everyday complications, such as trying so hard to make myself understood in Italian.

We knew it was easy to get around inside the historical walled city; it was almost traffic-free, a pleasant relief from the urban madness of the never-ending traffic, cars and people that we had been experiencing.

There were many churches, cathedrals, museums, and towers to help us occupy our time, though I wasn't interested in joining the swarms of tourists. One thing I loved about Lucca was that I could lose myself in the labyrinth of narrow streets inside the walls, or relax on the expansive, grassy spaces outside the walls, or stroll along the tree-lined, four-kilometer 17th-century wall surrounding the city. The residents of Lucca have their evening *passeggiata* along the top of the wall that is wide enough to drive a vehicle.

We were desperately relieved and thankful to have a place like Lucca, as we needed time to recuperate and to make sense of what we had been through after our hellish walk into Marina di Massa.

We had plenty of questions. What had gone wrong? Why were we having such difficulty? Why were all these bad things happening to us?

After leaving Vercelli, we had gotten lost regularly, either because of the lack of signs, too many signs, or misinterpreting signs. Because we could no longer rely solely on our homemade map and guidebook, we often flip-flopped between them, people's directions, various other signs, and our intuition. Missing signs aside, sometimes we had to walk on busy roads and navigate ourselves through busy cities, dealing with crazy drivers who honked their loud horns at us as if we were endangering their lives.

Each phase of the journey had become a major decision and a major effort. The continuous challenges and frustrations over the past thirty days had taken their toll. We had become miserable and grumpy and prone to harsh arguments that would erupt at a moment's notice. We blamed each other when things went wrong.

To make matters worse, after leaving Fidenza, we felt somebody or something was deceiving us or playing tricks on us. It was as if we were no longer thinking rationally; we had lost track of reality and common sense, foolishly believing that strange spirits were cursing us.

We certainly felt that we were no longer on a cultural and culinary walking tour through Italy. There had been so many times that we were just too mentally and physically exhausted to enjoy the history and culture, or to search out a good restaurant to enjoy a traditional culinary experience. Instead, it had been a chore just to keep up with our daily tasks of finding a bed and a meal, doing laundry, and then getting food and planning our route for the following day.

At this point, the entire walk along the Via Francigena so far just felt too bloody complicated, too ugly, and I was tired of it all. I couldn't imagine continuing.

༺ஒஐ༻

For the next few days, I either relaxed in my haven or busied myself with little tasks, so I wouldn't have to think about the past or future. Neville went off and did his own thing, going off to cafes, sampling numerous *gelati* (Italian ice cream), or spending time at the Internet cafe.

I caught up on everyday tasks like laundry, shopping for snack foods, mailing extra stuff home, and writing in my journal. It had been five days since I had last written anything, and there were large gaps prior to that. Perhaps journaling would help answer some of the questions I had.

I also desperately wanted to reduce the load I was carrying. My pack felt too weighty, physically and mentally. I thought I had packed as lightly as I could before I left home, but it still felt too heavy. Even though I wasn't sure if we would continue the walk, it didn't matter; psychologically I had to get rid of something. I went to the post office and bought a box. Then I went through my pack and selected my extra pair of underwear (I didn't need three; I could wash one and wear the other), my extra pair of socks, papers and receipts I had collected, one completed journal, and my toque and gloves (the weather would only be getting warmer now).

The hardest item to send home was my recorder. It was something I treasured on my walks and looked forward to playing in special places. But even though it was fairly light, it weighed more than all the other items combined. I kept putting it into the box and taking it out, and then I finally relinquished it.

At the post office, I discovered the box only weighed one kilogram. It may not sound like a lot, but every gram mattered. I felt lighter.

My time outside the room, beyond going to the post office, was spent eating or walking. I relaxed in various bars sipping an *espresso* and nibbling on a *dolce* (sweet). I investigated the numerous *trattorie* (eating establishments less formal than restaurants), *osterie* (inns or taverns), and *enoteche* (wine bars) and some of the local food shops. I strolled along the top of the ancient wall, which gave me the comforting feeling of being close to nature while remaining close to my sanctuary.

After dinner one evening, we returned to the B&B and found Hilde in her office.

"Good evening, you're working late?" I asked her from the hallway. On our way out to dinner, I had seen her working late to prepare a guest room, but it was now almost 9:30 pm.

"Guests are on their way, but they were held up in traffic because of an accident. They will arrive late, perhaps close to midnight."

"Oh," I said, shocked. "That's too bad you must stay up so late."

She shrugged. "I know, but that's the way it is."

She motioned us inside her office to carry on our conversation.

"You had a good evening, yes?"

"It was okay." I added that the wine was good, but dinner was only average. She asked where we had gone. I showed her the card and she said, "Yes, but only for wine, not to eat." She explained that the food at the restaurant next door to the B&B had good, reasonable food.

We spent a half hour talking with Hilde. We asked her if any other pilgrims had stayed at her B&B.

"Yes, some have stayed here. I can usually tell now, by the way they look." Then she told us about a man she remembered well, who had arrived at her door late one afternoon.

"He was an older man, maybe in his 70's. He was covered in dirt from head to toe, and his clothes were torn. He was wet and tired, his hands and face were a mess, and he had cuts on his arms and legs."

"What happened to him?" I asked, curious.

"He got lost, stumbling through the woods, looking for the trail, trying to find his way out. Somehow, he eventually found Lucca. He stayed three days to recuperate."

"*Oh, my gosh, the poor man.*" I thought about how this old man's appearance must have been a shock for Hilde, just as we must have been a shocking sight for the man at the recycling plant when we walked up to his window to ask for help.

"He had been walking from the Netherlands."

"So did he continue his walk?" I asked.

"Yes," Hilde said. "He had to. It was as if somebody or something was pushing him. He was determined to make it to Rome."

Then she asked, "You two are walking to Rome, yes?"

We both looked at each other. "Well…"

"You know…I have great respect for people who can go on a long walk. I could not. I cannot even read a map."

She explained that for two years after moving to Lucca, she had a problem finding her way around the city. She would often get lost and frustrated because she couldn't find her way out beyond the walls. She commented that the streets were like a bowl of spaghetti, and with the high buildings and towers, she couldn't determine what direction she was walking in.

"I think it is incredible people choose to walk such distances," she continued. "I had a friend who walked the Camino de Santiago, but I could never imagine doing it myself. I like to sit and drive."

᚛᚜

NEVILLE

The next day Julie and I met up for lunch at Trattoria da Gigi, a tiny eatery Julie had found during her misadventures when trying to find the post office. We ordered two plates of pasta and half a carafe of wine. The place was soon busy with mostly locals and a few tourists who had discovered this little gem of a place. We discussed the story that Hilde had told us about the hapless Dutch pilgrim stumbling into her place tired and hungry.

"Sometimes when you're down and feeling sorry for yourself, you only need to hear a story about somebody else worse off than you to appreciate how fortunate you really are," I said to Julie.

It got us thinking about our situation.

We recounted many memorable moments. There were simple situations like getting cold bottles of water from the bouncer at an outdoor disco in the middle of the countryside en route to Piacenza. Or meeting the old man with his two grandchildren (home from school) and watching their eyes bulge out when we told them we were walking to Rome. Or the guy that allowed us to use his mobile phone to telephone and reserve our beds for the night.

And then there was Maria. We had first met Maria at Gran San Bernardo and again at Aosta. Then she surprised us in Orio Litta, and again in Piacenza, and once more in Fiorenzuola. She was a symbol of the mystery of the Via Francigena.

And there were the incredible sites, cities and towns we had seen—like Aosta, Arnad and Vercelli—steeped in the ancient history of many cultures. We felt honored to have walked through regions, hamlets, and villages that many foreigners and even Italians had never seen.

While at times we survived only on simple food like pizza, more often we enjoyed all kinds of tasty, traditional, and occasionally unique dishes. Sometimes when the food wasn't the best, the meal was still memorable because of the company we kept.

The more we reminisced, the more the bad memories faded away, and the pleasant and funny memories surfaced to replace them.

I even chuckled about the incident involving the bullpen that had been built right in the middle of the trail. Clearly, the bulls could have gored me, but looking back, I could laugh at the ridiculousness of it.

"And I guess one of the positive outcomes of getting lost on the way to Ivrea was meeting the old woman, the widow with her dog. I should be grateful for that," Julie added.

We left the restaurant feeling that we had experienced many good things on the walk so far.

❧

JULIE

Our last dinner in Lucca was at Trattoria Canuleia, a little restaurant tucked in a tiny laneway off the main street and behind the amphitheatre. After much indecision, we ordered *antipasti: fagottino di gamberi e melanzane su passatina de pomodoro* (bundle of shrimp and eggplant in tomato sauce). The *primo piatto* was *ravioli di piccione con ristretto di porto* (homemade pigeon ravioli with port sauce), and the *secondo piatto* was *petto di faraona con verdurine di stagione* (breast of guinea fowl with seasonal vegetables). Dessert included a dish of *torta al cioccolato fondente con salsa di frutta di bosco* (semisweet chocolate mousse torte with wild berry sauce). We finished off

Torta al cioccolato fondente con salsa di frutta di bosco – Lucca

the meal with a bottle of *rosso* house wine.

As we nourished ourselves with food and drink, we also nourished our souls with all the positive and delightful things we remembered about the walk. We were grateful for the people we had met and the stories we had shared with others, and the things we had experienced—all of which were the reasons we had wanted to do the walk in the first place.

"I *don't* really want to give up, Nev."

"I don't either. It's not the cultural and culinary journey we expected; it's a different kind of a journey," Neville said.

"So I guess this means that we are not only just *adventurous walkers* but also *pilgrims*?" I offered.

"We're *modern-day pilgrims*, following the medieval pilgrims before us," agreed Neville. "Besides, the worst part is behind us! We are in Tuscany now."

We had been looking forward to walking in Tuscany, especially the region south of Lucca, which was one of our favorite places in Italy.

"You're right, it should be easier now," I replied.

"Okay, so we'll continue!" we said in unison.

"*Yes*, we will just accept the way things are, try to let go of expectations, and go with the flow," Neville added.

"There is no right or wrong," I declared. We'll welcome the events and experiences we have, no matter what path or direction we take; we'll just go with whatever feels right."

We also agreed to try really hard to practice the "John and Ingrid principle" for the balance of the walk. The Aussie couple we had met in Pontremoli had adopted a "rule" when traveling—to limit any blaming, bickering or fighting. They would alternate responsibility and decision-making each day. If it was Ingrid's day, John could offer suggestions and comments, but ultimately Ingrid would make the final decision and they would both "live with it." It seemed fair and logical, and definitely worth trying.

So with this decision, we poured ourselves another glass of wine and toasted our new beginning.

Salute! Cin, cin! To the Via Francigena! To us!

XIV

Bella Toscana

"The sum of the whole is this: walk and be happy; walk and be healthy. The best way to lengthen out our days is to walk steadily and with a purpose."—Charles Dickens

JULIE

We left Lucca Sunday morning, feeling comfortable about being modern-day pilgrims. I was recharged and excited about continuing our journey to Roma.

We felt like pilgrims when we passed through Altopascio, a town south of Lucca. Altopascio has a rich medieval history of hospitality, catering to pilgrims and unfortunates who passed through the town. It is also home of the Knights of the Tau, one of the earliest Christian institutions, combining armed protection and assistance for pilgrims with the staffing of hospitals.

Dressed in our well-worn and dreary clothes, we watched elegantly dressed locals stroll by and gather at the Chiesa di San Jacopo Maggiore in the *centro storico*. I wondered how they felt now about modern-day pilgrims passing through their town.

After leaving Altopascio, I quickly got into a good walking rhythm. I was happy we had decided to continue. My spirit was renewed and I almost felt like I had when we first left Martigny.

As I tromped along in my own little world, I found myself singing a tune:

> *It feels so good…to be walking once again*
> *It feels so good…to be walking once again*
> *With a good rest in Lucca for the body and mind*
> *A great reprise from all that grind*
> *Of too many cars and barking dogs*
> *And all that madness, like being in a fog*
> *But now we've left all those frustrations and troubles behind.*

Just before Galleno, we walked along a beautiful, stone-cobbled path that then turned into a grassy path cutting through a patch of forest. It was magical and tranquil. On one side of the path were beautiful colorful flowers. As we walked, I imagined we were medieval pilgrims walking through a medieval forest. I remembered reading in our guidebook that this was one of the most beautiful sections along the Via Francigena.

Suddenly we saw two dogs running towards us. Given our previous experience with wild dogs, we braced ourselves, expecting the worst. I got my walking stick ready to fend off the dogs.

We stopped and waited as they ran toward us. The dogs simply stopped in front of us. To our complete surprise, they then trotted off together like two amigos out on a saunter. They were just two happy, carefree dogs. Strangely enough, the same two dogs returned about 15 minutes later. Again they stopped in front of us, grinning and wagging their tails, and then carried on down the trail.

"They were out on their rounds. Perhaps they were checking out the forests for evil spirits, or maybe they were trying to tell us that we had nothing to worry about," I said to Neville.

❧

As we reached San Miniato, the landscape changed. The town

is strategically located atop three small hills, overlooking the lower Arno Valley. In medieval days, San Miniato was at the intersection of the former Via Francigena, the Florence-Pisa road and the Lucca-Siena road. At that time, anyone who wanted to go anywhere in Italy probably passed through San Miniato, which is why it is considered the heart of Tuscany. For centuries, San Miniato was central to a constant flow of both friendly and hostile armies, traders of many goods and services, and other travelers from afar.

Today San Miniato is a member of the Italian organization *Cittaslow* (Slow Town). According to *Cittaslow's* promotional brochure:

> "...where 'slowness' and 'typical local foods' were instead features of a good lifestyle, and so...'Slow Town' came to life. San Miniato is part of this association as it has managed to preserve all its traditions, despite achieving undeniable industrial and economic development at the same time. Here the visitor can enjoy artistic and natural beauty, appropriate service, and simple genuine hospitality."

I asked the staff at the tourist office how the town had earned the *Cittaslow* label. She told me it was based on a number of characteristics, including the quality of life, the number of restaurants, the quality of service, and recreation. Apparently, the designation is reassessed every two or three years.

I wondered how they determined quality of life, and I thought perhaps they forgot to consider the number of cars that passed through the old town center every minute. I found it extremely frustrating having to maneuver around the constant flow of cars that whizzed along the narrow roads.

Today, San Miniato is not only a center of arts and culture, but also of flavors. Aside from the typical extra virgin olive oil, various pork products, and wines, it is home to the esteemed *tartufo bianco* or white truffle.

As per the town marketing literature:

> "...for more than a century, truffle hunters from San Miniato have been coming out at night with their dogs, following paths snaking between the trees, intent on capturing the minimal and faint fragrance to dig some holes and find the precious tuber."

Truffles are found in the surrounding hills of San Miniato, picked during the last four months of the year, starting in September, with the peak period being November and December. Also known as *tubers*, a type of fungi that grows underground, the Italians and French, and others who are serious about their food, hold them in high esteem. They are selected for quality and size and have a light yellow or green exterior and soft brown interior. Ranging in size from a small corn kernel to an orange (though this is rare), they have a strong aroma and unique taste and can be cooked or eaten raw. They are shaved and added to pasta, eggs, or soups to provide a subtle and delicate taste. It's important not to overpower any dish with too much truffle and it takes a well-trained cook or a long tradition of making dishes with truffles to know just the correct amount to use.

I was looking forward to trying one of San Miniato's famous white truffles. Regrettably, it was Monday and almost all the reasonably priced restaurants and those with local foods were closed. Arriving at my last and maybe only choice, I perused the menu. They offered a simple, tiny antipasto of *crostini al tartufo bianco* for 19 euro each.

"Forget this, Nev. That's way beyond our measly pilgrim's budget," I complained.

Disappointed, we returned to the Convento di San Francesco to eat a simple but hearty dinner. Two middle-aged Italian women and one young Spanish man joined us, and at the table beside us sat four or five monks and what we assumed were support staff working at the convent.

The Spaniard, who spoke some Italian and English, was in his late 30's. He had walked the Camino de Santiago, and now he was planning to walk to Rome. The next day, he planned to walk all the way to San Gimignano, about 40 km. But like us, the two women were going to take it slower. They expected to reach Gambassi Terme, only 25 km away.

We talked and ate, sharing stories about our caminos, over a dinner of pasta, oxtail in tomato sauce and salad, with fruit for dessert. We were obviously too busy talking because one of the monks walked over and asked us to finish our meal. I couldn't understand why—were they on a schedule?

Moments later, another older monk interrupted our dinner again as he passed out a little prayer book, neatly organized into a prayer for each day of the week. He began reading the prayers aloud and the rest of the monks joined in. We tried to follow along, but soon lost our place. After the prayer session, the support staff and the monks left us behind in the dining room to finish our meal.

⸎

We left San Miniato under cloudy skies, but I didn't mind, because it was already warm by 8:00 am. It was a beautiful walk, mostly on dirt tracks passing centuries-old hamlets. The wonderful Tuscan landscape was getting closer! We were leaving behind a busy and crowded network of roads, industries, manufacturers, and modern towns. Ahead lay a vast area of vineyards and farms scattered among gently rolling green hills and woods of oak, linden, and willow.

By late morning, I was getting hungry and thought a snack would soon be in order. Within minutes, we stumbled upon a fork to the right of the trail, and then saw a sign "Coiano Winery." Coiano is a little hamlet straddling a spot where the Via Francigena intersects with a small country road.

Impulsively, I announced, "Okay, let's just go and see if we can have a sample of their wine. This might be a good place to have a snack." We wandered up the driveway, waiting for someone to appear, but there was no one around. "Maybe they have a little tasting room," I suggested, and we proceeded ahead. We passed some sheds on the left and approached a building that looked like a house on our right. Then, as we walked toward another building, we heard someone behind us. We turned and saw a middle-aged man approaching us.

I greeted him. "*Buon giorno. Per favore, è possibile avere una degustazione di vino?*"

He asked us to wait a minute, then went away and came back with an older man. The older man motioned us to follow him and guided us through a cement arch, unlocked a door, and led us into the cellar. It was cold, damp, and dark.

He hesitated, and looked at us.

"We would like to try some wine," I told him in Italian.

He pulled out three different bottles and opened them: two bottles of red and one white. We sampled each one. We liked them all, but were particularly fond of one.

Neville and I both thought it would be wonderful to buy a glass each and sit outside on their patio, sipping our wine with lunch and enjoying the Tuscan landscape. So I asked the man if we could do this. He just shrugged his shoulders—the Italian response that means "Whatever—it doesn't matter."

I told him, "We like this one," pointing to the bottle we wanted to have with our lunch. I told him we would like two glasses, and I asked him how much.

"*Per la bottiglia sono 2,50 euro,*" he replied.

"*Solo un bicchiere di vino per favore, una bottiglia è troppo per noi. Quanto costano due bicchieri di vino?*" I replied (No, only a glass, no bottle; how much is two glasses of wine?).

He looked at me in wonder. I was not sure what was going through his mind other than maybe, "You dumb tourists, you only want a glass?"

The old man repeated slowly and purposely, "*Una bottiglia di vino euro 2,50, un bicchiere di vino euro 3,00.*"

"*No, no grazie, una bottiglia è troppo, vogliamo solo due bicchieri*— No, thank you, that's too much wine for us, only two glasses for us," I said.

Then Neville and I looked at each other. Why buy a glass for 3.00 euro when we could buy the entire bottle for 2.50 euro?

"Just buy the bottle. We'll just leave whatever we don't finish," Neville suggested.

"*Va bene*," I said to the old man. "*Una bottiglia e due bicchieri. Grazie.*"

He handed us the bottle and two glasses with a smirk on his face.

We walked outside to the bench on their grand patio, plunked our backpacks down on the ground and reclined on the bench. The old man locked the door of the wine cellar behind us and disappeared around the back of the building.

I dug out our food for lunch while Neville poured the wine. We savored the flavors of our lunch of local cheese, bread, and grapes that I had bought earlier in San Miniato and slowly sipped our bottle of Coiano wine.

I reflected on our morning walk from San Miniato while gazing at the Tuscan landscape before us. We had walked along a small country road past the tiny hamlet of Calenzano, and then, at Canneto, we had veered off to follow a well-marked, dirt farm track straight south through the rolling hills of northern Tuscany, passing farmhouses and little hamlets.

We were feeling truly mellow, sitting on the bench alone and enjoying our food and our wine, the smell of the flowers, the fresh air, and the sun. Looking over the Tuscan landscape of low rolling hills, we were completely absorbed by our surroundings. It was a classic Tuscan experience and one we would cherish for a long time.

We were happy pilgrims.

It was just about noon when we reluctantly pulled ourselves up from the bench. When we reached the end of the driveway, we were shocked to see a middle-aged couple standing there.

They had stopped for a water break and they were equally as astonished to see us.

The man spoke first, asking us in English, "You don't speak English, do you?"

"Ah…yes," we both replied enthusiastically.

"We're walking the Via Francigena. Are you two walking the Via Francigena?" he asked.

"Yes we are. We stopped to try some red wine and then decided to have a bottle with our lunch."

"I couldn't do that, drink before noon and then go walking," he said.

I laughed. "I know, normally I wouldn't drink and walk either. I always said I could never do that. But it just happened and I feel great!"

The man shrugged his shoulders. "I guess you're just two crazy people like us, hiking the Via Francigena. Where are you from?"

"Canada," we replied.

"Where? We're from Canada too, from the Kitchener area. I'm David and this is Mary, my better half."

What a small world! I hadn't expected to meet another Canadian couple walking the Via Francigena.

That afternoon we walked together through the hills, sharing our stories and stopping every few minutes to snap photos of the beautiful scenery. Ahead of us lay rolling hills of recently harvested wheat fields. The ground was tilled, exposing the multicolored soil juxtaposed against the bright colorful houses perched on top of the hills.

I pinched myself. I couldn't believe we were now walking in Tuscany.

Bella Toscana moment – Picnic wine lunch – Coiano Winery

❦

We left Gambassi Terme early next morning, after stopping at a local *panificio* to pick up some baked goods for breakfast and lunch. We followed a narrow side road for a short distance and then swung off onto a dirt track. Ahead of us, as the morning mist slowly lifted, the early morning sunlight revealed the beauty of the Tuscan countryside—low hills, cypress trees, and vineyards.

We caught up with David and Mary later that morning when they stopped for a midmorning snack. They told us they were only hiking to San Gimignano and had reserved a room at the three-star Hotel La Cisterna. Since we had chosen to spend the night at the monastery, we agreed to meet in San Gimignano later that afternoon for coffee.

As we got closer to San Gimignano with its 14 remaining towers (there were once 72) looming in the distance, we caught up with a German walking tour group and stopped to talk to them. They had taken a bus from San Miniato to Gambassi Terme and now were doing the short hike to San Gimignano. When we told them we had walked from Switzerland, a couple of them expressed both surprise and delight at our efforts.

Coming upon a walking tour group was a sure sign that we were getting nearer to the tourist centers of Tuscany. For many foreigners, Tuscany is the most beautiful destination in all of Italy. Tourist places beget tour groups, and tour groups lead to…well…more tourists. At some places, tourists exceed residents, and San Gimignano was one of those places. The problem was so severe in the city that the locals were considering measures to limit the number of tourists that could visit the old historical center each day.

In any case, we decided to stay close to the German tour group, as it seemed the group leader knew all the shortcuts to San Gimignano. We followed the group as he led them off the main road and walked along the edge of the vineyard rows through private property. I wondered if the owner would let pilgrims walking the Via Francigena tramp through his vineyards. As we got close to San Gimignano, Neville and I had the identical thought: it was time to pass the group; we were pilgrims on a mission.

Upon reaching the *centro*, we asked for directions to the *monastero*. We learned it was down a road to the left, shortly after entering the gate. We walked down, only to discover it had closed at noon and would not open again until 3:30 pm, if we were lucky.

We had no interest in waiting around so we wandered through some backstreets in search of another place to stay. Along the way, we passed many homes and apartments with a sign on their door: *Affittacamere*—rooms to rent.

I impulsively stopped at one of the places and rang the doorbell. Initially, there was no answer but then we heard a voice. A middle-aged woman came to the door. We enquired if she had a vacant room.

"Yes I have a room," she replied. "You can have now for only 55 euro for the night."

She showed us a pleasant, rather large room overlooking the street below. It was luxury for us pilgrims, so we quickly accepted.

We cleaned up a bit and went out to try to find David and Mary at their hotel. They were having a nap so we agreed to meet them at 4:00 pm for coffee. We wandered around town, but the number of tourists strolling through the small narrow streets was overwhelming so we returned to our room. Not since Lucca had we seen so many people; it was even worse than Lucca.

❧

We returned later to the Hotel La Cisterna and asked the receptionist to ring David and Mary's room. She looked us up and down, as if we were "poor pilgrims."

Mary announced that she first wanted to go into one of the churches to see frescoes. For me, it was just another church, but not for Mary. Located in the Piazza del Duomo, the church originally known as the Duomo, is now officially the Collegiate Church of Santa Maria Assunta. In 1148, Pope Eugenio III, returning to Rome along the Via Francigena, consecrated the Duomo. The present façade dates from the 13th century.

As we approached the entrance, Mary explained to me that she had been to this church before, and that she loves to revisit it each time she returns to San Gimignano. "I like the simplicity of the façade—especially in comparison to the many highly decorated churches," she said. "And the long, wide flight of steps leading up to the church doors sets the cathedral apart from its surroundings, while at the same time the color and stone texture of the stairway blends in with the other buildings. It's a great place to sit and watch the world go by."

The interior of the church was almost completely covered with frescoes dating from the 14th century—Old Testament paintings by Bartolo di Fredi and New Testament paintings perhaps by either Barna de Siena or Lippo Memmi.

Mary whispered to me, "I love the literalness of the Old and New Testament frescoes. They are 'primitive' in the folk art sense, but a vibrant interpretation of the biblical stories. I think the frescoes offer an insight into the thinking of the time."

She pointed out that Domenico Ghirlandaio, in 1475, painted the frescoes in the Capella (chapel) de Santa Fina. She told me his art was a mixture of medieval and Renaissance styles, when artists were discovering new techniques for painting perspective. His perspectives were considered advanced and were enhanced by his use of architecture in his frescoes.

Admiring his work, she whispered to me, "I love Ghirlandaio's faces. Some are portraits of people living at the time—patrons, friends, and often, himself. I also like the towers of San Gimignano in the background of 'Obsequies of Santa Fina'—frescoes depicting the stories of Santa Fina."

After wandering about, I later found Mary standing and appreciating two sculptures at the back of the cathedral. They were carved in wood by artist Jacopo della Quercia (1367–1438). In 1406, Jacopo was commissioned to do a new fountain in Siena's Piazza del Campo, in rectangular white marble. However, it is not certain whether it, or a replica, is in the *piazza* today.

Mary particularly liked the carving of the Virgin, dated 1421. "Her face is exquisite and the proportions are lovely. I also like the warm colors and the graceful flow of her gown," she enthused.

We left the church and found a café in one of the main *piazzas* to chat over coffee. We asked David and Mary why they were walking the Via Francigena. "David had drunk too much red wine, just after returning from Italy, and decided he needed to walk from the Alps to Rome," Mary laughed.

David added, "we were looking for a hiking challenge, and since we love Italy, I knew it wasn't going to be the Camino de Santiago in Spain."

The towers of San Gimignano

They set off with a plan to walk a section for two to three weeks each year. But just before they left on their second trip, only then did they learn about the Via Francigena.

Before we parted, Mary invited us to meet them for dinner in the hotel restaurant; they planned to have *cinghiale* (wild boar). It was tempting—we loved *cinghiale* and were happy to eat it anytime—but we thought the restaurant would be beyond our pilgrim budget. Besides, I sensed that David was looking forward to having their dinner alone, just the two of them, to reminisce about their previous visit there many years earlier. Neville told them we would think about it and maybe see them later.

We walked around town and came upon a bookstore stocked with plenty of Via Francigena books and maps. We spent the rest of the evening ambling through the bookstore. We bought a topographical map and used the Internet for the first time since Lucca.

Near the bookstore, we discovered a narrow laneway with a set of stairs that led to the top of the ancient walls. Up top, we had great views of the nearby towers and surrounding countryside. The sun was slowly setting and producing a wide range of reds, yellows and oranges against the landscape. As it got darker, the tourists disappeared, and we stood there alone with the spectacular sunset colors reflecting off the historic towers.

We decided to let Mary and David enjoy their dinner alone, and we had an inexpensive dinner outside the walls of the old city. It was a welcome relief to be away from all the tourists.

The food was good and reasonably priced. We both ordered *zuppa di verdure* (a thick green stew) and *anatra alla vernaccia* (duck made with a local white wine sauce). Over dinner, we talked about David and Mary, and how lucky we were to have met two other "crazy Canucks" with whom to share our stories and dreams. We hoped we would see them again.

After dinner, we wandered back into the old part of the town. The streets were quiet and empty, but tomorrow more tourists would arrive for the day. Just as certain as the sun rises each day, it was certain that new busloads of tourists would pour into the streets to admire the rich history of San Gimignano. But for now, we were relishing the solitude.

"It's actually a pretty little town, and it has a very different feel now, compared to the daytime, don't you think Neville?" He agreed.

I was happy and proud that we had walked to, and would walk from, this famous Tuscan town. And I was glad we had chosen to stay the night. I think to really experience and appreciate the history of San Gimignano you have to stay overnight. I liked the way Mary described it:

> "As a Canadian, where the landscape seems to change frequently in cities and towns, where esthetics is ignored in favor of efficiency and cost, and where concrete and asphalt reign supreme, I really love visiting San Gimignano where everything is as it was centuries ago. The proportions of buildings relate to a human scale, the colors of the stone are warm, and the twisting, winding streets lead me to surprising vistas of the valley below, or a spacious, welcoming square."

I was grateful for having met Mary. It was her passion for the town and the art of the Collegiate Church that left me with a true appreciation for San Gimignano. I recalled Mary's words from our conversation over coffee:

"I can always go into the Collegiate in San Gimignano and say hello to my favorite art works!"

XV

Siena: The Good City

"When you look at a city, it's like
reading the hopes, aspirations and pride
of everyone who built it."
— Hugh Newell Jacobsen

NEVILLE
I was gently awoken to a woman singing a sweet melody.

Tiptoeing downstairs from the bedroom loft to the main floor, I gazed out the window. I saw the sun gradually spread its rays across the old city, lighting up building after building, as if I was watching a stage show. From the window, I could see all the way over to the Campo and the famous Torre del Mangia, which shone brightly against the morning sun. Across the valley, a light morning mist cloaked the church of Sant'Agostino, making the scene look dreamy and surreal. I felt as if I was in a scene from the movie 'Room with a View', but I was in Siena.

⁘

Most historians agree that the Etruscans founded Siena and the Romans later ruled it, but when the Lombards invaded the region, Siena became an important center. At the time, the existing Roman roads of the Via Aurelia and the Via Cassia passed through areas controlled by the Byzantine Empire. So the Lombards built a new route through the center of Tuscany, which passed right through Siena. The city became an essential stopping point along the Lombard Way, later called the Via Francigena.

What I found interesting about Siena was that, during the Middle Ages, the city's leaders had a simple philosophy that hospitality, charity, and "Good Government" were important factors in order for Siena to be a "Good City." It would become a community where all people were welcomed and treated with respect, and the city would flourish, prosper and grow. This was a novel initiative because, until then, Italy was a land of city-states based on medieval feudalism, and it was only the monasteries that provided hospitality and a safe shelter for people of all ages and classes. It was unprecedented for a governing body of a medieval city to come up with this idea.

Being a numbers guy, I also discovered an interesting and amusing piece of information. Nine was a significant number in Siena's evolution as a medieval city, beginning with the development of the Piazza del Campo, Siena's cultural center.

Before the 14th century, Siena was nothing more than a swampy hollow surrounded by three hillside communities—Castellare, San Martino and Camollia. The Governo dei Ventiquattro, a council of aristocratic members who governed the city from 1236 to 1270, converted this empty bog into a huge market square to be utilized for fairs and public events. It attracted people from throughout the region and later it would be known as the Campo.

And this is where the number nine came into the picture.

The "*Noveschi*" or "Nine" replaced the Governo dei Ventiquattro and governed Siena at the height of its medieval power between the years 1287 and 1355. The Council of Nine was really a complex, self-defined group of six to twelve individuals. Each member of the council was selected by other council members from the merchant population of Siena (that excluded the traditional feudal nobility), but only after meeting strict requirements. Each member of the council would then serve for a defined period of time.

This was one of the most peaceful periods in the city's history, resulting in an economical and cultural renaissance. Between 1327 and 1349, the Campo was paved with red bricks laid in a fishbone pattern with ten lines of travertine tiles. They divided the Campo into nine sections, which symbolically represented the rule of the Nine. The Campo became one of Europe's greatest medieval squares.

But the *Noveschi* did more. As part of their major public works program, they set out to improve the city's water supply, make buildings safer, restore the Duomo, and erect the Palazzo Pubblico and the Torre del Mangia. The latter three works of construction were administrated under the watchful eye of three officials, the praetors, who were appointed to a yearly term.

In line with their belief that good government led to a good city, the *Noveschi* commissioned Ambrogio Lorenzetti to paint a series of frescoes lining three walls of the room in the Palazzo Pubblico (town hall) where the *Noveschi* held their meetings. The frescoes, known as the "Allegory of Good and Bad Government," are symbolic visual representations of the good and bad regimes and their impact on the city and the countryside.

The *Noveschi* promoted a belief that strong, socially focused governance led to social stability and cooperative security for its citizens. They believed that bad, weak governance, along with greed and power, resulted in more crime, disease, poverty, and social unrest.

By the 15th century, there was a steady, sometimes heavy stream of pilgrims, travelers, and merchants passing through and stopping in Siena. One report suggested that in the Jubilee year of 1450, more than 4,000 pilgrims passed through the city walls each night, stopping and staying at one of the city's 90 hotels. Pilgrimage tourism was big business, with various agencies offering medieval religious packages.

At that time, Siena had reached its zenith as a medieval tourist destination and it has never looked back. Today it is still the geographical and cultural center of Tuscany.

❧

JULIE

Siena and its citizens certainly bestowed their hospitality and charity on us as modern-day pilgrims. For one, our friend Antonella, graciously lent her Siena apartment to us. It was located three hundred meters from Siena's famous Campo, offering a postcard view across the old city. From the living room window, the Torre del Mangia and other buildings shifted in color and appearance as the light changed throughout the day. The bright afternoon sunlight shone directly into the living room, making it ideal for me to bask in its warm rays. The apartment was a perfect location for experiencing all that Siena had to offer. I appreciated Antonella's generosity—and the free entertainment of a resident opera singer was a bonus!

On the night we arrived, we decided to go with Antonella's recommendation that we have dinner at a nearby trattoria La Torre. It was only a short walk from her apartment and just a few steps from the Campo. We followed her instructions, but in the dark, the little narrow laneways all looked the same. We finally stumbled on the *trattoria*, tucked away between two shops, after passing a young couple kissing in the nearby laneway.

It was a small place with only a dozen or so tables and a small open kitchen where we could watch two cooks preparing the meals. With its red brick ceiling, it looked like it might have been an old cave or wine cellar. The owner, Alberto, a portly man of sixty or so years, greeted us at the entrance and showed us to a table. There was no printed menu. Instead, Alberto, with his deep voice, proceeded to recite the menu of the day—names of pasta, sauces, and meat dishes rolled off his tongue as if he was reciting a prayer.

As soon as we heard *cinghiale* (wild boar), Neville and I looked at each other and the decision was made. Neville selected the *tagliatelle con cinghiale* (similar to fettuccine but made with egg) and I ordered one of my favorite dishes, *pici con cinghiale* (rolled, elongated rustic spaghetti-like pasta local to this area of Tuscany made with *un ragù* of tomato, garlic, and ground wild boar meat). Alberto reminded me that cheese is normally not included with the pasta if the sauce contains garlic.

"This is the best *cinghiale* I have ever tasted," I said to Neville. "I really like this little place; it's so unpretentious."

For our *secondi piatti*, Neville ordered a plate of *anatra* (duck), and I ordered *vitello arrosto* (roasted veal). We left the *trattoria* feeling as if we had eaten in a friend's large family dining room. We were delighted that we had broken our normal rule of avoiding restaurants close to tourist attractions or the city center; the result was one of the most delicious and memorable meals we experienced on the Via Francigena.

⁓

NEVILLE

The following morning I let Julie (who had succumbed to a cold bug) sleep in and rest while I went out into the streets and explored the city.

Walking through the old streets and passing narrow laneways, I could see clearly Siena's medieval past. Already people were out and about, and many had stopped to admire the Campo, which was more impressive than I had imagined. I joined them and sat down on the terra-cotta brick cobbled surface, soaking up the morning sun and enjoying the sights, sounds, and goings-on. There were the obvious groups of tourists, but among the crowds were young couples, families with kids playing and chasing balls, and older women and men sitting in one of the many cafes that lined the Campo.

Three-story pastel-colored buildings and outdoor *ristoranti, trattorie* and shops lined the perimeter. In medieval days, these same buildings were called the "*palazzi signorili,*" or plaza mansions, and housed Siena's three wealthiest families at that time: the Sansedoni, the Piccolomini and the Saracini.

Il Campo – Siena

It is easy to appreciate why the Campo remains the cultural heart and community center of Siena. What is difficult to imagine is the Campo full of horses and people. It is the site of the Palio di Siena, known simply as "Il Palio," a twice-yearly horse race held every July 2 and August 16. Ten jockeys, dressed in outfits representing ten of the seventeen *Contrade*, or city wards, race their horses bareback, circling the Piazza del Campo three times along a narrow, sloping dirt track. The entire race lasts less than a few minutes and it is not unusual for the occasional horse to finish the race without its rider.

I noticed a small sign on each of the fountains around the Campo. It stated that it was "illegal to eat and drink in the Campo." Another one stated that playing Frisbee and kicking soccer balls were also illegal. However, I spotted people either tossing a Frisbee or eating an ice cream. There was another sign warning that "topless sunbathing is illegal" but regrettably nobody was ignoring this law.

⌘

Julie

When Neville returned to the apartment, he found me relaxing on the sofa, doing what I like best: soaking up the sunlight beaming through the window and eating a pastry. I had taken a break from catching up on my journal writing.

"Are you ready to explore the city?" Neville asked enthusiastically, but afraid I might decline.

"Yes, I would like to visit the *Ospedale di Santa Maria della Scala*," I replied, surprising him.

Legend states that Beaton Sorore, a cobbler turned monk, founded the *Ospedale*, or hospital, in the 9th century. Sorore mended shoes for the poor and for pilgrims walking the Via Francigena as they passed through Siena. His workshop became a place where pilgrims would rest and receive comfort and aid. Wealthy families of Siena began to give him sums of money to support his relief work, and with this money, Sorore built the hospital.

Officially, records show that the Cathedral Canons (council of Roman Catholic bishops) founded the hospital in March 1090 to provide shelter and hospitality to pilgrims. Travelers in the Middle Ages, often injured or preyed on by bandits, and at constant risk of contracting contagious diseases, found not only a bed for the night but also doctors and nurses. The services expanded to include aid for the city's poor, as well as shelter and education for abandoned children. By the 15th century, the hospital came under the control of the city. Ospedale di Santa Maria della Scala is one of Europe's oldest hospitals (and hospices), and along with Siena's Palazzo Pubblico and Cathedral, is considered a major artistic monument.

Since the early 1980's, the hospital has been a large, intriguing museum complex containing chapels, several halls of museum collections, Sienese collections on the history of art and medicine, an archaeological museum, various rooms for exhibitions, and the church of Santa Maria Annunziata, which dates back to the 13th century. There were two areas of the museum that left me with a lasting impression.

On the lowest level is the Oratorio de Santa Caterina della Notte (Oratory of the Company of Saint Catherine of the Night). It is considered the heart of the hospital where St. Catherine would go to pray and comfort the sick. As I walked into the first room of the Oratorio, I noticed how dark it was. Only lighted candles or small lights hung on the walls, offering just enough light to read the plaques. Several arches divided the chapel into small sections, each ornately decorated with a painted blue ceiling. There were many pieces of artwork, sketches and paintings, probably from the 13th and 14th centuries, some depicting St. Catherine's life.

Curious, I wandered further into the depths of the chapel. Behind the chapel was a small room with many plaques engraved with names and dates. There were four hooks on the wall on one side of the room and seven hooks on the other side, and from each hook hung a long thick string of beads with a cross at the bottom. I imagined these were used during prayer, and although they looked old, it seemed as if they had been used only yesterday.

Then I discovered yet another archway leading into another small room. This last room looked to be the least touched by restorers. Dark and simply decorated, with walls painted black, white and gray, it felt very mysterious. On one of the walls hung a couple of gigantic wooden boards titled something like "...*ruolo di fratelli...della compagna d' este Caterina della notte dal 1792 a pace...*" I assumed it was a memorandum and inscription, including the names of the Brothers of the "Company of Saint Catherine of the Night" and what appeared to be dates of their deaths, from 1792 to 1946.

I returned to the main chapel and sat for a few minutes in solitude, while Neville went off to explore the balance of the museum.

A strange feeling—that I find difficult to put into words—overcame me. It was as if I could feel the heaviness of the place—for the pain that many people might have suffered and the sacrifices made by those who cared for these people. Yet at the same time, it had a feeling of love and peacefulness and serenity. I truly felt the soul of the place.

The other feature of the hospital that stood out for me was the illustrations of the hospital's daily life and activities depicted in the *Sala del Pellegrinaio*, or Pilgrim's Hall, in the "Pilgrimage" series of frescoes painted between 1441 and 1444. In a massive open space, the walls on both sides of the hall were covered in frescoes and included a wide range of scenes: abandoned children being received into the arms of wet nurses; the feeding, weaning, and education of the children; children being provided with grain from farms belonging to Santa Maria della Scala scattered all over Senesi territory; a surgeon assisting a patient onto a stretcher; a youth with a cut on his thigh being washed by an attendant before being operated on; a monk hearing a confession while two attendants carried a stretcher; and workers distributing bread to children, pilgrims, and beggars.

Governed from the beginning by the regulatory and statutory laws of the region, the mission of the hospital was "to provide hospitality and means and usefulness to the old and poor veterans of the city..." They were supposed to receive "all things they were in need of according to the means of the hospital." This also included looking after the reception, care, education, and marriage of abandoned children who were expected to be "received kindly and graciously and given milk and food at the expense of the hospital." Furthermore, the hospital assisted these children throughout their lives, giving them an opportunity to choose whether they wanted to dedicate themselves to helping others within or outside the hospital, or simply forming a family on their own.

❧

NEVILLE

That evening Julie became *"Über (Super) Italian Cook."* She assembled a simple but fine homemade Italian dinner. The *antipasti* included fresh red plump tomatoes, sliced *coppa* ham, *salame* and *prosciutto,* and large fresh artichokes topped with shaved *pecorino* cheese. The *primo piatto* was a bowl of *pici*, the local pasta, topped with a light sauce of fresh Italian herbs and *pecorino* cheese. Naturally, I provided a bottle of Tuscan *Sangiovese* red wine to wash it all down.

After dinner, we took a slow saunter around the Campo. People were out enjoying the final moments of the autumn evening and drinking and talking in the outdoor cafes. Surprisingly, even though the sun had set and the balmy rays of the day were long gone, there was a sense of warmth in the air.

Siena still has that small-town community feel to it, similar to what we had experienced in Aosta. But unlike some of the great Roman cities like Pavia, Piacenza, and even Lucca, Siena is more picturesque, like a Leonardo da Vinci painting.

I thought more about the idea of "Good Government" and "Good Cities" and wondered why our elected leaders in today's society had forgotten about this important constituent of social good. Clearly, it had worked well for Siena in the past and, from our current observations and experiences, it is still working well.

Into the Light

*"...there is a poetic approach to the sacred
journey, a highly developed picture of the
goal—healing, rebirth, peace itself—
that draws the traveler forward."*
– Phil Cousineau

NEVILLE

From Siena to the border of Tuscany and Lazio, there is a region best described as the "badlands" of Tuscany—a 120-kilometer expanse of barren rolling hills.

South of Siena, the Via Francigena gently winds along the River Arbia and through the Val d'Arbia. Leaving behind the charming green Siena vineyards, the trail drifts through the dry, gray, clay crags of the "Crete Senesi." It is a moonscape-like countryside characterized by lone stone villas perched on barren white clay outcrops and jagged slopes, and surrounded by juniper and cypress trees. The clay, known as "*mattaione*," is composed of sediments of the prehistoric Pliocene Sea, which covered the area between 2.5 and 4.5 million years ago. Erosion has played a major role in the landscape, forming weathered hillsides known as "*calanchi*" and clay knolls called "*biancane*" or "*mammelloni*."

The Via Francigena continues through the villages of Grancia di Cuna, which is a wonderfully preserved medieval fortified farm, then to Isola d'Arbia and Monteroni d'Arbia, home to a stunning fortified watermill from the 14th century, and on to Buonconvento, an important agricultural center.

Much further south, at San Quirico d'Orcia, the Via Francigena crosses into what is one of my favorite locations in all of Italy—the Val d'Orcia. If there is a place to find tranquility and peace, this is it.

ᏩᎨᏍᎤ

On the first day we crossed into the Val d'Orcia. Almost immediately, I experienced a feeling of calm and serenity. Slipping away, were the angry feelings of the past, the struggles of the weeks before, the arguments between Julie and me, and between us and other "demons."

The isolation, the empty spaces, the radiance of the sun, and the sheer expanse of the countryside invoked a sense of enchantment and solitude. Ahead of us was a landscape of hills, interspersed with streams, rivers, deep ravines, and craggy outcrops. It felt as if time simply slowed down.

For centuries, the Via Francigena has intersected the Val d'Orcia, guiding travelers, wayfarers and pilgrims through this natural and man-made landscape. Ahead lay freshly tilled gray and golden undulating hills that blended easily with the dark green vegetation lining the rocky cliffs. The vineyards, in flowing lines of red, green, and orange, merged with the silvery gray of the olive groves. While the morning light was crisp, the afternoon light melted the pale blue sky into the hills. The evening sunsets were fiery red, and always present in the distance was the majestic grandeur of the Monte Amiata, an extinct volcano.

Val d'Orcia fascinated the grand Sienese painters of the Renaissance, mesmerized the romantic writers of England, France, and Germany, and has provided a backdrop of grandeur for travelers of many eras. Today, the beauty and charm of the Val d'Orcia continues to attract photographers, writers, and travelers alike.

⸻

A few years ago, I developed Guillain-Barré. In technical terms, it is a rare, acute, inflammatory autoimmune syndrome affecting the peripheral nervous system, usually triggered by an acute infection. Initially, I had tingling sensations and weakness that started in my legs and then spread to my arms and upper body. I was almost paralyzed when I entered the hospital. In roughly 20% of cases, the paralysis leads to permanent disability; for a few unfortunate souls, it results in death. Recovery is slow, taking months, sometimes even years.

I spent twelve days in hospital in the neurosciences unit. When I first arrived, I could barely walk. Over the following days, my condition continued to worsen to a point where I could not get up out of bed or even go the bathroom without help. Days later, I could only consume fluids and only if somebody held the plastic cup for me.

As bad as it was, about a week later, I started to improve, and after two weeks I was able to convince the hospital staff to send me home to fend for myself. A month later, I was able to walk with the aid of a cane, and two months later I could walk five kilometers without stopping.

Not once during that time did I ever think I would lose the battle, that I might become permanently disabled or even die. I had read that many people who come close to death or have near death experiences report seeing "a bright light" that becomes more intense closer to death, pulling them into the afterlife or another world. Many people report feeling intensely positive and reaching a point of acceptance, forgiving any wrongs in their past and becoming at peace with themselves and those around them.

However, while I was lying in my hospital bed, I cannot say this ever happened to me. Instead, whatever was responsible for this rare and horrible condition, it became my destiny to fight it and fully recover from it.

Yet in Val d'Orcia, for the next three days, "a bright light" shone upon me. As we slowly walked through this region of Tuscany, there was little in the way to distract me and I could become lost in my personal thoughts. It was warm and pleasant and peaceful. As I reflected on the past five weeks, I took the time to clear my mind of any regrets, anger, frustrations, disappointments, and failed expectations. It was a time of liberation, and any doubts that I had, disappeared.

⌒⌒⌒⌒

As we ambled along, faint images of lone hilltop villas and rows of cypress trees lining the driveways faded away in the hazy vapor of the afternoon sun. Our only guiding landmark was Monte Amiata in the distant west, resting like an old paternal grandfather watching his family brood. The trail snaked around and over the hills in an easterly direction away from San Quirico d'Orcia. Near Bagno Vignoni, we stopped to talk to a lone man walking by himself along one of the many farm tracks.

"We are walking the Via Francigena to Rome," we told the man, as we had told many before him.

"It's the walk, the journey, and not the destination that is most important," the man advised us.

Etruscans and Romans and kings and queens bathed in the primitive thermal waters of Bagno Vignoni, later named after the famous 11th-century castle situated on a hill above the village. Pilgrims traveling the Via Francigena en route to Rome would also rest and soak in the spa waters to heal and cleanse themselves in preparation for their arrival in Rome. In honor of pilgrims past, we felt we should do the same.

In the center *piazza* of Bagno Vignoni, a plaque with an inscription by Sienese scholar Lattanzio Tolomei states (loosely translated) the following:

"Oh, Nymphs living in these vapors, liberating the eternal fire among the waves, restoring life to those who suffer, I salute you and gift you with copious waters. Spring forth and bring health to the infirm, and to the healthy, a sweet bath. For both, we will be grateful."

We booked a room at the Hotel Posta Marcucci, one of the original spa hotels in Bagno Vignoni owned and managed by the Marcucci family that has lived in the region since 1700. Like most people in the area, they were simple farmers. In the 1950s they built the hotel, which has 36 rooms and an outdoor pool filled with precious mineral water. Overlooking the Orcia River, it offers a wonderful view of Rocca di Tentennano. Indoors, the "Water Rooms" include a thermal spa pool, a hydro massage bathtub, and a Turkish bath to regenerate body and mind.

We changed and went downstairs to try out the pools and baths. I had nubile nymphs on my mind.

The outdoor thermal pool appeared old; the water was barely warm—not what I would call a thermal pool. We tried the indoor "Water Rooms" but the experience was disappointing. The hydro massage bathtub was cool, the Turkish bath was small and cramped, and the tiny sauna was not working. The Hotel Posta Marcucci had seen better days. And I didn't see any capricious nymphs or other shadowy beings.

On the second day, we left Bagno Vignoni, prepared to tackle the next stage of our journey. After climbing a steep hill to the *frazione* (hamlet) of Rocca d'Orcia, we could see in the distance the Rocca di Tentennano, the same castle that we had seen from our hotel room window. The castle stands on a pinnacle high above the Val d'Orcia with the small village of Rocca d'Orcia just below. The castle is built of limestone and, like so many other castles in the area, it played a role in the endless territorial conflicts between Florence and Siena. Originally used as a military lookout and defensive position, the castle was also famous as a refuge, beginning in 1377, for Saint Catherine of Siena, who taught people to read and write.

Further on, we turned onto a dirt farm track that led down a gentle valley away from the road. It was good to be finally walking along a gravel path instead of a secondary paved road, and there were wide-open views to the east over the Val d'Orcia. Julie and I spoke little; we were both feeling peaceful and in harmony with our surroundings and ourselves.

Castiglione d'Orcia and Rocca d'Orcia served as our guides, leading us away from Bagno Vignoni. To our right, Monte Amiata still watched over us, and on the distant horizon we could see, perched on top of a single rocky knoll, the fortress town of Radicofani. As far away as we were, we could see the Rocca di Radicofani. Dating back to before the year 1000, the mighty castle sits on a daunting basaltic cliff almost 900 metres high, above the Val d'Orcia and between Monte Cetona to the east and Monte Amiata to the west.

By early morning, it was already getting hot, even for October. There were no sounds except for a distant farm tractor and the occasional bird. It was a steep climb towards Campiglia d'Orcia, 400 meters over the next four kilometers, and in the hot mid-afternoon sun, it was slow going. As we struggled up the hill, our drinking water rapidly disappeared. In the distance we could still see Rocca d'Orcia but it was disappearing in the afternoon haze.

We continued to Abbadia San Salvatore, a small community that lies on the periphery of broad chestnut woods covering the eastern side of Monte Amiata. Built around the monastery of the same name, it is one of the best-preserved medieval centers in Italy and a popular summer and winter resort. The Lombard King Ratchis founded the abbey in 743, and it is one of the oldest monasteries in Tuscany.

Abbadia San Salvatore was an important stopping point for us, as it had been for pilgrims in the past. High up on the east side of Monte Amiata, surrounded by deep forests, the old town provided a welcome reprieve from the intensity of the bright light, humidity and heat of the day. Time went backwards as we wandered through the village, sauntering past the well-preserved outer walls and streets and the medieval and Renaissance houses of gray stone. The streets and buildings were decorated with chestnut branches and leaves, local produce, and ornaments, in celebration of an autumn festival.

On the third and final day of our journey through Val d'Orcia, we left Abbadia San Salvatore and headed for Proceno and the Lazio-Tuscany border, where there was nothing but many kilometers of chalky white, dusty farm tracks and the barren rolling hills.

As we descended a steep hill, mist and a light drizzle shrouded our view. The bright, hazy sunlight that we had experienced the first two days was now replaced by a narrow beam of light that sliced through the mist and fog. It was initially faint, as the morning fog and mist swirled around it, and I almost didn't notice it. But it grew in intensity.

It was so powerful that we were unable to stare at it for long. Somewhere down in the valley there was a beacon, a brilliant guiding light.

We descended further along a small paved road. By now the rain had stopped and the mist had lifted enough to suggest that beyond were farms and rural countryside. About a kilometer later, the road reconnected to a provincial road and we continued our walk, criss-crossing a series of smaller paved side roads.

As we continued walking towards the narrow beam of light, the fog and mist burned off and the sun came back out. But when we arrived at where the light should be, it was no longer there. It had disappeared, as if it never had been there at all.

Once we started to climb the last set of hilly slopes and enter Lazio, we could no longer see Monte Amiata. The landscape to the west had faded in the afternoon haze. In the distance, the town of Radicofani was fading away too. I stopped and looked around, realizing that the burnt landscape of Val d'Orcia was disappearing. The afternoon sunlight was soft, less harsh, and the surroundings were changing; it was greener, hillier, and treed, as if we were crossing into another world.

Leaving Val d' Orcia en route to Proceno

The town of Proceno came sharply into focus. Sitting on a small rocky outcrop above the valley, it was not hard to miss. It was as if we had come upon a magical fairy tale castle, a hilltop shrine surrounded by lush green forest.

Legend has it that Lars Porsenna, sometimes known as Lucumone Porsenna, a 6th century BC Etruscan king, once went boar hunting in the woods where Proceno stands today. At this location, a colossal, vicious wild boar attacked him. Neither surprised nor frightened, the king killed the boar. In those times, it was common to read the liver of wild animals that one had killed. A "Haruspices," an Etruscan diviner or "entrails observer", did the reading. The outcome of this particular reading was that King Porsenna should establish a town in this location to celebrate his lucky escape.

We walked along a quiet road that followed the ridge up to the castle. On a number of previous occasions, whenever we had entered a town, an old man would take it upon himself to greet us and guide us to our accommodation. I fully expected this to happen

Our personal cane di guida del Proceno

at Proceno, but instead a small, black-and-white, shorthaired dog greeted us at the entrance. I chuckled. He reminded me of a dog that had greeted us when we were walking the Camino de Santiago in Spain. He had a happy-go-lucky expression on his face, and his mouth was slightly open, as if he was smiling at us.

"Come, follow me and I'll show you the way," the dog seemed to say.

"Perhaps he is Saint Peter in disguise (like St. James would be in Spain), or maybe one of the many dogs that are here to guide us through the pearly gates of heaven," I joked with Julie.

Oddly, the dog assumed the role of a local resident guide as he walked ahead of us into the town, looking back every so often to ensure that we were following him. Not sure where we were going and what we expected to find, we followed him, hoping to discover the answers later.

Our Proceno guide dog continued up the hill, passing the town gates and leading us up the main street higher and higher towards the main square. We passed the Castello di Proceno that today is a small boutique hotel with several rooms and apartments for rent. A little further, we passed a couple of bed and breakfasts and the occasional shop. Otherwise, the town was small and nearly deserted.

When we reached the main square of the town, we saw an open café-bar, so we entered and ordered a couple of cold drinks, our first cold refreshment on this hot day.

After, as we continued to walk the narrow lanes, exploring the tiny town of Proceno, our little black-and-white guide dog stayed close to us, guiding us here and there. He still had his happy-go-lucky expression, as if he knew everything would be okay.

I chuckled to myself once again. I thought about my run-in with Guillain-Barré a few years ago, and I thought about the "bright light" that had beckoned to us this morning, shining so intensely through the morning mist. I felt so calm and peaceful. Maybe the Val d'Orcia was really heaven.

XVII

Tuscia

"Here laughs the Etruscan, one day,
as he lay, with eyes to the ground
watching the sea…"
— *V.Cardarelli*

NEVILLE

I was at a small café-bar sitting outside and enjoying a late afternoon *espresso*. Perched on a puny-sized chair with an equally puny-sized table, I watched the street scene unfurl in front of me. As I glanced down the road, I could not help but notice the woman in the small black dress slowly walking towards me. Her dress was so petite that her ample bosom poured over the upper fringes of her outfit, revealing voluminous, darkly tanned flesh. She stopped occasionally to speak to people as she sauntered up the street. As she passed my little table, she sweetly smiled down at me and continued by as I savored the last of my dark rich *espresso*.

Italians have an infatuation with the human female breast. It symbolizes different things—from motherly love and maternal affection, to the erotic and the scandalous.

In Italy, you will find an ongoing overt display of female breasts. Flaunted bare breasts promote ferry trips from Naples to Sicily and appear in Italy's top satirical TV show "*Striscia la Notizia.*" They appear in Roman mythology, best depicted by Artemis of Ephesus, the many-breasted goddess symbolizing female nourishing power and fertility—*dal petto viene il cibo della vita*—from the breast springs forth the food of life. They appear in paintings such as Giambattista Tiepolo's "The Truth Unveiled." This famous 254-year-old painting, originally handpicked by Italy's Prime Minister Silvio Berlusconi as a backdrop for ministerial press conferences, was replaced with a copy whereby the offending naked left breast was covered up with a white veil, thus offending almost every serious art lover in Italy.

Italians' fascination with the female breast may stem from the Etruscans, considered by some to be the original Italians. They were primeval peoples that came before the Romans and lived in this region between the 8th and 3rd centuries BC. The Etruscans lived as far north as the Po River, but by some accounts, northern Lazio—a prehistoric, volcanic hotbed—was the heart of the Etruscan empire.

Etruscans were fun-loving folks, who had a passion for life that included elaborate banquets—even at funerals—featuring copious wine consumption and sensuous music and entertainment. They enjoyed a hedonistic, uninhibited sexual lifestyle that some describe as scandalous and amoral. Theopompus of Chios, a Greek historian from the 4th century BC, stated that:

> "...it was commonplace for Etruscans to engage in sexual activities with numerous partners; the sharing of wives was an established custom. Women took particular care of their bodies and exercised often, sometimes along with the men. They did not only share their couches with their husbands but with the other men who happened to be present. There was no embarrassment in being naked, and sexual acts frequently occurred in public for all to see. It was common to partner swap and for women to engage in gymnastic sexual positions."

When not playing pleasure-seeking games, the Etruscans focused on the supernatural. Religious ceremonies and funeral rites were common and of supreme importance. They built tombs resembling their dwellings and placed household objects beside the bodies of their deceased relatives for them to use in the afterlife.

"Here laughs the Etruscan, one day, lying down…" This is the beginning of a poem by the famous poet Vincenzo Cardarelli from Tarquinia. It describes the Etruscans' vision of life and death: that it is a passage into another world beyond this one, where time never changes.

D. H. Lawrence, in his book Etruscan Places, suggested that Etruscans considered death as simply the transition between life here on earth and the afterlife; the latter was the prolongation and celebration of life.

Etruscans settled Acquapendente, formerly known as Acquapendentem, meaning "pending water." When we arrived in Acquapendente, it was dark and therefore difficult to see the street signs as we struggled through the tight, narrow laneways of the old city center, desperately praying that we would find a place to crash for the night. We finally found the Albergo Ristorante Toscana, smack in the middle of the old center in the Piazza Nazario Sauro. With our heavy packs, we clomped upstairs and found our room. In the center of the large bedroom was a plush king-sized bed covered with numerous oversized pillows. In the bathroom was one of those antique, deep, freestanding claw foot tubs. The entire place was wonderfully huge and gloriously decked out with cherry wood flooring. It was an unexpected godsend for weary pilgrims.

Later that evening, we enjoyed a deep luxurious bath together. As I lay there in the bath with my arms wrapped around Julie, I thought about the Etruscan view of life, sexuality, death, and the afterlife. From death springs forth life and we are reborn, was what they believed. After the bath, we crawled into that soft, warm and cozy bed, buried ourselves deep under the covers, and slowly rocked ourselves to bliss, and eventually sleep. It felt like a new beginning, a rebirth, exciting and even a tad bit scandalous!

❧

We left Acquapendente, taking the state road and making our way to the hamlet of San Lorenzo Nuovo, a tiny community of fewer than 3,000 people just north of Lake Bolsena. It would be easy to miss it if you were blazing your way to Rome. The Etruscans built the original village before 770 BC and it was then known as San Lorenzo alle Grotte, named after the abundant caves or grottos in the area. Walking along a series of mule tracks and passing various farms, we were now renewed, energized, and excited as we got closer to Rome.

Leaving San Lorenzo, we climbed a dirt path and were treated to majestic views of Lake Bolsena. Once known as Lacus Volsiniensis, it is the remains of a large volcanic crater formed almost 400,000 years ago from the Vulsini volcanic complex. Historical records state that volcanic activity occurred in 104 BC, and the entire region, even today, is still semi-active. The Via Francigena sweeps along the eastern flank of the lake, and the soil along this section of the trail is layered in deep crimson, volcanic lava rock.

Approaching Bolsena, we passed the ruins of the Roman city of Volsinii. To confuse matters, Volsinii is the name of two ancient cities in Tuscia. In 265 BC, Rome destroyed the Etruscan Volsinii, also known as Velzna and considered by some to be the present-day Orvieto. The surviving inhabitants were imprisoned, moved to the east side of Lake Bolsena, and then assimilated into the new city of Roman Volsinii, or Volsinii Novae, now present-day Bolsena.

We arrived at La Rocca Monaldeschi della Cervara, a large, square fortress complex with corner towers that dominated the town and overlooked the lake. The fort was built between the 11th and 14th centuries and today houses the Territorial Museum of Lake Bolsena. I asked a woman for directions to the *convento*. I was not sure what she said but she pointed us towards a road to the left. Another man approached us and then walked with us down a series of steps to a lower part of the town and through the main *piazza*. He stopped and pointed, suggesting we needed to climb a big hill to reach the *convento*.

It was a long, tough climb that felt like it went on forever. I saw a large building that appeared to be the *convento*, so I raced ahead of Julie, opened the large door, and waited for her to arrive.

A young, pleasant woman who barely reached the height of my waist greeted us. Even though she was expecting a large group that night, she had one room left for us. She waved us in and led us down a hallway. The *convento* was more rustic than I had expected. There were construction men working as we walked through, and it was obvious the entire *convento* was in a state of restoration that had been going on for some time. She led us upstairs with her three-year-old daughter clinging to her leg and showed us to our room. It was basic but comfortable and we settled in, had a quick hot shower, and went out looking for our dinner.

Convento Santa Maria del Giglio was built in the 1600s. Legend has it that a group of Franciscan monks living on the nearby island of Bisentina, the largest of two islands in Lake Bolsena, found their conditions too dangerous and difficult, and thus decided to move to the mainland and build the convent that exists today.

For almost 400 years, the Franciscan monks lived at this new location. During the 1700s, the *convento* expanded to include two west wings and a second floor was added in the 19th century. By this time, the convent was providing shelter to seventy permanent residents. After WWII, the convent went into a decline as the number of monks living in the convent decreased. In 1997, the Association "Punti di Vista" took over and they still manage the present-day guesthouse.

～

JULIE
We had difficulty finding a place to eat that evening but finally we located the small La Tavernetta Stefania. We ordered *insalata mista*

(mixed salads), a plate of *Coregone alla griglia* and a plate of *Trota piccante alla griglia,* both local fish specialties from Lake Bolsena. And a bottle of Est!Est!!Est!!!, the unique local white wine from Montefiascone. We finished off the meal sharing a dish of the house dessert, a moist chocolate torte. Since arriving in Lazio, this was our second wonderful meal. Our culinary and cultural adventure through Italy was finally coming back to life again.

The next morning we returned to the main *piazza,* hoping to get our morning *caffè* and *dolce* and buy some food for lunch. Our walk of the day was from Bolsena to Montefiascone, mostly dirt paths through woods and farms fields, so we thought there might not be anywhere to buy food.

While Neville went to the café to get our coffees, I went into the *forno* (bakery) across the *piazza* to buy our supply of buns for lunch. While I waited in a very long line with numerous local women, I surveyed the display case and counters to see if there would be anything interesting to have with our coffee. Because I felt I needed a big breakfast, I left the shop with some *focaccia* bread for lunch and a 10-inch square prune *crostata* for breakfast.

"Look what I got Neville, my favorite. Here, there's plenty for us to share."

"But I already bought something for myself," he replied.

Along with a couple of *caffè lungo* (similar to *caffè Americano,* a "long" *espresso*), he had bought a large chocolate-covered Italian *brioche.*

"Oh, that looks good! How come you didn't get me one?" I asked.

"Well, you already have something," he replied.

"But I'd love to have one of those too—besides I got the *crostata* to share with you," I said, staring wildly at his massive chocolate-covered *brioche.* So back he went to the café-bar to purchase another one for me.

By the time we were ready to leave, we were both stuffed silly. While Neville went into a *tabacchi* shop to buy some water, I went across the *piazza* to a small *alimentari* and bought some sliced cheese and meat to accompany our *focaccia*. With well-stocked stomachs and backpacks, we were finally ready to push off.

⁂

NEVILLE

Outside Bolsena, the trail turned sharply left and climbed a steep hill, passing through a grove of trees and then breaking out onto a short section of the old cobbled-stone Roman road. We walked along the road, past expensive homes—mostly owned by non-Italians, I assumed—that commanded breathtaking views of Lake Bolsena.

The trail climbed steeply again and disappeared into another grove of trees, slowly circling back into the Parco Archaeologico Naturalistico di Turona. The park was home to the Etruscan city of Civita di Arlena and got its name from one of two small channels that border it—although some argue that the name is a symbolic reference to the Etruscan Goddess Turan, the goddess of love and beauty. As we entered the park, we could easily appreciate the idea: it was an exotic, richly treed, enchanted forest.

We passed an old stone water foundation and basin. I could only imagine the Goddess Turan bathing in the cool waters. Conjuring up the Etruscan spirit, I jokingly suggested to Julie, "this is a great place for you to strip off naked and cool yourself."

She turned to me and gave me one of those sly, suggestive looks that husbands sometimes get from their wives. "Fat chance I'm going to strip off here," she said.

We arrived at Montefiascone, once believed to be the Etruscan Temple of Fanum Voltumnae, the chief sanctuary and geographical and spiritual center of the Etruscan universe. We came upon the La chiesa di San Flaviano, built in 1032. Inside the church are 14th century frescoes, discovered in the year 1896. Julie went to investigate and then called me to come inside. For a single euro coin, the lights came on, allowing us to admire the wonderful frescoes for a few brief minutes.

Also at the church is a gravestone, immortalizing John Defuk, and the legend of the famous wine of Montefiascone:

> There is an old story about a man named Martin who was traveling ahead of the imperial group heading to Rome for the coronation of Henry the Fifth. The group included squires, prelates, nobles, knights, pilgrims, merchants, and a wine lover named John Defuk. Martin acted as sommelier, inspecting the different wineries along the way to find good wine. Whenever he found a good one, he would write the word "Est!" above the door, meaning "It's here!" When he found an excellent wine, he would write "Est!Est!!" When he reached Montefiascone, after tasting the local *moscatello*, he immediately wrote "Est!Est!!Est!!!"—an affirmation of the superb quality of the wine.
>
> As the story goes, when Defuk arrived several days later, this recommendation did not escape him and, indeed, on his way back from Rome he decided to stay in Montefiascone for the rest of his life, eventually dying there—it is thought from too much wine drinking.

❧

JULIE

It had been a long, hot day, and I was exhausted. As much as I wanted to crash on the bed and sleep when we arrived at the Monastero Suore Benedettine, I forced myself to shower and change my clothes. I tried out all six beds in the room and finally picked the best one. Even though it felt like I had just sunk into a hammock, I was comfortable. I just wanted to stay and sleep until morning.

"I don't feel like dinner, I don't have the energy," I said to Neville.

"Well, you have to eat something," Neville rationalized, thinking I wouldn't make it through the night without food.

"*No I don't.* I'm *not* interested in food. I don't feel like eating *anything.* I have some snacks in my bag. I'll be fine until morning. Just let me *sleep!*"

After indulging in a massive chocolate pastry and an equally large fruit *crostata* for breakfast, and then plenty of cheese, *prosciutto*, and bread for lunch, I had had enough!

Neville kept prodding me, trying to convince me to go out. I knew that he didn't want to go out alone. Tired and lazy as I was, I got fed up listening to him, so I finally gave in.

"Okay, okay, I'll come, but give me 20 minutes. And I don't want to walk all over town looking for just the right place."

We walked the streets searching for a restaurant. I suggested one place but Neville didn't like it. He scanned the menu posted outside the wall of the restaurant.

"It's written in German and there are no prices—it's probably a tourist restaurant," Neville claimed.

We continued towards the *porta*, where we had first entered the old town. After walking outside the arches and surveying the surrounding cafes, bars and restaurants, I was overwhelmed. "I don't have the energy to walk around checking out menus," I pleaded.

Just on the inside of the *porta* we noticed a *ristorante pizzeria.* I scanned the menu and suggested, "Let's just go into this one. They have some local foods. They even have lentil soup, which will be perfect for me; that's all I can handle."

I managed to eat the soup and drink lots of water. I slept well that night; in fact, it was one of the best sleeps ever, even with the sagging mattress.

The next morning was another cool, misty one as we walked into the old *piazza* in search of coffee and breakfast. The eerie mist cloaked the *piazza,* and people and buildings faded in and out; we felt like we were back in medieval times. The atmosphere reminded us of our time in O Cebreiro in Spain when we hiked the Camino de Santiago.

Morning Mist – Montefiascone

We climbed a series of stairs and reached the Rocca dei Papi, a large fortress park that, in its heyday, had been the Pope's summer vacation home. On a clear day, you could see 360 degrees around, but this morning it was so foggy we could barely see in front of our feet.

The path descended alongside a high rock wall, past the old fortress, and through the gates of Porta Roma. Soon the trail became a dirt path that led out into the countryside.

⌘

NEVILLE
I smiled at Julie. "This should be fun!"

I had visions of naked young Etruscan women lying around patiently waiting for my arrival at the famous Bagnaccio hot springs. For more than 2,000 years, the baths have been freely open to anybody to use. The site is still marked by the Roman ruins of Bagnaccio, a small bath complex on the same narrow unpaved *strada bianca*, the ancient Via Cassia, which is also the road to Viterbo.

But there were no nude, sensuous, pleasure-seeking Etruscan women. This was modern Italy and all around us were many obese, deeply suntanned Italians in skimpy bathing suits.

There were three smallish pools, each big enough for about a dozen people. The hottest pool was the closest to the source of the hot spring water; the middle pool was temperate; and the far pool was almost cool. There was a large wading pool and one dry pool with kids playing around in it. Clearly, we must have been a sight with our packs and hiking boots as we sauntered into the pool area. We found some picnic tables towards the back of the area, discreetly changed into our bathing suits, and slipped into each of the pools to try them out. After bathing for half an hour, we returned to our table to have lunch.

A group of young Italian boys were playing nearby. They walked over to a picnic table behind us and started setting up for a picnic lunch. One by one, they returned, bringing whatever they could carry: plates, cutlery, and food from their parents' car. Then the parents showed up with more kids, repositioned the table and settled in for their picnic.

The father motioned to us, asking where we were from.

"We're from Canada. We're walking the Via Francigena—from Switzerland," we proudly proclaimed.

He had this all too common, surprised look and turned to tell the young boys in Italian what we had just said. The boys' eyes widened.

"It's a four-day walk from here to Rome. Would you like to join us?" I asked one of the young boys.

"It's only one hour by car, and for most Italians, especially my kids, if it takes more than one hour to walk, it's too far," the father replied, laughing.

After lunch, we saddled up, and before long, Julie was racing ahead of me. She got one of her rare bursts of energy, getting into a fast walking rhythm. It was another four kilometers to Viterbo and within minutes Julie was ahead of me by half a kilometer. I soon lost sight of her and then spent the next hour trying to catch up, finally reaching her just before we arrived in Viterbo.

She was sitting on a cement curb, smiling at me.

"Hi, slowpoke," she said.

"Looks like you got a second wind," I replied.

"Yeah, I guess I was on a high, just like I was on the *meseta* along the Camino in Spain. I suddenly got my burst of energy, and I felt alive and healthy and strong."

We walked through and beyond the historical center of Viterbo and found the Instituto Adoratrici Sangue di Cristo, our home for the next two nights and conveniently located on the east side, just outside the walls of the old town center.

That evening we ambled back into the old town. There is much debate about the origins of Viterbo, and if Etruscans in fact founded the city, but what remains today is mostly medieval. Almost four kilometers of massive walls, built between the 11th and 12th centuries, surround the old center. Access is still through a number of ancient gates set deep into the walls, some of them unchanged from medieval times. Viterbo's walls and towers, as well as its fountains and historic *palazzo*, were built using "*peperino,*" a local volcanic stone whose shades of gray contribute to the town's picturesque air of antiquity.

The center was jam-packed with people and cars. We were witnessing Viterbo's Sunday *passeggiata*. Carloads of people were arriving, and from each car emerged couples, grandparents, babies, children, buggies and small dogs. They converged into a mass of humanity that quickly filled the center. Soon, the café-bars and shops were stuffed with people talking, laughing and milling around. By 6:00 pm, it was almost impossible to walk through any of the streets, let alone drive. I started to think that half of Rome had decided to visit Viterbo this Sunday evening.

We found a small restaurant, Ristorante Tre Re. We ordered the Viterbese specialty, *Lombrichelli all'Etrusca* (handmade thick spaghetti made with spicy tomato sauce, with chicory and anchovies), and grilled vegetables and *zuppa de castagna e ceci* (chestnut and chickpea stew). The highlight was the dessert of fresh ricotta with *cacao* and chestnuts served with a warm chocolate sauce.

Our dinner was yet another surprise, full of textures and flavors. We were pleased that we were once again able to easily find delicious local cuisine.

Halfway through the meal Julie suddenly blurted out, "You know what Neville? I had this incredibly comfortable feeling today that everything is going to work out. Rome is getting closer; I feel like we're really going to finish."

XVIII

The Gods Laughed

"You want to hear God laugh?
Tell him your plans."
– Yiddish proverb

JULIE
We were sitting at the table, eating our usual breakfast of dry crispy toast, *biscotti* and coffee (standard items served when breakfast was included with our accommodation), looking over our maps, and discussing our departure from Viterbo and the rest of the day's walk.

A gentleman dressed in casual clothes walked into the breakfast room. He looked to be in his early 60s. With light gray, slightly frizzy hair and a full, graying beard, he was shorter than I was, lean and fit looking.

"*Buon giorno,*" we called to him. "*Come sta?*"

"*Bene grazie, e voi?*" the man replied.

"*Molto bene, grazie. Sta facendo la Via Francigena?*" we asked.

"*Si, e voi?*"

"*Si, e noi.*"

"*Bene,*" he replied.

We invited him to sit with us.

"Where are you from?" he asked us in English.

"Oh, you speak English well," we both said, surprised.

"*Si, grazie,*" he replied with a smile on his face.

We asked one another the usual questions, shared our stories about our journey so far—where we had started from and how long we had been walking. His name was Cesare. He told us he had started walking from Parma, where he lived, taking a route that connected with the Via Francigena before the Cisa Pass. He had just arrived in Viterbo the night before.

This is funny, I thought. How ironic, after commenting over dinner that we did not expect to find any Italians walking the Via Francigena—and now we were talking to one, and a senior at that!

Following the official Via Francigena route meant walking to Veltralla along the busy Via Cassia, something I loathed to think about. Neville had suggested there might be another route that went east along Lake Vico to Capranica. To ensure we would not finish up walking another busy paved road, Neville wanted a better map of the region, but he had not been able to find one in Viterbo. Frustrated, he had decided the best choice was to take the bus to Veltralla. From Veltralla, we would pick up the "official trail" and walk to our next destination, an *agriturismo* just outside of Capranica. I was disappointed that we were not going to take the alternate route.

I peppered Cesare with questions: Was he leaving today? Which way was he walking—the official route or the alternate route? He said he was leaving this morning and believed the alternate route along the lake would be a better path.

We compared maps. Cesare's map showed the route as a road too, but a different category of road. Neville showed Cesare his maps and explained he thought it would be busy. Cesare agreed, but still believed it was the better route to walk. How adventurous of this older man, I thought, to try this route, even though he was not sure if it would be quiet or full of cars.

Unfortunately, Cesare's positive thinking did not rub off on Neville. Neville still thought we should take the bus to Veltralla.

We bid goodbye to Cesare and wished him well, hoping to see

him again in Capranica. But we assumed we probably wouldn't. On the Via Francigena, we had met only a handful of people and we rarely saw them again. Still, we had cherished this opportunity to talk to another pilgrim.

At the bus stop, I looked across the street and there was Cesare. He was tramping along, looking happy and content in his own little world, oblivious that we were on the other side of the street. There was something about Cesare and the way he walked, as if he knew that he would find the alternate route an enjoyable one.

I watched him round the corner at the traffic light and continue down the sidewalk on the busy road leading out of town. I secretly wished that I was walking that way with Cesare. After all, why would anyone not believe an Italian walker?

❦

We arrived in Capranica about noon, hungry. The *agriturismo* that we had selected was another three kilometers beyond the town, so I suggested to Neville that we have a big, filling lunch, so we would not have to walk back into town later. That way we could get to the *agriturismo* early, and I could just relax and write in my journal.

We wandered into the old town center in search of a place open for lunch. We found a *trattoria* with a few locals inside and decided that it would be as good a place as any; besides, the food smelled good. Normally, I have a rule about not having pasta for lunch unless I want a real siesta, because it makes me sleepy. When I have to do a lot more walking in the afternoon, I usually choose something else to eat. This time we knew we would be staying here, and three kilometers wasn't far, so I broke my rule and indulged. We each ordered a pasta dish, a meat dish, a salad, and of course a glass of wine for digestion.

After a very full and satisfying lunch, I asked the owner of the *trattoria* for directions to the *agriturismo*. It was more than three kilometers away, but in the direction from which we had come!

"Oh man! Too bad we didn't think about asking before we sat down to eat," I said to Neville.

"I don't want to walk back three kilometers or more, and then have to walk back here again in the morning," Neville remarked.

"No, I don't either," I agreed.

"Maybe there's other accommodation close by; I'll go check out a town map while you watch our packs," Neville suggested.

Neville returned unhappy, "I found a crude, useless town map on a large metal display sign but there was nothing to suggest places to stay."

"Well...let's go ask someone then," I suggested.

We went back to the old center searching for someone to ask. We stopped in the middle of the street; nobody was around, and nothing was open. Standing in front of the town hall, I said, "Why don't we go inside...maybe there's someone we can ask. The door is wide open; there must be someone in there."

On the ground level we found an empty hall but no rooms, so we climbed the stairs to the next floor. We walked around and called out *"Buon giorno, mi scusi."* All we could hear was the echo of our footsteps. The doors to all the rooms were wide open, but no one was around.

"It's definitely siesta time. I doubt we're going to find anyone around here now." I said.

"Well, I don't want to wait another hour until someone returns," Neville said.

We went outside to the square, looking around for some clue, feeling like lost pilgrims. "Hmmm...Is this starting to feel like déjà vu?" I asked. I suggested we go next door and ask the police. Neville's chuckle was tinged with sarcasm, but I ignored him and walked into the station.

A balding male *poliziotto* (police officer) greeted us pleasantly. I asked him, *"Mi scusi, per favore,* can you help us. We would like to find a place to stay tonight?"

He only knew of the same place that was three kilometers away in the opposite direction. We told him that we wanted to find something on the way to Sutri instead.

Neville showed him the name of the place he had in mind, in the direction we were going. He didn't know it, but offered to phone. We waited with anticipation while he talked on the phone for several minutes. He hung up the phone and told us, "*No, è chiuso.*"

"Crap! It's closed for the season," Neville said.

"So there's really nowhere for us to stay here," I said to Neville. "I guess we'll have to walk on to Sutri." It was another five kilometers at least.

"Well then, ask him to phone the monastery in Sutri to make sure they're open, and ask for directions," Neville prodded me.

The police officer phoned the monastery. I wished it to be open. What could a poor pilgrim do? I listened closely to the conversation; it sounded like he was getting directions.

After five long minutes, he hung up and said, "*Bene, ci sono i letti per voi.*" Good, they have beds for you.

The officer drew a map and gave us directions to the monastery. We thanked him profusely.

So, after spending two hours in Capranica, stuffing ourselves with a heavy pasta meal and wasting time trying to find a place to stay, we now had another hour or more of walking in the hot, late afternoon sun. But at least we knew we had a bed for the night.

I think I heard the Gods laughing.

⌘

NEVILLE

Upon arriving in Sutri, we followed the police officer's directions, but we could not find anything that resembled a monastery.

"How could this be happening again? I was sure this is what he told us," Julie said.

We walked up and down the street, stopping and asking people for directions. Nobody knew where the monastery was.

I spotted a butcher shop on the corner. "This guy must know," I said.

The butcher told us to continue on the main road, past the first arch that we had walked under earlier, then through the second old arch to the old town center and it would be on our left.

"So easy," Julie said to me, smiling. I was getting a sense of déjà vu.

At the Monastero Santissima Concezione, we buzzed the main door and were let in, finding ourselves standing in a small foyer that was no more than three meters square. I found myself expecting somebody to appear and escort us through another set of doorways, past a series of little arches, past a sunny, airy cloister, and then up a flight of stairs to a series of rooms, just like the ones we had stayed in at so many other *conventos* during our journey.

Instead, a short nun greeted us from behind a dark wooden latticed window. In front of her was a wooden turnstile, like a "lazy Susan." Beside this window was a wooden door. She stood a few paces back in the shadows, making it almost impossible to see her face. I had no idea how old she was, but given the state of the building, I figured she must be old.

We told her we were here for one night. She placed a piece of paper on the wooden turnstile and then swung it around; on the piece of paper was the price of a bed. I dropped some bills and swung the wooden turnstile around so the nun could pick them up again on the other side. We repeated the process for the passing of the keys.

The nun told us that we would receive breakfast when we returned the key.

"Okay, if we have to return the key in order to get breakfast; where is breakfast being served?" Julie whispered in my ear.

The nun said goodbye—shooed us out the front door—then quickly shut the little wooden window and disappeared.

Stepping outside Julie asked, "Nev, okay, where do we sleep?" I pointed to another doorway in the adjacent building.

"*What*...! you mean we're going to sleep inside *that* building?"

In front of us was a run down, gray, crumbling cement structure with slanted walls that had chunks of plaster missing.

"*Oh my God, I can't believe this!* What kind of place is this?" Julie cried out.

"I think one key is for this outside front door and the other one is for the bedroom door." I said.

I tried the first key to open the front door to the building—no luck. Then I tried the second key—this time I had success.

"Good, step one accomplished," I said to Julie, smiling.

We squeezed through the narrow door and slowly walked up the stairs to a small tight landing. It was dark but I could see there were four doors. I couldn't help but notice the crumbling, decaying walls inside the hallway, and I hoped—well, prayed—that maybe it wouldn't be so bad once we were inside our room.

I tried the key to the room number, but it didn't work.

"Are you sure it's the right one? Maybe she said this one," Julie said, taking the keys away from me. She tried both keys and all four doors, thinking there must be a technique that I hadn't figured out.

"Come on Neville, it's gotta work," Julie cried out, obviously agitated. But it didn't. "Well, maybe she gave you the wrong key." Julie said in a huff.

I bounded down the stairs to the outside with Julie following behind me, and we returned to the main door of the *monastero*. We rang the buzzer and the door opened. We walked in and waited. The same nun appeared at the window.

Julie explained to the nun that the key "*no functiona.*" The nun looked puzzled, then went away for a second, came back, apologized and gave us a new set of keys.

We returned to the same building and put the key into the lock of the heavy front door. This time neither key would open the front door.

"Alright, what is going on here? How stupid is *this*?" I complained.

We went back to the *monastero* and once again sheepishly told the nun, "*no functiona.*"

I was sure she must have thought, "I have had enough of these silly foreign pilgrims."

Seconds later, the door beside the wooden turnstile flew open, and the short nun emerged. For a fleeting second or two, our eyes met, and I saw in front of me a very attractive young woman. I was speechless as she grabbed the keys from me and rushed out the main entrance into the street, and then hurried over to the building next door. As we followed, I heard her mumble, "*Io vi accompagno ma non è corretto, non dovrei fare questo,*" which I took to mean something like "I go with you, but it is not right; I should not do this."

The nun tried to open the front door of the building, but it wouldn't open. We both tried hard not to laugh. But the nun continued, this time incorporating a few special techniques, and the door finally opened.

"*Bene, grazie,*" we said.

Once inside and in our bedroom, we discovered a series of rooms. There were, in fact, three separate bedrooms, a shared kitchen, a separate bathroom, and a lounging room. The only window was in the bathroom that faced the inside center of the building. We had a comfortable bed each, it was quiet, clean, and we had a hot shower. We were weary but happy pilgrims.

This time we heard the Gods laughing.

⌀⌀⌀

JULIE

As we sat around relaxing, thankful to have landed in a peaceful, spacious room, we were reminiscing about Maria, specifically about when we had crossed the Po River and left her behind, not knowing if we would ever see her again.

We heard the front door opening downstairs.

We both looked at each other. "Could that be Cesare?" I asked.

We rushed to open the bedroom door and looked down the stairs. It *was* Cesare! He was slowly climbing the stairs carrying a white plastic grocery bag. We were overwhelmed with delight to see him again.

"*Buona sera! Come va?*" I asked.

"*Stanco, molto stanco,*" he slowly replied. He was tired, very tired. He had walked around the lake, covering a total distance of 35 km—the long way to Capranica. He discovered, as we had, that there was no place to stay in Capranica, so he took the last bus to Sutri. "But it was a beautiful walk around the lake."

He looked weary, and I asked him if he wanted to use our shower, since the room he had been assigned didn't have one. He declined, but suggested we have dinner together. We discovered a restaurant in the old part of town, a *pennetteria* (a restaurant that serves a large variety of pasta). It was an odd restaurant for the size of the town. It looked more like a banquet hall, and it was empty. It felt strange to sit inside such a gigantic place, just the three of us.

We were presented with an extensive menu offering every conceivable type of pasta, pizza, and salad. Cesare was hungry for pasta. He had only eaten a few snacks from his white plastic bag during the day. As he surveyed the menu, he started to explain the traditional pastas because he knew we were interested in eating local food.

"*Basta pasta Cesare, l'abbiamo già mangiata a pranzo,*" I told him.

Unfortunately, we did not feel like pasta, having eaten our fill at lunch. I think we disappointed him when we each ordered a large salad. To make amends, we did take him up on his suggestion of *pizza bianca*.

It was like a naked pizza, topped with garlic and salt and drizzled with olive oil. "Oh! What a treat!" I exclaimed. Thank you Cesare! This is very tasty, I love the crispiness."

I commented to Cesare how strange the monastery was. "What does it mean?" I asked.

"It's a 'closed *monastero,*' home to the Carmelite nuns who are 'cloistered' nuns. That means the nuns observe 'papal enclosure rules,' whereby their monasteries typically have walls and grilles separating them from the outside world. The nuns are not allowed to have contact with anybody from outside the monastery, though occasionally they may meet visitors in specially built parlors."

Now it all made sense. I told Cesare about the nun who was forced to go outside to help us with the door.

"Oh, that's not allowed!" he said, surprised. We all laughed.

The next morning I found the answers to my questions about breakfast. The three of us walked in together. As the men returned the keys, using the same lazy Susan method, I looked to the left and was shocked at what I saw. About four feet away was a small table with three chairs. The table was set with a small jug of orange juice, a small carafe of coffee, three small juice glasses and three cups, three plates and three sets of utensils, a small dish of marmalade—and nothing else.

"Well, I have seen everything now," I whispered to Neville, chuckling. It certainly was a unique breakfast experience.

◦◦◦

We left Sutri, stopping briefly at the Etruscan ruins outside the old town center and along the main road. Thin, white rays of light from the early morning sun shone down though a heavy mist, making for an eerie atmosphere at the ancient burial site. As I stood looking at the four-meter-long caves dug into the walls of *tufa* cliffs—clay created from volcanic ash—I felt like I had entered the Etruscan afterlife.

We walked together for most of that morning and arrived in Monterosa in search of some lunch. Cesare pointed out a *forno* where we could buy bread, and across the same narrow street was an *alimentari* where we could buy meat and cheese. Cesare came with me and helped me order some cheese and roasted marinated peppers. There were tables outside the *forno*, so I assembled the sandwiches while Neville went to order two coffees. Cesare remained in the *alimentari*, asking the shopkeepers if they knew about the route along the highway to La Storta.

Julie and Cesare at lunch – Monterosa

After ten minutes he came out to get his map book, saying, "I think it better we take the bus." He went back into the shop. Ten minutes later he returned and said, "I think it is possible for us to walk. There's a small shoulder along the highway and a barrier to separate us from the traffic."

Neville and I, wary of Italian drivers, were not keen about walking on the highway. Getting closer to Rome meant it would be even crazier. Cesare was not keen either, but we agreed we would investigate the highway first, and then decide.

We sat down to eat, Neville and I snacking on a cheese and roasted red pepper sandwich and a sweet tart, while Cesare pulled out plain packaged biscuits and cakes stashed in the white plastic grocery bag he had carried since Sutri.

We walked to the entrance of the highway to get a closer look at the small shoulder along the highway. The highway was busy, noisy, and I could not imagine walking on it. It was akin to walking on a major North American highway, like Toronto's Hwy 401 or the I5 in the United States.

"So, what do you think, Nev?" I asked, as cars zoomed by at breakneck speed.

"No, I don't think so. I really don't want to walk on this," Neville replied. I didn't either.

We asked Cesare what he was going to do.

"I go–I try it," he said. He didn't think it would be that bad.

"Are you sure?" I was stunned.

We wished him a safe journey and hoped we would meet again. And he was off like a brave soldier. We watched him walk down to the highway, merging with the chaos, keeping close to the side of the barriers, and carrying his plastic grocery bag.

"How brave he is," I said to Neville. "God, I hope nothing happens to him." Perhaps he was used to it or understood something about dealing with crazy Italian drivers zipping past him that we never would.

Sad to leave Cesare fending for himself on the highway, we backtracked to the bus depot to catch a bus to Campagnano di Roma.

Buses came and went. Each time a bus arrived, I would step up to the door and ask the bus driver, "Campagnano di Roma?" And each time the bus driver replied "no," or just shook his head.

There was no timetable posted. We just hoped for the right bus to come along. But time ticked by and every moment I got more anxious. "What the heck are we doing here? We could be waiting here forever," I moaned.

"I can't believe it. I'm sure one of these buses must go there," I said, sulking, after I had asked the fifth bus driver. "Maybe I'm not pronouncing the name of the town correctly. Maybe they don't understand what I'm asking."

We waited and waited. After an hour of waiting, I was getting short-tempered and cursing the bus system.

More buses came and I got the same response. "This is *insanity*," I told Neville. "We could have been at Campagnano di Roma by now. Cesare is probably already there. We should have just walked after all!"

The more I thought about our situation, the more annoyed I became. I hollered, "I hate waiting around for a bus when we don't even know if it's coming today."

Neville walked away from me saying, "I don't want to be around you when they come and take you away!"

Soon afterward, I calmed down and started to think. "All right, the next bus that comes in, I'll ask if it goes to Settevene, and if it does, we can get on and walk from there." A few minutes later, another bus arrived. I asked about Settevene, which was a closer destination, and he nodded his head yes. I yelled to Neville to get on!

After a ten-minute ride, the bus dropped us off at a pullout alongside the highway. It was a rather strange place, not at all what I had expected. Was this the town? It was just several buildings, shops, and kiosks, lining the highway on either side as the traffic hummed by. I felt annoyed that we were dropped off in the middle of nowhere, on a busy highway.

We spied a pedestrian bridge about 200 meters ahead and shuffled over to it, dragging our backpacks. We stopped at the foot of the bridge to get saddled up. While Neville examined his map book to find out how to access the trail from here, I thought again what a strange place it was as I scanned up and down the highway, trying to identify something that looked like a trail. And then…suddenly, about half a kilometer down on the opposite side of the highway, walking in our direction, I saw a man. I stared, and when I saw the white plastic bag, I knew it was him.

"I see Cesare!" I yelled to Neville.

I sprinted to the top of the bridge, waving my blue and white scarf high in the air like a half-crazed woman who hadn't seen anyone for decades. I called out Cesare's name, knowing perfectly well he wouldn't hear me above the roar of the traffic. At first, he didn't acknowledge me, but finally he gave me a little wave back, as if he was too embarrassed to admit he knew me.

We were all pleased to see one another. Cesare looked tired, but the only thing he said was, "It was not so bad; there was a good shoulder." We started to explain our challenge of getting a bus out of Monterosa, but Cesare motioned us on; he just wanted to keep walking.

How ironic. For all the frustration we experienced and the time we wasted, we ended up at the very spot where Cesare appeared. And as if that wasn't enough, we still had another kilometer of walking the busy highway to Campagnano di Roma. I knew then we would be walking together all the way to Rome.

The Gods were laughing at us again.

❦

Cesare had hopes of sleeping at the Hotel Righetto, but they were not taking overnight guests. However, they invited us all back for dinner.

The Hotel Righetto has been owned by the same family for years. The current owners had originally lived in Milano, teaching at the university, but both had retired from their professional careers to take over the restaurant. We ordered a local pasta dish and shared a dish of meat and vegetables, and then spent the evening checking out all the memorabilia and photos of special events and famous people that lined the walls.

We agreed to have coffee together the next morning before we started our trek. Shortly after leaving Campagnano di Roma, we entered Parco di Veio, which is 15,000 hectares of deep, lush forests wedged between the Via Cassia to the west and Via Flaminia to the east, with Campagnano di Roma to the north and Roma to the south. The territory covers the so-called Agro Veientano, a region of land that surrounds the Etruscan city of Veio, named after the Etruscan goddess Vei, patron of agriculture and vegetation. The park is home to a diverse range of animals and plants found in the woods, deep gorges, and streams.

We had heard about a park with bike and walking paths that could potentially lead us all the way into Roma. I relished the idea. After looking at our maps, I felt sure we could walk through this beautiful park all the way to the city.

Walking through Parco di Veio felt like walking through Sherwood Forest. We followed a beautiful, easy walking trail that passed under large sprawling oak-like trees. In the distance, wild white horses and *Chianina* cows roamed the open fields and meadows. It was a magical place and it would have been a beautiful way to finish our journey. But that's not what the Gods had in store for us.

After leaving a section of park to walk along a dirt track through farmers' fields, we didn't re-enter the park as I had expected. Instead, we found ourselves on a trail that broke out onto a main road. I looked around, bewildered. "Okay, where is the park?" I asked the guys. I felt like some entity had transported us somewhere we didn't want to be. "Darn, maybe the park continues on the other side of the highway," I suggested.

We followed the Via Francigena signs and crossed over the highway. Both Neville and Cesare knew of the alternate route that crossed over a bridge above a river, and went through another park, thus avoiding the busy provincial road.

"Somewhere up ahead we should see signs for the other path," Neville claimed.

We continued down the provincial road, passing a café-bar and looking out for the path. Up ahead we saw what looked like a small dirt path, so we agreed to walk to it. Yet when we arrived, it was a wide driveway to somebody's home.

"Maybe the path is further on; this wouldn't be the first time the maps were unreliable," I suggested. We agreed to walk further down the busy road, still looking for the alternate route.

Ahead lay a narrow provincial highway with no shoulder to walk on. None of us wanted to walk on this road but we believed the alternate path would eventually appear. Meanwhile, the crazy Italian drivers whizzed by us at lightning speed. I used my walking stick to force the cars to move away from us as we walked down the road. Feeling heroic, and having the biggest protection, I took the lead. I felt it was my duty to protect Cesare since all he had was his white plastic bag.

I kept my stick out. "Crazy Italian drivers," I yelled out. "God, they are ruthless. And they have the nerve to honk at us, as if we were the inconsiderate ones!"

I heard Cesare say something, but I couldn't hear him, so I stopped. When he caught up, he scolded me, "Julie, it is not safe to do this."

"No, no it's okay," I replied.

Cesare wasn't happy with me, so he took the lead, using his white plastic bag as a guard. I chuckled at the thought of his plastic grocery bag keeping the cars away. He held it out away from his body, fending off the cars; he seemed fearless.

A few minutes later I cringed as I watched a motorcyclist almost clip him. "*Oh man, oh God, that was too close!*" I cried out. "God, where is that trail, anyway?"

I wondered if Cesare felt my dread. But he just soldiered on, seemingly unfazed by the incident. He must have Caesar's blood in him, I thought. Hail Cesare! Hail Caesar!

For me, it was ugly, beyond nerve wracking. But even though I felt my life flash before me several times, I plodded on, prayed, and hoped for safety soon. I tried my best to absorb some of Cesare's fearless energy.

Finally, after walking a horrific four kilometers, we arrived at an intersection. "Thank God, a reprieve! *Now* what do we do?"

I collapsed on the curb while Cesare stopped to ask a motorist for directions. When he returned, he told us there was no other way to get to La Storta except to walk the Via Cassia—the busiest road and the one that I feared most of all.

By this time I was a wreck and nearly in tears. I did not want to go on. I couldn't stand the thought of walking on a highway that was even busier and noisier than the one we had just walked.

Cesare and Neville both tried to reassure me. "Come on, Jul, you can do it, only two or three kilometers left till the *convento*," Neville urged.

And Cesare added his encouragement in a straightforward, no-nonsense way: "Giulia, yes, we must go, it is the only way."

I mumbled under my breath how much I dreaded the thought of walking on the Via Cassia, as I slowly picked myself up. How much of this could I take? Was this another test?

Neville took the lead. He rounded the corner of the cement wall to make his was up to the Via Cassia. I just cringed and held my breath.

"God, please have mercy on me. I can't handle this anymore."

Neville looked back at me, yelling something. I couldn't hear what he said, but he was smiling. Then, as I rounded the corner, I knew what Neville was saying. I saw, much to my amazement and joy, a sidewalk—a big wide one. *Oh God—grazie.*

For all my fears about walking on the Via Cassia, it turned out far better than I had expected. Though we were in a noisy, busy, industrial section, we had a three-meter-wide sidewalk to walk along in safety. I was so thankful.

When we arrived at our refuge, the Istitutio Figlie del Sacro Cuore in La Storta, a nun showed us to our room and I collapsed on the bed, exhausted.

❦

NEVILLE

Before dinner, Cesare and I met at the front desk, hoping to get information about getting to Mount Mario, also known as Mount Joy or Mons Gaudii. While we were standing there, one of the nuns asked Cesare if he or I was the person who had fallen into the river!

Later that evening during dinner, we met the man who had fallen into the river. He told us his story while we dined over a satisfying meal of *penne* with *ragù*, green salad, eggplant with fresh anchovies, and baked pork cutlets. Apparently, he had found and taken the mysterious alternate path, the same route we were so determined to find into La Storta. He had come upon a river but couldn't find a bridge to cross the river. So he decided to wade through the river in knee-deep water. Unfortunately, he lost his balance and fell in, soaking himself from head to toe and drenching his pack and all his equipment.

"I had to walk for two hours soaking wet. I hope my camera card still works," the man said, smiling ruefully.

At least he was smiling; I was sure he must have felt differently at the time. But still, he seemed unfazed by the experience. I thought, "What situations we pilgrims get ourselves into!"

We finished off our meal with a plate of sweet ice cream, accompanied with cheese. And we laughed along with the man who had fallen in the river, and at ourselves.

❦

JULIE

We stood on top of Monte Mario, looking across to the Vatican and the sprawling city of Rome. Here we were: steps from our final destination and the end of our journey, just like the many pilgrims before us. It was a bittersweet feeling.

A heavy morning mist cloaked the landscape and draped like a veil over the Vatican City. Even with the haze, I could appreciate the enormity of the city.

"Can you see any of the famous landmarks?" I asked Neville. Before he could respond, Cesare pointed toward some of them. "If it was clearer, you could see the Seven Hills of Rome, and Villa Borghese, and the Coliseum," he said.

I was flooded with a jumble of emotions—relief, sadness, pride, regret, satisfaction, and joy.

The longer I stood there, above the magnificent city, having trekked nearly 1000 kilometers, the more I appreciated our struggles and our perseverance.

"I still can't believe it, we've made it!" I shouted excitedly to Neville and Cesare.

The morning light started to break through the haze, and the mist slowly lifted, unveiling the treasure of Rome in all its magnificence. Any vestiges of frustration, disappointment, dismay, anger, or insanity that I was still harboring slipped away with the mist.

With the bright rays of the sun, the landscape and buildings became clearer. And now so did our journey—with its trials and tribulations—it all made sense. I felt proud and grateful.

○⸜⸝○

NEVILLE

The Vatican was busy and chaotic. We negotiated our way along the busy sidewalks to the Piazza San Pietro (St. Peter's Square), walking alongside the tall, massive wall that encircled the Vatican, as tourists stood in line-ups with hundreds of others to visit the Vatican museum. Others swarmed around the souvenir kiosks that lined the main street, which led to the main entrance of the square and the Vatican. We passed under one of the many arches, and I was about to enter the center of St. Peter's Square, when I simply stopped to take it all in. Of course I had seen photographs, but standing there, it was overwhelming.

As we stood at the gates of St. Peter's Square, it could well have

Julie and Neville in Piazza San Pietro – Città del Vaticano

been the "Pearly Gates of Heaven." I waited for Saint Peter to make a special appearance to welcome us and invite us in.

But alas, there was nobody to greet us. When we had walked the Camino de Santiago in Spain, we met so many other pilgrims along the way, which meant that, when we finally reached our destination—Santiago—there were other pilgrims waiting to greet and congratulate us with hugs and tears and laughter.

Here in St. Peter's Square, it was different. We were lone pilgrims in the midst of masses of strangers and tourists—three weary adults wearing backpacks. We walked over to the Opera Romana Pellegrinaggi, the pilgrim office. The officials, imperious and unsmiling, promptly and efficiently issued our *Testimonia*, the certificate of the authenticity of a pilgrimage, and sent us on our way.

To be fair, the staff in Santiago, Spain had not shown much excitement either. But then there had been a lineup of 100 pilgrims behind us, all wanting their *Compostela*, with many more to come before the end of the day. Here in Rome, we were only three pilgrims, and quite possibly the only three that would show up today, or even this week.

We were *"I tre moschettieri pellegrini*—the three pilgrim musketeers," having arrived at the Vatican after journeying for many weeks and many kilometers. Clutching our hard-earned *Testimonia*, we felt special.

❧

JULIE

That afternoon, we dined in a nearby restaurant, Il Papalino, which Cesare had frequented when he visited Roma during his working years.

"You should try the typical Roman pasta," he suggested.

"Oh yes," we said, "what do you recommend?"

"*Bucatini all'Amatriciana*—pasta with a special pork sauce. It's a little zesty."

"Perfect, we'll have that."

"*Vino?*" he asked. Neville and Cesare examined the wine list and selected a bottle of red wine, Duca de Ceri, Cerveteri Rosso 2007. And Cesare ordered *due bottiglie di Acqua di Nepi*.

"It's a sparkling water; I think you will enjoy it," he said. I was hesitant because I didn't really like fizzy water. But Cesare had always made good choices, so I thought what the heck.

When the server brought our pasta dishes, I couldn't believe my eyes; the plates were piled high.

"Nev, we could have shared this. I don't know if I can finish this."

We dug in. I finished every bite.

Bucatini all'Amatriciana is a signature Roman dish. There is a debate about its origins. Some argue that the dish originated from Amatrice, a small town that was once part of Abruzzo. The sauce is made with *guanciale,* or salted pork, prepared using pig's jowl fried in olive oil (traditionally lard), with chunks of chili pepper and tomatoes and grated *Pecorino Romano* cheese.

With the first bite, I could see why it had become a tradition. It was hearty, salty, and spicy, tantalizing the taste buds. *Bucatini* was something like *spaghetti*, but with fatter noodles and a narrower hole, so that when I bit into it, it was squishy.

I was not expecting to like the *Aqua di Nepi*, but I was pleasantly surprised. It was not too fizzy and had a refreshing, light, sweet flavor that quenched one's thirst after the saltiness of the pasta. In fact, it was one of the best bottled waters I had ever tasted.

"Great," I said. "I have another item to add to my culinary list. *Molte grazie,* Cesare."

Cesare also introduced us to another classic traditional food, a special Roman treasure called *puntarelle* (meaning little tips). It is a special dish, available only at certain times of the year, and considered a great delicacy for those who have acquired a taste for it. Often mistaken for a weed, *puntarelle* is a member of the chicory family, a spear-like endive that requires special preparation. The leaves and shoots are removed; then the stalks are split, pared into strips, and traditionally soaked in water overnight. This makes them crisp and curly, while removing the natural bitterness. Finally, the stalks are dressed with a paste of raw garlic, anchovies, and vinegar, left to sit for thirty minutes, and served with olive oil and a pinch of salt. It can be a laborious process; however, the longer the preparation, the better the outcome.

Puntarelle is crisp on the outside and tender on the inside and has an unusual flavour of pepper and fennel—a perfect complement to the rich and hearty *Bucatini all'Amatriciana.*

In many ways, *puntarelle* was like our journey through Italy on the Via Francigena—an extraordinary experience with a bitter undertone, but with time, sweet, spicy, and delicious.

The End

About the Authors

Julie has always loved walking, eating and traveling, but not necessarily always in that order. She is passionate about food that is local, fresh, natural, organic, safe, nutritious and tasty. She dreams of one day wandering foreign countrysides collecting long forgotten traditional food recipes and sharing them with others.

She enjoys the simple things in life: good food, and being out in nature, and she wishes we could all live in harmony with nature and ourselves. She strongly believes that walking is good for the soul and that "everyone should go on their own 'camino.'"

Neville, like most native Australians, was born with the urge to explore and has been going on "walkabouts" since he was five, at which time he and the family dog would "escape" and disappear for the day. In 1993, Julie and he spent almost a year traveling through Europe, SE Asia, New Zealand and Australia. It was during this period, while hiking in the Austrian Alps, that the "seed" to walk across a large expanse of land was planted.

In 2007, he and Julie walked the famous Camino de Santiago in Spain. Walking through Italy is their latest adventure.

CPSIA information can be obtained
at www.ICGtesting.com
Printed in the USA
BVHW071704011218
534532BV00001B/63/P